200
FUN THINGS
to Knit

200 FUN THINGS to Knit

DECORATIVE FLOWERS, LEAVES, BUGS, BUTTERFLIES, AND MORE!

Edited by Victoria Lyle

St. Martin's Griffin
New York

200 FUN THINGS TO KNIT
Copyright © 2017 by Quarto Inc.
All rights reserved. Printed in China.
For information, address St. Martin's Press,
175 Fifth Avenue, New York, N.Y. 10010.

www.stmartins.com

Library of Congress Cataloging-in-Publication Data available
upon request

ISBN: 978-1-250-11172-2

Our books may be purchased in bulk for promotional,
educational, or business use. Please contact your local
bookseller or the Macmillan Corporate and Premium
Sales Department at (800) 221-7945, extension 5442,
or by e-mail at MacmillanSpecialMarkets@macmillan.com.

First U.S. Edition: January 2017

10 9 8 7 6 5 4 3 2 1

Conceived, designed, and produced by
Quarto Publishing plc
The Old Brewery
6 Blundell Street
London N7 9BH
www.quartoknows.com

QUAR: FNTK

Additional designs: Jan Eaton, Caroline Sullivan
Pattern checkers: Betty Barnden, Lucia Calza, Susan Horan,
Lucille Kazel
Illustrators: Kuo Kang Chen, Coral Mula, John Woodcock
Photographers: Simon Pask, Phil Wilkins
Art director: Caroline Guest
Creative director: Moira Clinch
Publisher: Sam Warrington

Printed by 1010 Printing International Ltd, China

Note

The patterns in this book have previously appeared in:

- *100 Flowers to Knit & Crochet* by Lesley Stanfield
- *75 Birds, Butterflies & Little Beasts to Knit & Crochet*
  by Lesley Stanfield
- *75 Seashells, Fish, Coral & Colorful Marine Life to Knit*
  & Crochet by Jessica Polka
- *50 Sunflowers to Knit, Crochet & Felt* by Kristin Nicholas
- *75 Floral Blocks to Knit* by Lesley Stanfield

Caution

Designs that are stiffened with wire, incorporate pins or
hairpins, or are decorated with beads or sequins are not
suitable for babies and young children. When making
items for youngsters, always use top-quality, clean stuffing
marked as suitable for toys, and sew on any small parts
(such as petals) very securely.

CONTENTS

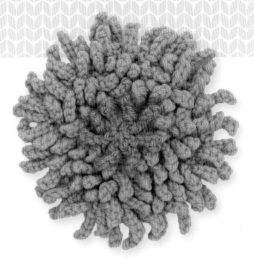

ABOUT THIS BOOK

This book provides a delightful collection of 200 fun things to knit, from flowers and plants to fish, bugs, and other critters. Each of these gorgeous creations can be used to embellish garments and accessories. There is also a collection of floral blocks for creating afghans or other projects of your own devising. Begin by looking through the pattern selector (pages 7–29), which displays all 200 designs in miniature together, select your design, and then turn to the instructions page to create your chosen piece. At the back of the book you will find some tips on knitting techniques (pages 196–221).

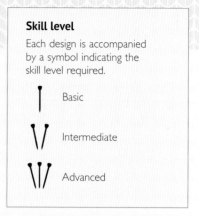

Skill level

Each design is accompanied by a symbol indicating the skill level required.

| | Basic

\\/ Intermediate

\\|/ Advanced

A knitting needle symbol indicates the skill level required, from 1 to 3.

The type of yarn and any other necessary extras are specified at the beginning of each pattern. Use standard needles unless specified otherwise in the pattern.

Full written instructions are provided for each design.

Charts are provided for intarsia, Fair Isle, and some lace designs to accompany the written instructions.

Mix and match suggestions are shown for a selection of the floral blocks.

Templates and assembly diagrams are provided where helpful.

Stitch symbols are explained next to the chart. Colorwork charts are accompanied by a color key for the different yarn colors used.

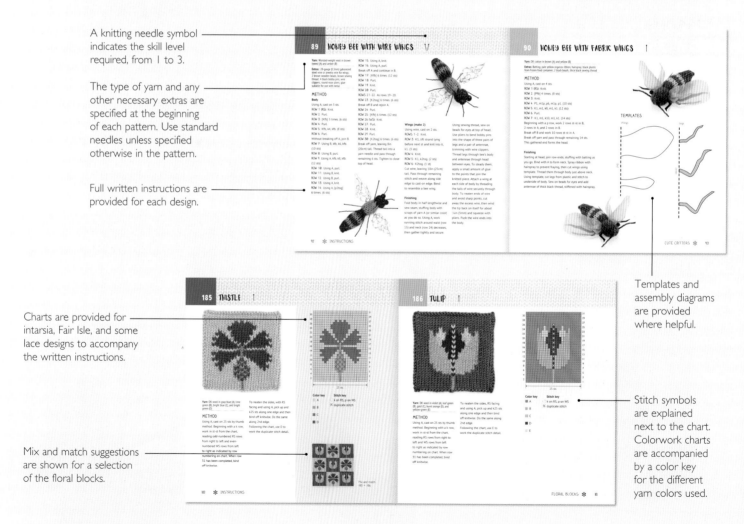

FLOWER GARDEN

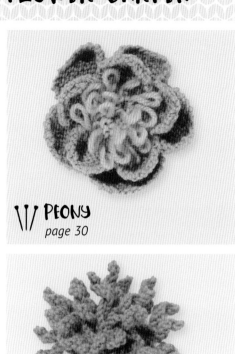

PEONY
page 30

CLEMATIS
page 31

SNOWDROP
page 31

CHRYSANTHEMUM
page 32

CAMPANULA
page 32

MORNING GLORY
page 33

ANEMONE
page 34

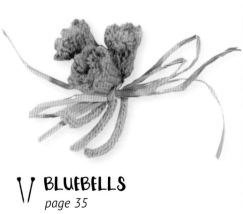

BLUEBELLS
page 35

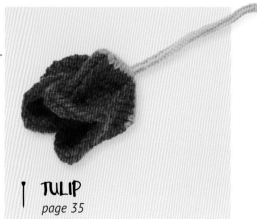

TULIP
page 35

FLOWER GARDEN

FIELD POPPY
page 36

CORNFLOWER
page 36

ARUM LILY
page 37

HOLLYHOCK
page 38

DOUBLE DAISY
page 38

LEMON BLOSSOM
page 39

LAVENDER
page 39

CARNATION
page 40

CLOVE CARNATION
page 40

PRIMROSE
page 43

CHRISTMAS ROSE
page 41

PETUNIA
page 42

DAHLIA
page 43

ROSE
page 44

ROSEBUD
page 44

TEA ROSE
page 45

POINSETTIA
page 46

FLORIBUNDA ROSE
page 47

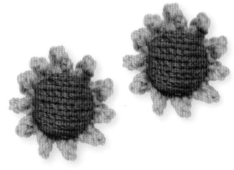

RUDBECKIA
page 47

SUNFLOWER MEADOW

COMMON SUNFLOWER
page 48

COCOA SUNDROP
page 48

SUNRAY SWIRL
page 49

WAGON WHEEL
page 50

CRÈME CARAMEL
page 51

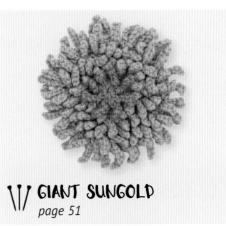

GIANT SUNGOLD
page 51

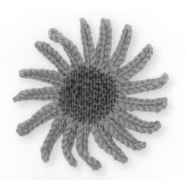

PRAIRIE GOLD
page 52

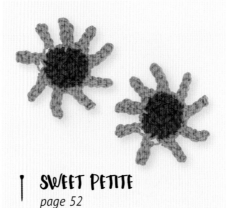

SWEET PETITE
page 52

SWIZZLE STICKS
page 53

\|/ POMPOM PUFF
page 54

\|/ CATHERINE WHEEL
page 55

\|/ POMPOM GEM
page 55

\|/ BOBBLE BEAUTY
page 56

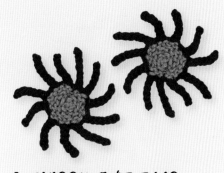

| CHERRY TWIZZLER
page 56

\|/ AMETHYST QUEEN
page 57

\|/ WOOLLY MAMMOTH
page 58

\|/ GOLD STRIPE
page 59

SUNFLOWER MEADOW

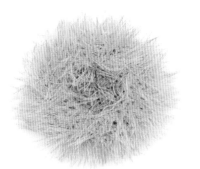

| TEDDY BEAR
page 60

| TOFFEE TWIST
page 60

|| LAZY DAISY
page 61

|| JOKER
page 62

| FIRECRACKER
page 62

| FLOWER BACK AND STEM
page 63

| CONCAVE PETALS
page 64

| GARTER PETALS
page 65

|| VEINED PETALS
page 65

PLANT LIFE

STALKED LEAVES
page 66

VEINED LEAVES
page 67

JAGGED LEAVES
page 68

MISTLETOE
page 69

CHERRIES
page 69

HOLLY LEAF AND BERRIES *page 70*

MAPLE LEAF
page 71

ELDER LEAF
page 71

PLANT LIFE

ELM LEAF
page 72

WHITEBEAM LEAF
page 72

BEECH LEAF
page 73

POPLAR LEAF
page 73

LOGANBERRY LEAF
page 74

LOGANBERRY
page 75

BLACKBERRY
page 75

LEMON
page 76

LEMON SLICE
page 76

CITRUS LEAF
page 77

OAK LEAF
page 78

ACORN
page 78

CARROT
page 80

FLY AGARIC
page 79

FIELD MUSHROOM
page 79

ASPARAGUS
page 81

CUTE CRITTERS

SWALLOWTAIL BUTTERFLY *page 82*

PEACOCK BUTTERFLY *page 84*

FRITILLARY *page 85*

LARGE BLUE *page 86*

COMMON BLUE *page 87*

ADONIS BLUE *page 88*

SLUG *page 89*

SMOOTH CATERPILLAR
page 90

STRIPED CATERPILLAR
page 90

WOOLLY BEAR CATERPILLAR *page 91*

HONEY BEE WITH WIRE WINGS *page 92*

HONEY BEE WITH FABRIC WINGS *page 93*

BUMBLE BEE
page 94

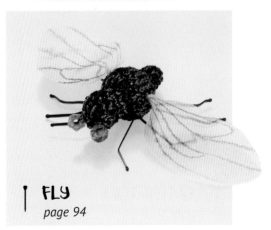

FLY
page 94

CUTE CRITTERS

LADYBUG
page 95

BLUE TIT
page 96

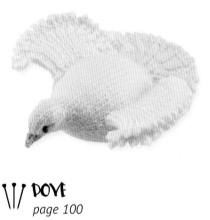

ROBIN
page 98

DOVE
page 100

EASTER EGGS
page 101

GRAY NEST
page 102

SWANSDOWN
page 103

UNDER THE SEA

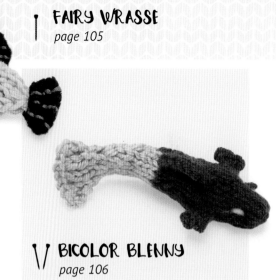

FAIRY WRASSE
page 105

\|/ **CLOWNFISH**
page 104

\/ **MYSTERY WRASSE**
page 105

\/ **BICOLOR BLENNY**
page 106

| **ZEBRA DARTFISH**
page 107

\|/ **ANGELFISH**
page 108

| **COURT JESTER GOBY**
page 109

\/ **SPRAT**
page 109

\/ **EEL**
page 110

| **LONGNOSE HAWKFISH**
page 111

UNDER THE SEA

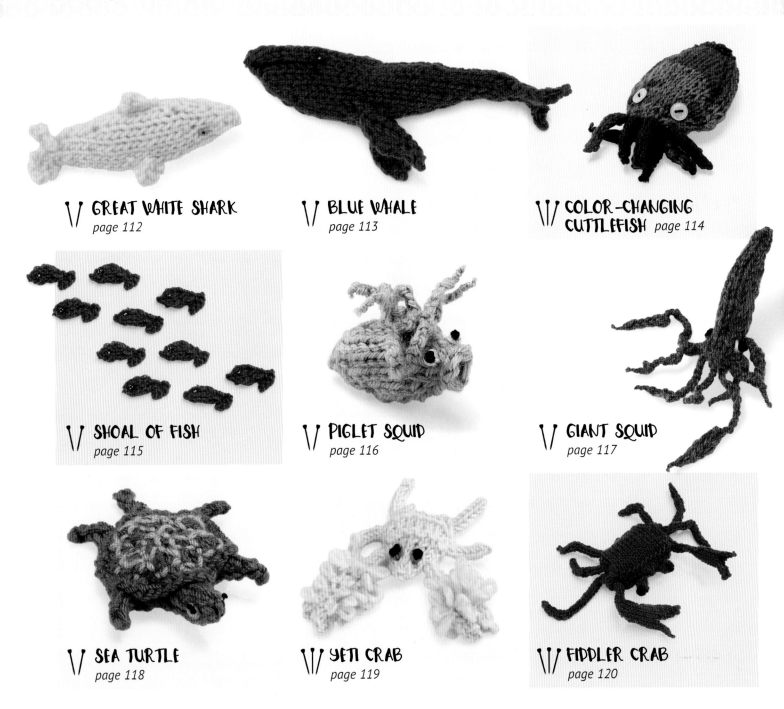

GREAT WHITE SHARK
page 112

BLUE WHALE
page 113

COLOR-CHANGING CUTTLEFISH *page 114*

SHOAL OF FISH
page 115

PIGLET SQUID
page 116

GIANT SQUID
page 117

SEA TURTLE
page 118

YETI CRAB
page 119

FIDDLER CRAB
page 120

RED STAR
page 123

BRINE SHRIMP
page 122

COMMON STARFISH
page 122

BRITTLE STAR
page 123

JELLYFISH
page 124

SIMPLE SEA ANEMONE
page 125

FANCY SEA ANEMONE
page 125

SNAIL SHELL
page 126

WENTLETRAP
page 126

CONE SHELL
page 127

UNDER THE SEA

| BARNACLE
page 128

\/ PLAIN SCALLOP
page 128

\/\/ STRIPED SCALLOP
page 129

\/\/ RED CORAL
page 130

| BRAIN CORAL
page 130

\/ BUTTONWEED
page 131

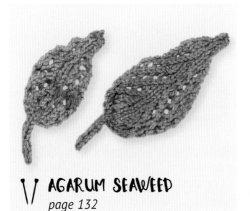

\/ AGARUM SEAWEED
page 132

\/ NEREOCYSTIS SEAWEED
page 133

| FAN SEAWEED
page 133

FLORAL BLOCKS

CROCUS
page 134

FORMAL FLOWER
page 135

SPRING BULB
page 136

POSY
page 137

LACE BOUQUET
page 138

BUTTONHOLE
page 139

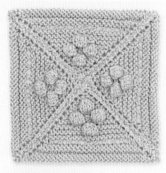

HYDRANGEA
page 140

LEAF QUARTET
page 141

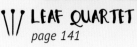

BUTTERFLY BLOOM
page 142

FLORAL BLOCKS

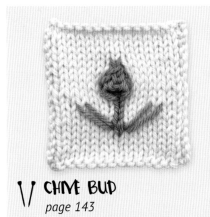

CHIVE BUD
page 143

SUNFLOWER OCTAGON
page 144

70s DAISY
page 145

MICHAELMAS DAISY
page 146

STAR FLOWER
page 147

POPPY
page 148

CORSAGE
page 149

CORD FLOWER
page 150

CORD LEAF
page 151

MAPLE LEAF
page 152

CLEMATIS
page 153

BOBBLE BOUQUET
page 154

BOBBLE BLOSSOM
page 155

FLOWER GARDEN
page 156

FLOWER BED
page 157

DAISY
page 158

SPRING LEAF
page 159

BLUE LEAF
page 160

FLORAL BLOCKS

MARIGOLD
page 161

FRAMED DAISY
page 162

DAISY MEADOW
page 163

RIBBED ROSE
page 164

BEGONIA LEAF
page 165

POMPOM FLOWER
page 166

FORGET-ME-NOT
page 167

WINDOW BOX
page 168

LILY
page 169

BUTTON FLOWER
page 170

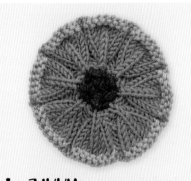

ZINNIA
page 170

60s FLOWER
page 171

HARVEST LEAF
page 172

AUTUMN LEAF
page 173

TEASELS
page 174

ANGELICA
page 175

FANTASY FLOWER
page 176

DREAM FLOWER
page 177

FLORAL BLOCKS

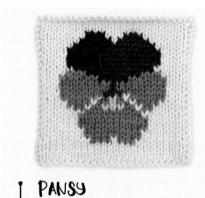

PANSY
page 178

FRITILLARY
page 179

THISTLE
page 180

TULIP
page 181

MOCK ORANGE
page 182

SNOWDROP
page 183

ROSE BUD
page 184

ROSE
page 185

FIG LEAF
page 186

OAK LEAF
page 187

ROWAN LEAF
page 188

LIME LEAF
page 189

TULIP TREE LEAF
page 190

CHEESE PLANT LEAF
page 191

ORIENTAL POPPY
page 192

IRIS
page 193

AMARYLLIS
page 194

GERBERA
page 195

PEONY

Yarn: DK wool in pink (A) and pale pink (B)

METHOD
SPECIFIC INSTRUCTION
Loop 1 = k1 but do not slip st off needle, bring yarn between needles to front, take it clockwise around left thumb and between needles to back, k same st on left needle again, this time slipping it off needle, on right needle slip 2nd st over st just made.

Outer petals (make 5)
Using A, cast on 6 sts.
ROWS 1 & 3 (RS): Knit.
ROW 2: [Kfb] 5 times, k1. (11 sts)
ROW 4: [Kfb, k2] 3 times, kfb, k1. (15 sts)
ROWS 5-12: Knit.
ROW 13: [K1, k2tog] 5 times. (10 sts)
ROW 14: Knit.
ROW 15: [K2tog] 5 times. (5 sts)
Leave sts on spare needle.

To join outer petals
NEXT ROW: Slip sts back onto working needle, k each set of 5 sts. (25 sts)
NEXT ROW: Knit.
NEXT ROW: K1, [k2tog, k2] 6 times. (19 sts)
NEXT ROW: Knit.
NEXT ROW: K1, [k2tog] 9 times. (10 sts)
Bind off.

Inner petals (make 5)
Using A, cast on 4 sts.
ROWS 1 & 3 (RS): Knit.
ROW 2: [Kfb] 3 times, k1. (7 sts)
ROW 4: K1, [kfb, k1] 3 times. (10 sts)
ROWS 5-10: Knit.
ROW 11: K1, [k2tog, k1] 3 times. (7 sts)
ROW 12: Knit.
ROW 13: [K2tog] 3 times, k1. (4 sts)
Leave sts on spare needle.

To join inner petals
NEXT ROW: Slip sts back onto working needle, k each set of 4 sts. (20 sts)
NEXT ROW: Knit.
NEXT ROW: [K1, k2tog, k1] 5 times. (15 sts)
NEXT ROW: Knit.
NEXT ROW: [K2tog] 7 times, k1. (8 sts)
Bind off.

Center
Using B, cast on 5 sts.
ROW 1 (RS): K1, [loop 1, k1] to end.
ROW 2: Kfb, k to last 2 sts, kfb, k1. (7 sts)
ROWS 3-4: As rows 1-2. (9 sts)
ROW 5: As row 1.
ROW 6: Knit.
ROW 7: Loop 1, [k1, loop 1] to end.
ROW 8: K2tog, k to last 2 sts, k2tog. (7 sts)
ROWS 9-10: As rows 7-8. (5 sts)
Bind off.

Finishing
Join each set of petals into a ring. Fasten off ends, using those at the base to secure one petal behind the next. Sew the inner petal ring inside the outer one. Gathering it slightly, stitch center in place.

2 CLEMATIS |

Yarn: DK wool in purple (A) and yellow (B)

METHOD
SPECIFIC INSTRUCTION

Loop 1 = see Peony (opposite).

Petals (make 6)

Using A, cast on 8 sts.
ROW 1 (RS): K2tog, k4, kfb, k1.
ROW 2: Knit.

Repeat rows 1–2 three times, then row 1 again.
Bind off knitwise.

Center

Using B, cast on 12 sts.
ROW 1 (RS): [Loop 1] 12 times.
Bind off, working k2tog across row.

Finishing

Leaving the center open, join petals to halfway along inner edges. Pinch a tuck at the inner corner of each petal and stitch. Join ends of center to make a ring and stitch it closed. Set center on petals.

3 SNOWDROP |

Yarn: Fine wool in white (A) and pale green (B)

METHOD
Petals (make 3)

Using A, cast on 4 sts.
ROW 1 (RS): Slip 1, k3.
ROW 2: Slip 1, p3.

ROW 3: Slip 1, m1, k2, m1, k1. (6 sts)
ROW 4: Purl.
ROW 5: Slip 1, m1, k4, m1, k1. (8 sts)
Beginning with a p row, work 5 rows st-st.
ROW 11: [K2tog] 4 times. (4 sts)
ROW 12: Purl.
Leave sts on spare needle.

Base

NEXT ROW (RS): Using A, k4 sts of each petal. (12 sts)
Beginning with a p row, work 3 rows st-st, then change to B and work 4 rows st-st.
Bind off, working k2tog across row.

Stem

Using B, cast on 18 sts. Bind off.

Finishing

Do not press. Join side seam of base. Insert stem in opening and secure.

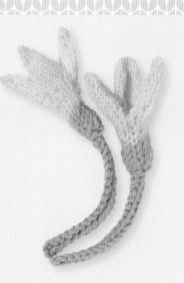

4 CHRYSANTHEMUM |

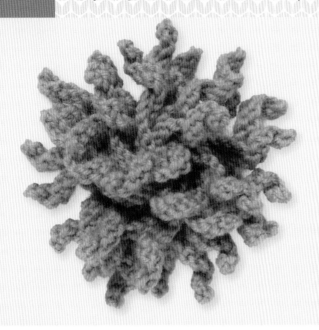

Yarn: Fine wool

METHOD

Cast on 20 sts, leaving an extra-long end for sewing up.
ROW 1 (RS): Bind off 16 sts, k to end. (4 sts)
ROW 2: K4, turn, cast on 16 sts by cable method. (20 sts)
Repeat rows 1–2, 29 times, then row 1 once again. Bind off.

Finishing
Beginning at cast-on edge and with RS to the outside, coil the strip of petals tightly. Use the first end of yarn to secure the base of the spiral as you go.

5 CAMPANULA \/

Yarn: Fine wool in blue (A) and green (B); DK wool in yellow (C)

Needles: 4 double-pointed needles

METHOD

Flower
Using A, cast on 7 sts. Slip sts onto 3 dpn.
ROUNDS 1-2: Knit.
ROUND 3: [Kfb] 6 times, k1. (13 sts)
ROUNDS 4-7: Knit.
ROUND 8: [Kfb] 12 times, k1. (25 sts)
ROUNDS 9-14: Knit.
ROUND 15: *K2tog, (k1, yo, k1, yo, k1, yo, k1) in next st, skpo; repeat from * 4 times. (45 sts)
ROUND 16: Knit.
Bind off.

Stem
Using B and 2 dpn, cast on 3 sts and knit a 1in (2.5cm) long cord. Do not bind off.

Base
Using 4 dpn, work in rounds:
ROUND 1: [Kfbf] 3 times. (9 sts)
ROUND 2: Knit.
ROUND 3: [K2, kfbf] 3 times. (15 sts)
ROUND 4: Knit.

Sepals
NEXT ROUND: [K3, turn, p3, turn, s2kpo, fasten off] 5 times.

Finishing
Sew base to flower and, using ends, catch each sepal to flower. Make three double knots on a length of C yarn. Coil and stitch them together, then attach inside bell of flower.

MORNING GLORY \|/

Yarn: Fine wool in white (A) and green (B)

Needles: 4 double-pointed needles

METHOD

Flower

Using A, cast on 5 sts. Slip sts onto 3 dpn.

ROUND 1: Knit.

ROUND 2: [Kfb] 5 times. (10 sts)

ROUNDS 3-6: Knit.

ROUND 7: [Kfb] 10 times. (20 sts)

ROUNDS 8-15: Knit.

ROUND 16: [K1, kfb] 10 times. (30 sts)

ROUNDS 17-20: Knit.

ROUND 21: [K2, kfb] 10 times. (40 sts)

ROUNDS 22-23: Knit.

ROUND 24: [K3, kfb] 10 times. (50 sts)

ROUNDS 25-26: Knit.

ROUND 27: [K4, kfb] 10 times. (60 sts)

ROUNDS 28-30: Knit.

BIND-OFF ROUND: Bind off 5 sts, *return st on right needle to left needle and cast on 2 sts**, bind off 8 sts***; repeat from * to *** 8 times, then from * to ** once again, bind off 2 sts. Fasten off.

Center

Using B, cast on 1 st.

ROW 1: (K1, yo, k1, yo, k1) in same st. (5 sts)

ROW 2: Purl.

ROW 3: Knit.

ROW 4: P5tog. (1 st)

Fasten off.

Stem

Using B and 2 dpn, cast on 4 sts and knit a 1¾in (4.5cm) long cord. Do not bind off.

Sepals

(K1, yo, k1, yo, k1, yo, k1) in each st of cord stem, turn. (28 sts)

Bind off.

Assembling flower

Sew center inside flower and join sepals to flower.

Leaf

Using B and pair of needles, cast on 3 sts.

ROW 1 (RS): Knit.

ROW 2 & ALL WS ROWS: Purl.

ROW 3: [Kfb] twice, k1. (5 sts)

ROW 5: K1, [kfb] twice, k2. (7 sts)

ROW 7: K2, [kfb] twice, k3. (9 sts)

ROW 9: K3, [kfb] twice, k4. (11 sts)

ROW 11: K4, [kfb] twice, k5. (13 sts)

ROW 13: K5, [kfb] twice, k6. (15 sts)

ROW 15: K6, [kfb] twice, k7. (17 sts)

ROW 17: K7, [kfb] twice, k8. (19 sts)

ROW 19: K8, [kfb] twice, k9. (21 sts)

ROW 21: K3, [slip 1 knitwise] twice, *lift 2nd st on left needle over first st and slip this st purlwise, lift 2nd slip st on right needle over purlwise slip st and return st to left needle**; repeat from * to ** once , k2, [kfb] twice, k3; [slip 1 knitwise] twice; repeat from * to ** twice, k3. (15 sts)

First side

NEXT ROW (WS): P7, turn.

NEXT ROW: K1, [slip 1 knitwise] twice; repeat from * to ** of row 21 twice, k2. (3 sts)

Bind off.

With WS facing, slip center st and work 2nd side as first side on remaining 7 sts.

Stem

Join B to center st and make 6-st chain. Fasten off.

Finishing

Join leaf stem to flower stem, weaving end into chain to strengthen leaf stem.

ANEMONE V

Yarn: DK wool in black (A), white (B), and purple (C)

METHOD

SPECIFIC ABBREVIATION

MB = make bobble: (k1, yo, k1, yo, k1) in next st, turn, p5, turn, k5, slip 2nd, 3rd, 4th, and 5th sts over first st.

Center

Using A, cast on 5 sts.

ROW 1 (RS): [K1, yo, k1] in each st. (15 sts)

ROW 2: Purl.

ROW 3: [Kfb, MB, kfb] 5 times. (25 sts)

ROW 4: [P1A, p3B, p1A] 5 times.

First petal

ROW 1 (RS): K1C, using B [kfb] twice, k1B, k1C, turn. (7 sts)

ROW 2: P2C, using B [pfb] twice, p1B, p2C. (9 sts)

ROW 3: Using C kfb, k2C, [k1B, k1C] twice, using C kfb, k1C. (11 sts)

Continue in C.

ROW 4: Pfb, p8, pfb, p1. (13 sts)

ROW 5: K1, [kfb, k2] 4 times. (17 sts)

Beginning with a p row, work 5 rows st-st.

ROW 11: [Ssk] twice, k9, k2tog twice. (13 sts)

ROWS 12 & 14: Purl.

ROW 13: K1, ssk, k7, k2tog, k1. (11 sts)

ROW 15: K1, ssk, k1, s2kpo, k1, k2tog, k1. (7 sts)

Working p2tog at each end of row and pulling yarn through last st for a smooth finish, bind off.

2nd, 3rd, 4th, and 5th petals

With RS facing, join yarn and work as first petal on each of 5 sts.

Finishing

Join row-ends of center and gather cast-on row. Work a few running sts around each bobble and pull up firmly.

8   BLUEBELLS   \\/

Yarn: Fine wool in blue (A) and green (B)

Needles: 2 double-pointed needles

METHOD

Flower

Using A, cast on 15 sts.

ROW 1 (RS): Knit.

ROW 2: Purl.

ROW 3: [K2tog, yo] 7 times, k1.
Beginning with a p row, work
3 rows st-st.

ROW 7: Join hem: [insert right
needle in next st, then in back
loop of corresponding st of cast-
on row and k2tog] 15 times.
Beginning with a p row, work
5 rows st-st.

ROW 13: [S2kpo] 5 times. (5 sts)

ROW 14: Purl.

Break off yarn and pass through
sts to gather them.

Stem

Using B and dpn, cast on
3 sts and knit a 2¼in (6cm)
long cord.

Finishing

Join seam of flower, setting in
stem at base. Using B, make
a small tassel and attach
inside flower.

9   TULIP |

Yarn: DK wool in deep pink (A), pale
pink (B), and green (C)

Needles: 2 double-pointed needles

METHOD

Flower

Using A, cast on 43 sts.

ROW 1 (RS): K1, [k2tog, k4, m1,
k1, m1, k4, ssk, k1] 3 times.

ROW 2 & ALL WS ROWS: Purl.
Repeat rows 1–2 five
times. Using B, repeat
rows 1–2 once, then
row 1 again.
Bind off purlwise.

Stem

Using C and dpn, cast on 3 sts
and knit a 4¾in (12cm) long
cord. Bind off.

Finishing

Pin out petal points and press.
Taking in half a st from each
edge, join side seam. On bound-
off edge, pinch a fold at point
formed by seam. Join two
diagonals of bound-off edge as
far as the increases of last row.
Pinch two remaining points and
join the two pairs of diagonals,
leaving a small opening in
center for stem. Insert and
attach stem.

10 FIELD POPPY

Yarn: DK wool in scarlet (A), green (B), and black (C)

METHOD

Petals (make 4)
Using A, cast on 7 sts.
ROW 1 (RS): Knit.
ROW 2: Kfb, k to last 2 sts, kfb, k1. (9 sts)
ROW 3: As row 2. (11 sts)
ROW 4: As row 2. (13 sts)
ROWS 5-8: Knit.
ROW 9: [Ssk] twice, k to last 4 sts, [k2tog] twice. (9 sts)
ROWS 10-12: Knit.
ROW 13: As row 9. (5 sts)
ROWS 14-16: Knit.
ROW 17: K1, sk2po, k1. (3 sts)
ROW 18: Knit.
Bind off.

Center
Using B, cast on 16 sts.
Bind off.

Finishing
Joining bound-off edges, sew petals together in pairs, then place one pair over the other in a cross formation and secure. Coil center into a tight spiral and sew base in the center of petals. Using C, work a ring of straight stitches around the center, then work French knots around these stitches. Maintain the petals in a cup shape with a small stitch behind pairs of petals.

11 CORNFLOWER

Yarn: DK wool in deep blue (A), mid-blue (B), and bright blue (C)

METHOD

Center
Using A, cast on 4 sts.
Without breaking off A, join B.
ROW 1 (RS): Using B, k3, turn, wyab slip 1 purlwise, k2.
ROWS 2-3: Using A, k all 4 sts. Repeat rows 1–3 nine times, then rows 1–2 once again. Bind off with A.

Petals
With RS facing and using C, pick up and k1 st from each stripe along long edge. (22 sts)
ROW 1: [Kfb] to end. (44 sts)
BIND-OFF ROW: *Cast on 3 sts by cable method, bind off 5 sts, transfer remaining st to left needle; repeat from *, ending bind off 4 sts.

Finishing
Join ends of center into a ring and gather the shorter edge tightly. Pin out petals and press.

ARUM LILY V

Yarn: DK wool in pale green (A), white (B), and yellow (C)

Needles: 4 double-pointed needles

METHOD

Stem

Using A and 2 dpn, cast on 3 sts and knit a 1in (2.5cm) long cord.

NEXT ROW (RS): [(K in front, p in back, k in front) of next st] 3 times. (9 sts)

Slip 3 sts onto each of 3 dpn and continue in B.

ROUND 1: Knit.

ROUND 2: [K1, (k in front, p in back, k in front) of next st, k1] 3 times. (15 sts)

ROUNDS 3-6: Knit.

Fill cavity with spare yarn.

ROUND 7: [K1, s2kpo, k1] 3 times. (9 sts)

Spathe

ROUNDS 8-11: Knit.

Turn and continue in rows but still using dpn.

ROW 1 & ALL WS ROWS: Purl.

ROW 2: K1, [m1, k1] 8 times. (17 sts)

ROW 4: K1, [m1, k1] 16 times. (33 sts)

Beginning with a p row, work 3 rows st-st.

ROW 8: [K2, k2tog] 4 times, k1, [ssk, k2] 4 times. (25 sts)

ROW 10: [K2, k2tog] 3 times, k1, [ssk, k2] 3 times. (19 sts)

ROW 12: [K2, k2tog] twice, k3, [ssk, k2] twice. (15 sts)

ROW 14: K2, k2tog, k2, s2kpo, k2, ssk, k2. (11 sts)

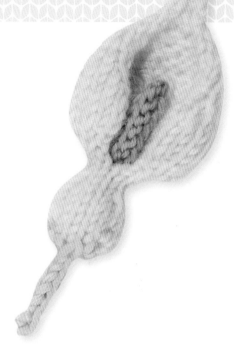

ROW 16: K2, k2tog, s2kpo, ssk, k2. (7 sts)

ROW 18: K2, s2kpo, k2. (5 sts)

ROW 20: K1, s2kpo, k1. (3 sts)

ROW 22: S2kpo. (1 st)

Fasten off.

Spike

Using C, cast on 10 sts.

ROW 1: Knit.

Slipping first st, bind off.

Finishing

Insert spike and secure.

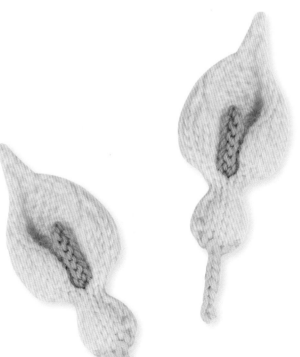

13 HOLLYHOCK |

Yarn: Fine cotton in deep pink (A) and pale pink (B)

Needles: 4 double-pointed needles

METHOD
Flower

Using A, cast on 6 sts. Slip 2 sts onto each of 3 dpn.

ROUNDS 1-2: Knit.

ROUND 3: [Kfb] 6 times. (12 sts)

ROUNDS 4-5: Knit.

ROUND 6: [Kfb] 12 times. (24 sts)

ROUNDS 7-10: Knit.

ROUND 11: [Kfb] 24 times. (48 sts)

ROUNDS 12-17: Knit.

ROUND 18: [Kfb] 48 times. (96 sts)

Change to B.

ROUNDS 19-26: Knit.

Bind off.

Finishing

Press lightly. Fold circle in half, pinch at center, and roll to form flower. Catch-stitch folds in place.

14 DOUBLE DAISY |

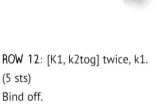

Yarn: DK cotton in white (A); fine cotton in white (B) and yellow (C)

METHOD
Lower petals

Using A, cast on 9 sts by cable method.

ROW 1 (RS): Purl.

ROW 2: Knit.

ROW 3: Bind off 5 sts purlwise, p2, turn, wyab slip 1 purlwise, wyif p2. (4 sts)

ROW 4: Knit.

ROW 5: Purl.

ROW 6: Kfb, slip these 2 sts onto left needle, cast on 4 sts by cable method, p all 9 sts.

Repeat rows 2–6 eight times, then rows 2–3 again. (10 petals) Bind off.

Upper petals

Using B, work as lower petals.

Center

Using C, cast on 5 sts by thumb method.

ROW 1 (RS): Kfb, k2, kfb, k1. (7 sts)

ROW 2 & ALL WS ROWS: Knit.

ROW 3: Kfb, k4, kfb, k1. (9 sts)

ROWS 4-10: Knit.

ROW 11: K1, k2tog, k3, k2tog, k1. (7 sts)

ROW 12: [K1, k2tog] twice, k1. (5 sts)

Bind off.

Finishing

Join ends of each strip of petals and lightly gather inner edges of rings, leaving a space in the center. Place upper ring of petals on lower one and stitch together, leaving petals free. Padding it slightly with spare yarn, set the center in place and sew on RS with small running stitches, 1 st in from the edge. Work a few stitches across the space at the back.

15 LEMON BLOSSOM \\/

Yarn: Fine cotton in white (A) and yellow (B)

METHOD

Petals

Using A, cast on 4 sts.
ROW 1: K4.
ROW 2: (K1, p1, k1, p1, k1) in first st, turn, k5, turn, p5, turn, k5, turn, [p2tog] twice, p1, wyab slip 2nd and 3rd sts on right needle over first st to complete petal; *p2, turn, slip 1, k2.
ROW 3: P4.
Repeat rows 1–3 three times, then rows 1–2 to *.
Bind off purlwise.

Finishing

With st-st on the outside, join cast-on and bound-off edges. Slightly gather center. Using B, stitch a ring of small loops around center, anchoring each with a backstitch on WS. Cut loops and trim them.

16 LAVENDER \\/

Yarn: Fine wool in mauve (A) and green (B)

Needles: 2 double-pointed needles

METHOD

NOTE: The flower head is worked from the top downward.

Flower head

Using A, cast on 3 sts.
ROW 1 (RS): [Kfb] twice, k1. (5 sts)
ROW 2: Purl.
ROW 3: [Kfb] 4 times, k1. (9 sts)
ROW 4: Purl.
ROW 5: K1, [cast on 3 sts by knitted method, bind off 3 sts, k1] 4 times.
Gently tug each tail to straighten it.
ROW 6: Purl.
Repeat rows 5–6 five times.
ROW 17: [Sk2po] 3 times. (3 sts)
Change to B.
ROW 18: Purl.
Using dpn, cast on 3 sts and knit a 4in (10cm) long cord. Bind off.

Finishing

Working on the RS using mattress stitch and taking in half a st from each side, join the row-ends of the flower head.

17 CARNATION

Yarn: DK wool in pink (A) and green (B)

Needles: 2 double-pointed needles

METHOD

Flower

Using A, cast on 7 sts.

*ROW 1 (RS): Purl.

ROW 2: Cast on 3 sts by cable method, bind off 3 sts, k to end.

Repeat from * 28 times.

Bind off purlwise.

Pin out petals and press.

With reverse st-st on the outside, roll remainder tightly and stitch closed.

Base

Using B, cast on 9 sts.

**ROW 1 (RS): Purl.

ROW 2: Cast on 1 st, bind off 1 st, k to end.

Repeat from ** 6 times.

Bind off purlwise.

With reverse st-st on the outside, join into a tube around the base of the petals.

Stem

Using B and dpn, cast on 3 sts and knit a 2¼in (6cm) long cord. Gather the base of the flower around the top of the stem.

18 CLOVE CARNATION

Yarn: Fine wool in pale pink (A), mid-pink (B), red (C), and green (D)

Needles: 4 double-pointed needles

Extras: Crochet hook

METHOD

Flower

Using A, cast on 51 sts.

ROW 1 (RS): K1, ssk, *k2, (k1, yo, k1) in next st, k2, s2kpo; repeat from * 4 times, k2, (k1, yo, k1) in next st, k2, k2tog, k1.

Change to B.

ROW 2: Purl.

Continuing in B, work row 1.

Change to A, work rows 2 and 1.

Change to B, work rows 2 and 1.

Change to C, work rows 2 and 1.

Using crochet hook, continue in C.

BIND-OFF ROW: [Ss in next st, 3ch, ss in same st] to end.

Fasten off.

Stem

Using D and 2 dpn, cast on 4 sts and knit a 1in (2.5cm) long cord.

Cup

Continue with 4 dpn.

ROUND 1: [Kfb] 4 times. (8 sts)

ROUNDS 2-6: Knit.

ROUND 7: [Kfbf] 8 times. (24 sts)

Bind off.

Finishing

Keeping points of chevron together, roll lower edge of flower tightly, curving outer row-ends down and stitching in place. Sew on cup, using yarn ends to fill it out.

Yarn: DK yarn in white (A); DK cotton in pale green (B) and yellow (C)

METHOD

NOTE: The petals are worked from the top downward.

Petals (make 5)

Using A, cast on 5 sts by thumb method.
ROW 1 (RS): Kfb, k2, kfb, k1. (7 sts)
ROW 2 & ALL WS ROWS: Purl.
ROW 3: K1, m1, k5, m1, k1. (9 sts)
ROW 5: K1, m1, k7, m1, k1. (11 sts)
ROWS 7, 9 & 11: Knit.
ROW 13: K1, ssk, k5, k2tog, k1. (9 sts)
ROW 15: K1, ssk, k3, k2tog, k1. (7 sts)
ROW 17: K1, ssk, k1, k2tog, k1. (5 sts)
Leave sts on spare needle.
When all petals have been completed, slip them onto one needle, WS facing, and bind off all 25 sts knitwise. Join both ends of the bind-off to make a ring.

Center

Using B, cast on 4 sts.
ROW 1: Knit.
ROW 2: P3, k1.
Repeat rows 1–2 nine times.
Change to C.

Stamens

ROW 1: Knit.
ROW 2: P3, k1.
ROW 3: Cast on 5 sts by knitted method, bind off 5 sts knitwise, k to end.
ROW 4: P3, k1.
Repeat rows 1–4, 14 times, or until, coiled, the strip fits the ring of petals.
Bind off.

Finishing

Starting at cast-on edge of center, coil the stamen strip with reverse st-st on the outside, stitch it through the base, and catch it down just below the stamens. Set the coil in the center of the petals, turn upside-down, and backstitch the bound-off edge of the petals around the base of the coil. Catch the last few rows of each petal to the next and catch these to the coil just below the stamens. Press the petals very lightly.

20 PETUNIA V

Yarn: Fine wool in purple (A) and pale mauve (B); DK wool in green (C)

Needles: 2 double-pointed needles

METHOD

NOTE: Slip stitches knitwise with yarn at back.

Flower

Using A, cast on 10 sts.

ROW 1 (RS): Kfb, k6, turn, slip 1, k to end. (11 sts)

ROW 2: Kfb, k5, turn, slip 1, k to end. (12 sts)

Change to B.

ROWS 3-4: Knit.

ROW 5: Kfb, k4, turn, slip 1, k to end. (13 sts)

ROW 6: Kfb, k3, turn, slip 1, k to end. (14 sts)

ROW 7: K2tog, k4, turn, slip 1, k to end. (13 sts)

ROW 8: K2tog, k5, turn, slip 1, k to end. (12 sts)

Change to A.

ROWS 9-10: Knit.

ROW 11: K2tog, k6, turn, slip 1, k to end. (11 sts)

ROW 12: K2tog, k7, turn, slip 1, k to end. (10 sts)

Repeat rows 1–12 four times. Bind off.

Sepals

Using C, cast on 6 sts.

*ROW 1 (RS): K4, turn, slip 1, k3.

ROW 2: K5, kfb. (7 sts)

ROW 3: Bind off 6 sts.

Transfer remaining st to left needle, cast on 5 sts by cable method, k all 6 sts; repeat from * 3 times, then rows 1–2 once. Bind off all sts.

With RS facing, along straight edge pick up and k3 sts from each sepal. (15 sts)

ROW 1: Knit.

ROW 2: [Sk2po] 5 times. (5 sts)

ROWS 3-5: Knit.

ROW 6: K2tog, k1, ssk. (3 sts)

Transfer these sts to a dpn and knit a 1¼in (3cm) long cord. Bind off.

Finishing

Pin out petal points and press lightly. With seam to outside, join cast-on and bound-off edges of flower. Weave in ends of A and B along fine stripes on outside. Join base of sepals and attach to base of flower. Using C, make a small knot in center of flower.

21 PRIMROSE |

Yarn: DK wool in pale yellow (A) and bright yellow (B)

METHOD
Petals
Using A, cast on 8 sts.
ROW 1 (WS): Purl.
ROW 2: Knit.
ROW 3: Bind off 4 sts knitwise, k to end. (4 sts)
ROW 4: K4, turn, cast on 4 sts. (8 sts)

Repeat rows 1–4 four times, ending with a row 3. (4 sts)
Bind off, leaving an extra-long yarn end.

Center
Using B, cast on 9 sts.
ROW 1 (WS): Purl.
ROW 2: K1, [yo, k1] 8 times. (17 sts)
Bind off knitwise.

Finishing
With reverse st-st on the outside, join petals into a ring and sew bound-off sts to first 4 cast-on sts. With st-st on the outside, coil center into a tight ring and secure cast-on base. Insert center in flower and stitch in place.

22 DAHLIA |

Yarn: DK wool

METHOD
Small petals
Cast on 8 sts.
ROW 1 (WS): Purl.
ROW 2: Knit.
ROW 3: Bind off 4 sts knitwise, k to end. (4 sts)
ROW 4: K4, turn, cast on 4 sts by cable method. (8 sts)
Repeat rows 1–4 seven times, ending with a row 3. (4 sts)
Do not bind off.

Medium petals
NEXT ROW: K4, turn, cast on 6 sts. (10 sts)
ROW 1 (WS): Purl.
ROW 2: Knit.
ROW 3: Bind off 6 sts, k to end. (4 sts)
ROW 4: K4, turn, cast on 6 sts. (10 sts)
Repeat rows 1–4 five times, ending with a row 3. (4 sts)
Do not bind off.

Large petals
NEXT ROW: K4, turn, cast on 8 sts. (12 sts)
ROWS 1 & 3: Purl.
ROWS 2 & 4: Knit.
ROW 5: Bind off 8 sts, k to end. (4 sts)
ROW 6: K4, turn, cast on 8 sts. (12 sts)
Repeat rows 1–6 five times, ending with a row 5. (4 sts)
Do not bind off.
Work 10 more medium petals, ending with a row 3. (4 sts)
Bind off.

Finishing
Beginning at the cast-on edge and with reverse st-st on the outside, coil petals, securing them as you go.

23 ROSE \/

Yarn: DK wool

METHOD

Small petals

Cast on 5 sts.
ROW 1: Kfb, k to end. (6 sts)
ROW 2: P to last 2 sts, pfb, p1.
(7 sts)
ROWS 3-4: Beginning with a
k row, work 2 rows st-st.
ROW 5: K1, k2tog, k to end.
(6 sts)
ROW 6: P to last 3 sts, p2tog, p1.
(5 sts)

Repeat rows 1–6 three times.
Do not break off yarn.

Medium petals

ROWS 1-4: Repeat rows 1–2
of small petals twice. (9 sts)
ROWS 5-8: Beginning with a
k row, work 4 rows st-st.
ROWS 9-12: Repeat rows 5–6
of small petals twice. (5 sts)
Repeat rows 1–12 twice.
Do not break off yarn.

Large petals

ROWS 1-6: Repeat rows 1–2
of small petals 3 times. (11 sts)
ROWS 7-12: Beginning with
a k row, work 6 rows st-st.
ROWS 13-18: Repeat rows 5–6
of small petals 3 times. (5 sts)
Repeat rows 1–18 twice.
NEXT ROW: K1, k2tog, k2. (4 sts)
NEXT ROW: P1, p2tog, p1. (3 sts)
NEXT ROW: K1, k2tog. (2 sts)
NEXT ROW: P2tog. (1 st)
Fasten off.

Finishing

Press. With reverse st-st on the
outside, roll up loosely from the
cast-on end. Lightly stitch the
straight edges together to form
a flat base, and then push up
center. Gather and stitch outside
edge at base. Turn back petals.

24 ROSEBUD \/

Yarn: DK wool in red (A) and green (B)
Needles: 2 double-pointed needles

METHOD

Petals

Using A, cast on 4 sts and work
as rows 1–10 of Rose's medium
petals (see above). (6 sts)
Repeat rows 1–10 twice. (10 sts)
Bind off.

Base

Using B, cast on 4 sts.
ROW 1 (RS): Purl.
ROW 2: Cast on 3 sts by knitted
method, bind off 3 sts, k3. (4 sts)
ROW 3: Purl.
ROW 4: Knit.
Repeat rows 1–4 four times.
Bind off.
With RS facing, pick up and
k12 sts along straight edge.

NEXT ROW: Purl.
NEXT ROW: [K2tog] to end. (6 sts)
Repeat last 2 rows once (3 sts).
Do not break off yarn. Slip sts
onto dpn and knit a 1½in (4cm)
long cord. Bind off.

Finishing

Press petals and coil them from
the bound-off end, with reverse
st-st on the outside. Gather

along straight edge and stitch.
Join the side seam of base
to make a cup and sew bud
inside it.

TEA ROSE

Yarn: DK wool in pink (A) and green (B)

Needles: 4 double-pointed needles

METHOD

First petal (make 2)

Using A, cast on 3 sts.

ROW 1 (RS): Knit.

ROW 2 & ALL WS ROWS: Purl.

ROW 3: K1, m1R, k1, m1L, k1. (5 sts)

ROW 5: K2, m1R, k1, m1L, k2. (7 sts)

ROW 7: K3, m1R, k1, m1L, k3. (9 sts)

ROW 9: K4, m1R, k1, m1L, k4. (11 sts)*

Beginning with a p row, work 3 rows st-st.

**ROW 13: Ssk, k7, k2tog. (9 sts)

ROW 15: Ssk, k5, k2tog. (7 sts)

ROW 17: Ssk, bind off 3 sts, k2tog,

slip 2nd st on right needle over first st.

Fasten off.

3rd and 4th petals

Work as first petal to *. Work 5 rows st-st,

then complete as first petal from **.

5th and 6th petals

Work as first petal to *. Work 7 rows st-st,

then complete as first petal from **.

Stem

Using B and 2 dpn, cast on 3 sts and knit a

1¼in (3cm) long cord.

Cup

Continue on cord stem using 4 dpn.

ROUND 1: [(K in front, p in back, k in front)

of next st] 3 times. (9 sts)

ROUNDS 2-5: Knit.

ROUND 6: [Sk2po] 3 times. (3 sts)

ROUND 7: [K1, yo, k1, yo, k1] in each st.

(15 sts)

First sepal

ROW 1 (RS): K5, turn.

ROWS 2 & 4: Purl.

ROW 3: Ssk, k1, k2tog. (3 sts)

ROW 5: Sk2po. (1 st)

Fasten off.

2nd and 3rd sepals

With RS facing, join yarn and work as first

sepal on each of 5 sts.

Finishing

Roll first petal tightly and secure. Arrange

other petals in a spiral around this, stitching

each in turn. Extend point of each sepal by

unfastening last st and working a few chain

sts. Stitch cup in place.

Yarn: Fine wool/cotton in red (A); DK wool in lime green (B) and yellow (C)

METHOD

Petals (make 6)

Using A, cast on 1 st.
ROW 1 (WS): Kfbf. (3 sts)
ROW 2: Knit.
ROW 3: Kfb, k1, kfb. (5 sts)
ROWS 4 & 6: Knit.
ROW 5: Kfb, k3, kfb. (7 sts)
ROW 7: Kfb, k5, kfb. (9 sts)
ROW 8: K2, p2, k1, p2, k2.
ROW 9: K4, p1, k4.
Repeat rows 8–9 four times.
ROW 18: K2, p5, k2.
ROW 19: K2, ssk, k1, k2tog, k2. (7 sts)
ROWS 20 & 22: K2, p3, k2.
ROW 21: Knit.
ROW 23: K2, sk2po, k2. (5 sts)
ROWS 24 & 26: K2, p1, k2.
ROW 25: Knit.
ROW 27: K1, sk2po, k1. (3 sts)
ROWS 28-29: Knit.
ROW 30: Sk2po. (1 st)
Fasten off (for tip of petal).

Center

Using B, cast on 5 sts.
ROW 1: K1, [yo, k1] 4 times. (9 sts)
ROW 2: Knit.
ROW 3: K1, [yo, k1] 8 times. (17 sts)
Bind off.

Finishing

Leaving a small hole in the center, join three petals. Do the same again, then stitch the 2nd set of petals on the first to form a star shape. Coil the center strip into a spiral, secure the base, and sew in the center of the star. Using C, make a ring of French knots around center.

27 FLORIBUNDA ROSE ┃

Yarn: DK wool

METHOD

Petals

Leaving an extra-long yarn end, cast on 10 sts.

ROW 1 (WS): K1, p5, k4.

ROW 2: K8, kfb, k1. (11 sts)

ROW 3: K1, p6, k4.

ROWS 4 & 6: Knit.

ROW 5: K1, p2tog, p4, k4. (10 sts)

ROW 7: Bind off 6 sts knitwise, k to end. (4 sts)

ROW 8: K4, turn, cast on 6 sts by cable method. (10 sts)

Repeat rows 1–8, 16 times, ending with a row 7. (4 sts)

Bind off.

Center

Leaving an extra-long end, cast on 4 sts. Work 38 rows garter stitch (k every row). Bind off, leaving an extra-long end.

Finishing

Beginning at the cast-on edge, coil center into a tight spiral, using the first end to secure it as you go. Beginning at the cast-on edge and with st-st on the outside, coil the petal strip around the center. Use the first yarn end to secure the petals and stretch the last few petals so that they are positioned between the petals of the previous round. End by catching down the bound-off edge.

28 RUDBECKIA ┃

Yarn: DK wool in orange (A) and yellow (B)

Extras: Domed button, 1in (2.5cm) diameter

METHOD

Center

Using A, cast on 7 sts.

ROW 1 (RS): Kfb, k4, kfb, k1. (9 sts)

ROW 2 & ALL WS ROWS: Purl.

ROW 3: Kfb, k6, kfb, k1. (11 sts)

Beginning with a p row, work 7 rows st-st.

ROW 11: K1, k2tog, k5, ssk, k1. (9 sts)

ROW 13: K1, k2tog, k3, ssk, k1. (7 sts)

Bind off purlwise.

Petals

Using B, make a slipknot on left needle. *Cast on 3 sts by cable method, bind off 3 sts knitwise, slip remaining st onto left needle; repeat from * 10 times (or number of times for required length). Fasten off.

Finishing

Stretch flower center over button and join opposite corners underneath. Take in fullness for a smooth finish. Pin petals around covered button and backstitch in place.

29 COMMON SUNFLOWER \\\

Yarn: DK wool in dark brown (A) and yellow (B)

METHOD
SPECIFIC ABBREVIATIONS
kpk = (k in front, p in front, k in back) of next st.

pkp = (p in front, k in back, p in front) of next st.

Center
Using A, cast on 5 sts.

ROW 1 (RS): Kpk, p1, k1, pkp, k1. (9 sts)

ROWS 2-4: K1, [p1, k1] to end.

ROW 5: Kpk, [p1, k1] 3 times, pkp, k1. (13 sts)

ROWS 6-14: As row 2.

ROW 15: K1, p3tog, [k1, p1] twice, k1, p3tog, k1. (9 sts)

ROWS 16-18: As row 2.

Bind off, working k1, p3tog, k1, p3tog, k1 across row.

Petals
With RS facing and using B, pick up and knit 1 st from edge, transfer this st to left needle, cast on 3 sts using knitted method, bind off 3 sts, *pick up and knit 1 st from edge, slip st already on right needle over it and then transfer new st to left needle, cast on 3 sts as before, bind off 3 sts; repeat from * around edge. Fasten off.

30 COCOA SUNDROP \\

Yarn: Worsted-weight wool in golden yellow (A) and maroon (B)

METHOD
Petals (make 8)
Using A, make 8 small concave petals (page 64).

Center disk
Using B and with RS facing, pick up and knit 3 sts from base of each petal. (24 sts)

ROW 1 (WS): [K1, ssk] 8 times. (16 sts)

ROW 2: Knit.

ROW 3: [Ssk] 8 times. (8 sts)

Break off yarn, leaving 8in (20cm) tail, and thread this through remaining 8 sts. Tighten to close center of disk, then sew side edges of disk together to form a circle.

Yarn: Worsted-weight cotton in yellow (A), green (B), and dark brown (C)

Extras: 33 round pale wooden beads, ¼in (6mm) diameter; brown sewing thread

METHOD

Petals (make 11)

Using A, cast on 13 sts.

*ROW 1: Knit.

Place marker at beginning of next row to indicate start of short-row shaping.

ROW 2: K4, turn.

ROW 3: K4 to end.

ROW 4: K8, turn.

ROW 5: K8 to end.

ROW 6: K11, turn.

ROW 7: K11 to end.

ROWS 8-9: As rows 4–5.

ROWS 10-11: As rows 2–3.

ROW 12: K13 to end.

Bind off 12 sts to complete first petal.

Slip remaining st onto left needle and cast on 12 sts using knitted method. (13 sts)**

Repeat from * to ** to make strip of 11 petals in total, binding off all 13 sts to complete the last petal. Either side of strip may be used as RS.

Center disk

Hold petal strip with unattached ends of petals hanging down. Using B and with RS facing, pick up and knit 7 sts from base of each petal along top edge of strip. (77 sts)

ROW 1 (WS): [K2tog, k13] 5 times, k2. (72 sts)

ROW 2: Purl.

ROW 3: Knit.

ROW 4: [P2tog, p7] 8 times. (64 sts)

Break off B and join C.

ROW 5 & ALL WS ROWS: Purl.

ROW 6: [Ssk, k6] 8 times. (56 sts)

ROW 8: [Ssk, k5] 8 times. (48 sts)

ROW 10: [Ssk, k4] 8 times. (40 sts)

ROW 12: [Ssk, k3] 8 times. (32 sts)

ROW 14: [Ssk, k2] 8 times. (24 sts)

ROW 16: [Ssk, k1] 8 times. (16 sts)

ROW 18: [Ssk] 8 times. (8 sts)

ROW 19: Purl.

Break off yarn, leaving 8in (20cm) tail, and thread this through remaining 8 sts. Tighten to close center of disk.

Finishing

Using tails of yarn, sew side edges of center disk together to form a circle. Using sewing thread, sew four beads along each yarn C ridge (formed by the decreasing) on center disk to create a swirling pattern. Sew one bead at center.

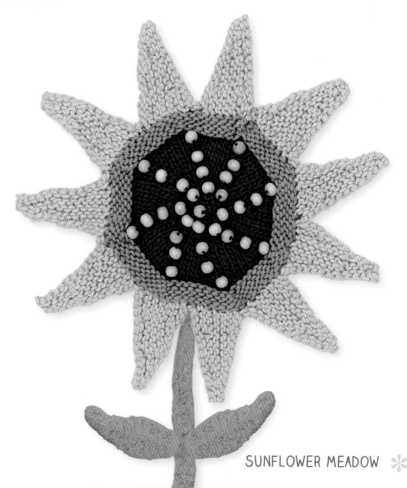

Yarn: Bulky-weight wool in golden yellow (A), brown (B), and orange (C)

Extras: 8 oblong dark wooden beads, ⅝in (15mm) long; orange sewing thread

METHOD

Petals (make 11)

Using A, cast on 7 sts.

*ROW 1: Knit.

Place marker at beginning of next row to indicate start of short-row shaping.

ROW 2: K3, turn.

ROW 3: K3 to end.

ROW 4: K5, turn.

ROW 5: K5 to end.

ROWS 6-7: As rows 4–5.

ROWS 8-9: As rows 2–3.

ROW 10: K7 to end.

Bind off 6 sts to complete first petal.

Slip remaining st onto left needle and cast on 6 sts using knitted method. (7 sts)**

Repeat from * to ** to make strip of 11 petals in total, binding off all 7 sts to complete the last petal. Either side of strip may be used as RS.

Center disk

Hold petal strip with unattached ends of petals hanging down. Using B and with RS facing, pick up and knit 6 sts from base of each petal along top edge of strip. (66 sts)

ROW 1 (WS): Knit.

ROW 2: Purl.

ROW 3: [K2tog, k31] twice. (64 sts)

Break off B and join C.

ROW 4: Knit.

ROW 5 & ALL WS ROWS: Purl.

ROW 6: [Ssk, k6] 8 times. (56 sts)

ROW 8: [Ssk, k5] 8 times. (48 sts)

ROW 10: [Ssk, k4] 8 times. (40 sts)

ROW 12: [Ssk, k3] 8 times. (32 sts)

ROW 14: [Ssk, k2] 8 times. (24 sts)

ROW 16: [Ssk, k1] 8 times. (16 sts)

ROW 18: [Ssk] 8 times. (8 sts)

ROW 19: Purl.

Break off yarn, leaving 8in (20cm) tail, and thread this through remaining 8 sts. Tighten to close center of disk.

Finishing

Using tails of yarn, sew side edges of center disk together to form a circle. Using sewing thread, sew beads evenly around center disk just inside circle of yarn B and in line with each yarn C ridge (formed by the decreasing).

33   CRÈME CARAMEL   \/

Yarn: Worsted-weight wool in caramel (A), magenta (B), and chartreuse (C)

METHOD

Petals (make 8)

Using A, make 8 small garter petals (page 65).

Center disk

Using B and with RS facing, pick up and knit 3 sts from base of each petal. (24 sts)

ROW 1 (WS): Knit.
Break off B and join C.
ROW 2: [Ssk, k1] 8 times. (16 sts)
ROW 3: Knit.
ROW 4: [Ssk] 8 times. (8 sts)

ROW 5: [Ssk] 4 times. (4 sts)
Break off yarn, leaving 8in (20cm) tail, and thread this through remaining 4 sts. Tighten to close center of disk, then sew side edges of disk together to form a circle.

34   GIANT SUNGOLD   \|/

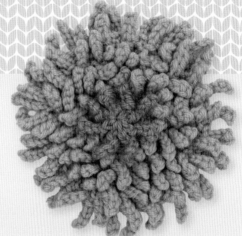
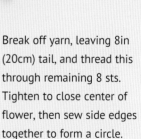
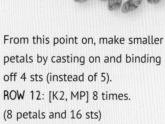

Yarn: Worsted-weight wool in golden yellow (A) and green (B)

METHOD

SPECIFIC ABBREVIATION

MP = make petal: cast 5 sts onto right needle using thumb method. Turn work and bind off same 5 sts. Leaving petal at RS of work, bring yarn to front between needles, slip remaining st from right needle onto left needle, and turn work so that WS is facing you.

Center disk and petals

Using A, cast on 48 sts.
ROW 1 (RS): Knit.

ROW 2: [K1, MP, k1] 24 times. (24 petals and 48 sts)
ROW 3: Knit.
ROW 4: [K2, MP] 24 times. (24 petals and 48 sts)
ROW 5: [K4, k2tog] 8 times. (40 sts)
ROW 6: [K1, MP, k1] 20 times. (20 petals and 40 sts)
ROW 7: [K3, k2tog] 8 times. (32 sts)
ROW 8: [K2, MP] 16 times. (16 petals and 32 sts)
ROW 9: [K2, k2tog] 8 times. (24 sts)
ROW 10: [K1, MP, k1] 12 times. (12 petals and 24 sts)
ROW 11: [K1, k2tog] 8 times. (16 sts)

From this point on, make smaller petals by casting on and binding off 4 sts (instead of 5).

ROW 12: [K2, MP] 8 times. (8 petals and 16 sts)
Break off A and join B.
ROW 13: [K2tog] 8 times. (8 sts)
ROW 14: [K1, MP] 8 times. (8 petals and 8 sts)
ROW 15: Knit.

Break off yarn, leaving 8in (20cm) tail, and thread this through remaining 8 sts. Tighten to close center of flower, then sew side edges together to form a circle.

35   PRAIRIE GOLD |

Yarn: DK or light worsted-weight wool in golden yellow (A) and orange (B)

METHOD

Petals (make 17)

Using A, cast on 10 sts.
Bind off 9 sts to complete first petal. (1 st remains)
*Slip remaining st onto left needle and cast on 9 sts using knitted method. (10 sts)
Bind off 9 sts. (1 st remains)**
Repeat from * to ** to make strip of 17 petals in total, then fasten off. Either side of strip may be used as RS.

Center disk

Hold petal strip with unattached ends of petals hanging down. Using B and with RS facing, pick up and knit 2 sts from base of each petal along top edge of strip. (34 sts)
ROW 1 (WS): Knit.
ROW 2: [K1, k2tog] 11 times, k1. (23 sts)
ROW 3: Knit.
ROW 4: [K2tog] 11 times, k1. (12 sts)
ROW 5: [K2tog] 6 times. (6 sts)
ROW 6: [K2tog] 3 times. (3 sts)

Break off yarn, leaving 8in (20cm) tail, and thread this through remaining 3 sts. Tighten to close center of disk, then sew side edges of disk together to form a circle. Using A, join ends of petal strip.

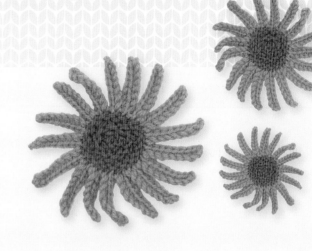

36   SWEET PETITE |

Yarn: Worsted-weight wool in pink (A) and maroon (B)

METHOD

Petals (make 9)

Using A, cast on 5 sts.
Bind off 4 sts to complete first petal. (1 st remains)
*Slip remaining st onto left needle and cast on 4 sts using knitted method. (5 sts)
Bind off 4 sts. (1 st remains)**

Repeat from * to ** to make strip of 9 petals in total, then fasten off. Either side of strip may be used as RS.

Center disk

Hold petal strip with unattached ends of petals hanging down. Using B and with RS facing, pick up and knit 2 sts from base of each petal along top edge of strip. (18 sts)

ROW 1 (WS): Knit.
ROW 2: [Ssk] 9 times. (9 sts)
ROW 3: [Ssk] 4 times, k1. (5 sts)
Break off yarn, leaving 8in (20cm) tail, and thread this through remaining 5 sts.

Tighten to close center of disk, then sew side edges of disk together to form a circle. Using A, join ends of petal strip.

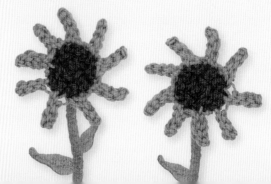

SWIZZLE STICKS

Yarn: Worsted-weight wool in pale gold (A), burnt orange (B), maroon (C), and pink (D)

METHOD

NOTE: Either side of petal layers may be used as RS.

Petals

TOP LAYER

Using A, cast on 5 sts.

Bind off 4 sts to complete first petal. (1 st remains)

*Slip remaining st onto left needle and cast on 4 sts using knitted method. (5 sts)

Bind off 4 sts. (1 st remains)**

Repeat from * to ** to make strip of 13 petals in total, then fasten off.

MIDDLE LAYER

Using B, cast on 8 sts.

Bind off 7 sts to complete first petal. (1 st remains)

*Slip remaining st onto left needle and cast on 7 sts using knitted method. (8 sts)

Bind off 7 sts. (1 st remains)**

Repeat from * to ** to make strip of 13 petals in total, then fasten off.

BOTTOM LAYER

Using C, cast on 11 sts.

Bind off 10 sts to complete first petal. (1 st remains)

*Slip remaining st onto left needle and cast on 10 sts using knitted method. (11 sts)

Bind off 10 sts. (1 st remains)**

Repeat from * to ** to make strip of 13 petals in total, then fasten off.

Center disk

Hold top layer petal strip with unattached ends of petals hanging down. Using D and with RS facing, pick up and knit 2 sts from base of each petal along top edge of strip. (26 sts)

ROW 1 (WS): [K11, ssk] twice. (24 sts)

ROW 2: [Ssk, k1] 8 times. (16 sts)

ROW 3: Knit.

ROW 4: [Ssk] 8 times. (8 sts)

ROW 5: Knit.

Break off yarn, leaving 8in (20cm) tail, and thread this through remaining 8 sts. Tighten to close center of disk, then sew side edges of disk together to form a circle.

Finishing

Pin middle petal layer behind top petal layer and sew to back around outer edge of center disk. Attach bottom petal layer in same way.

Felted variation with bottom petal layer omitted.

Yarn: Worsted-weight wool in variegated orange/rust (A), golden yellow (B), and orange (C)

Extras: Pompom maker, $1^3/_8$in (3.5cm) diameter; fabric glue (optional)

METHOD

Center disk

Using A, cast on 8 sts.

ROW 1 (RS): Knit.

ROWS 2, 4, 6 & 8: Knit.

ROW 3: [Kfb] 8 times. (16 sts)

ROW 5: [K1, kfb] 8 times. (24 sts)

ROW 7: [K2, kfb] 8 times. (32 sts)

ROW 9: [K3, kfb] 8 times. (40 sts)

ROWS 10-12: Knit.

ROW 13: [K3, k2tog] 8 times. (32 sts)

ROWS 14, 16 & 18: Knit.

ROW 15: [K2, k2tog] 8 times. (24 sts)

ROW 17: [K1, k2tog] 8 times. (16 sts)

ROW 19: [K2tog] 8 times. (8 sts)

ROW 20: Knit.

Break off yarn, leaving 8in (20cm) tail, and thread this through remaining 8 sts. Tighten to close center of disk.

Petals and pompoms

Using B and leaving 8in (20cm) cast-on tails, make 11 small concave petals (page 64). Using one strand each of B and C together, make 6 pompoms, leaving 8in (20cm) tails.

Finishing

Using tail of yarn, sew side edges of center disk together to form a hollow ball, leaving a small opening. Stuff with scraps of yarn A (or similar color), then close the opening. Using cast-on tails, sew base of petals evenly spaced around back of center disk. To attach a pompom, thread both tails separately through work at base of ring of petals. Tie the tails firmly with a flat knot and trim to about $^1/_4$in (6mm). Arrange the pompoms evenly around center disk. For extra security, paint the knots with fabric glue.

39 CATHERINE WHEEL

Yarn: Worsted-weight cotton in lemon yellow (A), red (B), and purple (C)

METHOD
SPECIFIC ABBREVIATION
MB = make bobble: (k1, p1, k1) in next st, turn, p3, turn, k3; lift 2nd and 3rd sts over first st and off right needle; push bobble through to RS of work and continue row.

Center disk and petals
Using A, cast on 48 sts.
ROW 1 (WS): [MB, k7] 6 times.

ROW 2: [K6, k2tog] 6 times. (42 sts)
ROW 3: [MB, p6] 6 times.
ROW 4: [K5, k2tog] 6 times. (36 sts)
ROW 5: [MB, p5] 6 times.
ROW 6: [K4, k2tog] 6 times. (30 sts)
ROW 7: [MB, p4] 6 times.
ROW 8: [K3, k2tog] 6 times. (24 sts)
ROW 9: [MB, p3] 6 times.
ROW 10: [K2, k2tog] 6 times. (18 sts)

Break off A and join B.
ROW 11: Purl.
ROW 12: [P1, p2tog] 6 times. (12 sts)
ROW 13: Purl.
ROW 14: [P2tog] 6 times. (6 sts)
ROW 15: Purl.
Break off yarn, leaving 8in (20cm) tail, and thread this through remaining 6 sts. Tighten to close center of disk.

Finishing
Using tails of yarn, sew side edges together to form a circle. Using double strand of C, work French knots around center disk.

40 POMPOM GEM

Yarn: Worsted-weight wool in red (A), golden yellow (B), and orange (C)

Extras: Pompom maker, 1³⁄₈in (3.5cm) diameter; fabric glue (optional)

METHOD
Petals (make 6)
Using A, make 6 medium garter petals (page 65).

Center disk
Using A and with RS facing, pick up and knit 5 sts from base of each petal. (30 sts)

ROW 1 (WS): [K2tog] 15 times. (15 sts)
ROW 2: Knit.
ROW 3: [K2tog] 7 times, k1. (8 sts)
Break off yarn, leaving 8in (20cm) tail, and thread this through remaining 8 sts. Tighten to close center of disk, then sew side edges of disk together to form a circle.

Pompom
Using one strand each of B and C together, make a pompom, leaving 8in (20cm) tails. Thread both tails separately through center disk, tie firmly with a flat knot, and trim to about ¹⁄₄in (6mm). For extra security, paint the knots with fabric glue.

41 BOBBLE BEAUTY \/

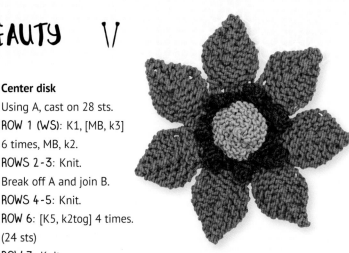

Yarn: Worsted-weight cotton in burgundy (A), green (B), and pink (C)

METHOD

SPECIFIC ABBREVIATION

MB = make bobble: (k1, yo, k1, yo, k1) in next st, turn, p5, turn, k5, turn, p5; lift 2nd, 3rd, 4th, and 5th sts over first st and off right needle; wyif slip remaining bobble st onto left needle; push bobble through to RS of work and turn to continue row.

Center disk

Using A, cast on 28 sts.
ROW 1 (WS): K1, [MB, k3] 6 times, MB, k2.
ROWS 2-3: Knit.
Break off A and join B.
ROWS 4-5: Knit.
ROW 6: [K5, k2tog] 4 times. (24 sts)
ROW 7: Knit.
ROW 8: [K1, k2tog] 8 times. (16 sts)
ROW 9: Knit.
ROW 10: [K2tog] 8 times. (8 sts)
ROW 11: Knit.

Break off yarn, leaving 8in (20cm) tail, and thread this through remaining 8 sts. Tighten to close center of disk.

Petals (make 7)

Using C and leaving 8in (20cm) cast-on tails, make 7 medium garter petals (page 65).

Finishing

Using tails of yarn, join side edges of center disk together to form a circle. If necessary, use tip of yarn needle to pull bobbles to RS of disk. Sew base of petals evenly spaced around back of center disk.

42 CHERRY TWIZZLER |

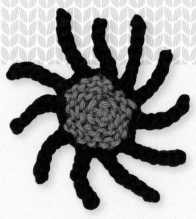

Yarn: Worsted-weight wool in red (A) and chartreuse (B)

METHOD

Petals (make 11)

Using A, cast on 8 sts.
Bind off 7 sts to complete first petal. (1 st remains)
*Slip remaining st onto left needle and cast on 7 sts using knitted method. (8 sts)
Bind off 7 sts. (1 st remains)**

Repeat from * to ** to make strip of 11 petals in total, then fasten off. Either side of strip may be used as RS.

Center disk

Hold petal strip with unattached ends of petals hanging down. Using B and with RS facing, pick up and knit 2 sts from base of each petal along top edge of strip. (22 sts)

ROW 1 (WS): [K3, ssk] 4 times, k2. (18 sts)
ROW 2: Knit.
ROW 3: [Ssk] 9 times. (9 sts)
ROW 4: [Ssk] 4 times, k1. (5 sts)
Break off yarn, leaving 8in (20cm) tail, and thread this through remaining 5 sts. Tighten to close center of disk, then sew side edges of disk together to form a circle. Using A, join ends of petal strip.

Yarn: Worsted-weight wool in burnt orange (A), dark gray (B), pink (C), and purple (D)

METHOD
SPECIFIC ABBREVIATION

MB = make bobble: (k1, yo, k1, yo, k1) in next st, turn, p5, turn, k5, turn, p5; lift 2nd, 3rd, 4th, and 5th sts over first st and off right needle; wyif slip remaining bobble st onto left needle; push bobble through to RS of work and turn to continue row.

Center disk

Using A, cast on 40 sts.
ROW 1 (WS): [K3, k2tog] 8 times. (32 sts)
ROWS 2-3: Knit.
Break off A and join B.
ROW 4: [K2, k2tog] 8 times. (24 sts)
ROW 5: K1, [MB, k3] 5 times, MB, k2.
ROW 6: Knit.
ROW 7: [K3, MB] 6 times.
Break off B and join C.
ROWS 8-9: Knit.
ROW 10: [K1, k2tog] 8 times. (16 sts)
ROW 11: Knit.
ROW 12: [K2tog] 8 times. (8 sts)
ROW 13: Knit.
Break off yarn, leaving 8in (20cm) tail, and thread this through remaining 8 sts. Tighten to close center of disk.

Petals (make 11)

Using D, make 11 large concave petals (page 64).
Using D and with RS facing, pick up and knit 7 sts from base of each petal. (77 sts)

ROW 1 (WS): Knit.
TO BIND OFF: [K2tog] twice (2 sts on right needle), lift first st made over 2nd st and off right needle, *k2tog (2 sts on right needle), lift previous st over new st and off right needle.** Repeat from * to ** to end.
Break off D, leaving 10in (25cm) tail, and pass through remaining stitch. Use tail to sew row-ends together to form a circle.

Finishing

Use tails of yarn, sew side edges of center disk together to form a circle. Sew circle of petals to back of disk.

WOOLLY MAMMOTH V

Yarn: Worsted-weight wool in green (A), golden yellow (B), chartreuse (C), and orange (D)

Extras: Batting (optional)

METHOD

Center disk

Begin with stalk at back as follows:

Using A and leaving 8in (20cm) tail, cast on 9 sts.

ROW 1 (RS): Knit.

ROW 2 & ALL WS ROWS: Purl.

ROW 3: Knit.

ROW 5: [K3, m1] 3 times. (12 sts)

ROW 7: [K4, m1] 3 times. (15 sts)

ROW 9: [K5, m1] 3 times. (18 sts)

ROW 11: [K6, m1] 3 times. (21 sts)

ROW 13: [K7, m1] 3 times. (24 sts)

ROW 15: [K4, m1] 6 times. (30 sts)

ROW 17: [K5, m1] 6 times. (36 sts)

ROW 19: [K6, m1] 6 times. (42 sts)

ROW 21: [K7, m1] 6 times. (48 sts)

ROW 23: [K6, m1] 8 times. (56 sts)

ROW 25: [K7, m1] 8 times. (64 sts)

ROW 26: Purl.

Break off A and join B.

ROWS 27-28: Knit.

ROW 29: Purl.

Repeat rows 28–29 three times.

ROWS 36-38: Knit.

ROW 39: [K6, k2tog] 8 times. (56 sts)

ROWS 40, 42 & 44: Knit.

ROW 41: [K5, k2tog] 8 times. (48 sts)

ROW 43: [K4, k2tog] 8 times. (40 sts)

ROW 45: [K3, k2tog] 8 times. (32 sts)

ROW 46: Knit.

Break off B and join C.

ROW 47: [K2, k2tog] 8 times. (24 sts)

ROWS 48 & 50: Purl.

ROW 49: [K1, k2tog] 8 times. (16 sts)

ROW 51: [K2tog] 8 times. (8 sts)

ROW 52: Purl.

Break off yarn, leaving 8in (20cm) tail, and thread this through remaining 8 sts. Tighten to close center front of disk.

Front with petals open

Back

Front with petals
curled around

Petals and leaves

Leaving 8in (20cm) cast-on tails, make
9 small veined petals using D (page 65)
and 2 thin veined leaves using A (page 67).

Finishing

Using tails of yarn, join seam of stalk at back
of center disk to form a hollow cone, leaving
a small opening. Stuff with scraps of yarn (or
use batting since this is quite a large flower),
then close the opening. Sew base of petals
evenly spaced around center disk, matching
cast-on edges of petals to first row in yarn B
on disk. The petals may be allowed to flop
outward, or stitched in place down center
so that they curl around disk. Sew a leaf on
opposite sides of stem, attaching at base
and with a few stitches halfway up center
of each leaf.

45 GOLD STRIPE \\/

Yarn: Worsted-weight wool in brown tweed (A),
golden yellow (B), and burnt orange (C)

METHOD

Center disk

Using A, cast on 42 sts.

ROW 1 (WS): Knit.

ROW 2: K1, [k3, k2tog] 8 times, k1. (34 sts)

ROW 3: K1, [(k1, p1, k1) in next st, p3tog]
8 times, k1.

ROW 4: Purl.

Without breaking off A, join B.

ROW 5: Using B, k1, [p3tog, (k1, p1, k1) in
next st] 8 times, k1.

ROW 6: Using B, purl.

Break off B and continue in A.

ROWS 7-8: As rows 3–4 (so ending with
a RS row).

Break off yarn and slip all sts onto other
needle, so next row will also be a RS row.

Join C.

ROW 9 (RS): Ssk, k to last 2 sts, k2tog.
(32 sts)

ROW 10: Knit.

ROW 11: [Ssk] 16 times. (16 sts)

ROW 12: Knit.

ROW 13: [Ssk] 8 times. (8 sts)

ROW 14: Knit.

Break off yarn, leaving 8in (20cm) tail,
and thread this through remaining 8 sts.
Tighten to close center of disk.

Petals (make 8)

Using C and leaving 8in (20cm) cast-on
tails, make 8 large garter petals (page 65).

Finishing

Using tails of yarn, sew side edges of disk
together to form a circle. Steam disk to
make it lie flat, without losing texture of
stitches. Sew base of petals around back
of row 4 of center disk, spacing them
evenly at angles created by the decreasing.

46 TEDDY BEAR \V/

Yarn: DK or light worsted-weight cotton in green (A) and chartreuse (C); fringed yarn in lemon yellow (B)

METHOD

Begin at center back as follows:

Using A, cast on 8 sts.

ROW 1 (RS): Knit.

ROWS 2, 4, 6 & 8: Purl.

ROW 3: [Kfb] 8 times. (16 sts)

ROW 5: [K1, kfb] 8 times. (24 sts)

ROW 7: [K2, kfb] 8 times. (32 sts)

ROW 9: [K3, kfb] 8 times. (40 sts)

ROW 10: Purl.

Break off A and join B.

ROWS 11 - 14: Knit.

ROW 15: [K3, k2tog] 8 times. (32 sts)

ROW 16: [K2, k2tog] 8 times. (24 sts)

ROW 17: [K1, k2tog] 8 times. (16 sts)

Break off B and join C.

ROW 18: Purl.

ROW 19: [K2tog] 8 times. (8 sts)

ROW 20: Purl.

Break off yarn, leaving 8in (20cm) tail, and thread this through remaining 8 sts. Tighten to close center of flower.

Finishing

Using tails of yarn, sew side edges together to form a hollow ball, stuffing lightly with scraps of matching yarn if desired. To shape flower center, stitch firmly through center point, joining front and back closely together; then stitch firmly all around center disk of yarn C through both layers of knitting.

47 TOFFEE TWIST |

Yarn: DK or light worsted-weight wool in burnt orange (A) and purple (B)

METHOD

Petals (make 13)

Using A, cast on 5 sts.

Bind off 4 sts to complete first petal. (1 st remains)

*Slip remaining st onto left needle and cast on 4 sts using knitted method. (5 sts)

Bind off 4 sts. (1 st remains)**

Repeat from * to ** to make strip of 13 petals in total, then fasten off. Either side of strip may be used as RS.

Center disk

Hold petal strip with unattached ends of petals hanging down. Using B and with RS facing, pick up and knit 2 sts from base of each petal along top edge of strip. (26 sts)

ROW 1 (WS): [K2tog] 13 times. (13 sts)

ROW 2: [K2tog] 6 times, k1. (7 sts)

ROW 3: [K2tog] 3 times, k1. (4 sts)

Break off yarn, leaving 8in (20cm) tail, and thread this through remaining 4 sts. Tighten to close center of disk, then sew side edges of disk together to form a circle. Using A, join ends of petal strip.

Yarn: Worsted-weight wool in green (A), taupe (B), pale gold (C), and orange (D)

METHOD

Center disk

Begin at center back as follows:

Using A, cast on 8 sts.

ROW 1 (WS): Knit.

ROW 2: [Kfb] 8 times. (16 sts)

ROW 3: Knit.

ROW 4: [K1, kfb] 8 times. (24 sts)

ROW 5: Knit.

ROW 6: [K2, kfb] 8 times. (32 sts)

ROW 7: Knit.

Break off A and join B.

ROWS 8-9: Knit.

Without breaking off B, join C.

ROW 10: Using C, [k3tog, (k1, p1, k1) in next st] 8 times.

ROW 11: Using C, knit.

Break off C and continue in B.

ROW 12: [(K1, p1, k1) in next st, k3tog] 8 times.

ROW 13: Knit.

Break off B and join D.

ROWS 14-15: Knit.

ROW 16: [K2, k2tog] 8 times. (24 sts)

ROW 17: Knit.

ROW 18: [K1, k2tog] 8 times. (16 sts)

ROW 19: Knit.

ROW 20: [K2tog] 8 times. (8 sts)

ROW 21: Knit.

Break off yarn, leaving 8in (20cm) tail, and thread this through remaining 8 sts. Tighten to close center of disk.

Petals (make 9)

Using C, make 9 medium concave petals (page 64).

Using C and with RS facing, pick up and knit 7 sts from base of each petal. (63 sts)

ROW 1 (WS): Knit.

ROW 2: [K2tog] 31 times, k1. (32 sts)

Bind off, leaving 10in (25cm) tail, and use this tail to sew row-ends together to form a circle of petals.

Finishing

Using tails of yarn, sew side edges of center disk together to form a hollow ball, leaving a small opening. Stuff with scraps of matching yarn, then close the opening. Sew circle of petals evenly spaced around back of center disk, joining to last row of disk worked in yarn A. Using double strand of D, work a 1in (2.5cm) long lazy daisy stitch at base of each petal.

49 JOKER \|/

Yarn: Worsted-weight wool in orange (A), maroon (B), and variegated orange/rust (C)

METHOD

Center disk

Using A, cast on 8 sts.
ROW 1 (RS): Knit.
ROWS 2, 4, 6, 8 & 10: Knit.
ROW 3: [Kfb] 8 times. (16 sts)
ROW 5: [K1, kfb] 8 times. (24 sts)
ROW 7: Purl.
ROW 9: [K1, k2tog] 8 times. (16 sts)
ROW 11: [K2tog] 8 times. (8 sts)
ROW 12: Knit.
Break off yarn, leaving 8in (20cm) tail, and thread this through remaining 8 sts. Tighten to close center of disk.

Long petals (make 9)

Using B and leaving 8in (20cm) cast-on tails, make 9 long veined petals, repeating rows 4–5 seven rather than five times (page 65).

Frilled petals (make 18)

Using C, cast on 5 sts.
Bind off 4 sts to complete first frilled petal. (1 st remains)
*Slip remaining st onto left needle and cast on 4 sts using knitted method. (5 sts) Bind off 4 sts. (1 st remains)**
Repeat from * to ** to make strip of 18 frilled petals in total.
Break off yarn, leaving 12in (30cm) tail, and pass through remaining stitch.

50 FIRECRACKER |

Yarn: DK or light worsted-weight wool in red (A) and chartreuse (B)

METHOD

Petals (make 24)

Using A, cast on 15 sts.
Bind off 14 sts to complete first petal. (1 st remains)
*Slip remaining st onto left needle and cast on 14 sts using knitted method. (15 sts)
Bind off 14 sts. (1 st remains)*
Repeat from * to * to make strip of 24 petals in total.
Break off yarn, leaving 10in (25cm) tail, and pass through remaining stitch. Either side of strip may be used as RS.

Center disk

Using B, cast on 3 sts.
ROW 1: Knit.
ROW 2: [Kfb] 3 times. (6 sts)
ROW 3: Knit.
ROW 4: [Kfb] 6 times. (12 sts)
ROWS 5-7: Knit.
ROW 8: [K2tog] 6 times. (6 sts)
ROW 9: Knit.
ROW 10: [K2tog] 3 times. (3 sts)
ROW 11: Knit.
Break off yarn, leaving 8in (20cm) tail, and thread this through remaining 3 sts. Tighten to close center of disk.

Finishing

Using tail of yarn, sew side edges of center disk together to form a hollow ball. If desired, stuff loosely with scraps of yarn B (or similar color) as you sew the side seam. Bring cast-on and bound-off edges together to

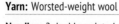
Finishing

Using tail of yarn, sew side edges of center disk together to form a hollow ball, leaving a small opening. Stuff with scraps of yarn A (or similar color), then close the opening. Using cast-on tails, sew base of long petals evenly spaced around back of center disk. Using bind-off tail, sew strip of frilled petals around disk, in front of long petals.

flatten the ball and stitch tightly through center. Run yarn tail of petal strip through edge of strip where petals are joined. Use tail to gather up edge to a length that will form a double coil to fit behind center disk. Secure the double coil with a few stitches through both layers, then sew center disk in place.

Yarn: Worsted-weight wool

Needles: 2 double-pointed needles, two sizes smaller than usual for the yarn

METHOD

NOTE: For a smaller cone to fit back of smaller flower, bind off after row 11, 15, or 19, or use finer yarn and correspondingly smaller needles. For a larger cone, see instructions below or use heavier yarn and correspondingly larger needles.

Stem

Using dpn, cast on 4, 5, or 6 sts, depending on how thick you want the stem to be, and knit a cord to length required. Bind off. To make a stem using ordinary single-pointed needles, cast on enough sts for length of stem required. For a flat stem, knit 2 rows and then bind off. For a round stem, knit number of rows required for desired width of stem, then bind off; fold stem in half lengthwise and sew long edges together.

Cone

Using single-pointed needles, cast on 6 sts.
ROWS 1-3: Knit.
ROW 4: [Kfb] 6 times. (12 sts)
ROW 5: Knit.
ROW 6: K1, [m1, k2] 5 times, m1, k1. (18 sts)
ROWS 7-9: Knit.
ROW 10: K1, [m1, k3] 5 times, m1, k2. (24 sts)

ROWS 11-13: Knit.
ROW 14: K1, [m1, k4] 5 times, m1, k3. (30 sts)
ROWS 15-17: Knit.
ROW 18: K1, [m1, k5] 5 times, m1, k4. (36 sts)
ROWS 19-21: Knit.
ROW 22: K1, [m1, k6] 5 times, m1, k5. (42 sts)
ROWS 23-24: Knit.
For larger cone to fit back of larger flower, continue in this way, working an increase row on 2nd and every following 4th row. Bind off, leaving tail of yarn for sewing to flower.

Finishing

Sew seam of cone, then sew top of stem to back of cone. Stuff cone with scraps of matching yarn and sew to back of flower.

Yarn: Worsted-weight wool

METHOD

NOTE: Do not press the petals because this will flatten the concave shape.

Small

Cast on 3 sts.
ROW 1 (RS): Knit.
ROW 2: Knit.
ROW 3: Kfb, p1, kfb. (5 sts)
ROW 4: P2, k1, p2.
ROW 5: K2, (k1, yo, k1, yo, k1) in next st, k2. (9 sts)
ROWS 6, 8 & 10: P2, k5, p2.
ROWS 7 & 9: K2, p5, k2.

ROW 11: Ssk, k1, p3, k1, k2tog. (7 sts)
ROW 12: P2, k3, p2.
ROW 13: K2, p3tog, k2. (5 sts)
ROWS 14 & 16: Purl.
ROW 15: Ssk, k1, k2tog. (3 sts)
ROW 17: Cdd. (1 st)
Fasten off.

Medium

Cast on 7 sts.
ROW 1 (RS): K2, p3, k2.
ROW 2: P2, k3, p2.
ROWS 3-4: As rows 1–2.
ROW 5: K2, m1, p3, m1, k2. (9 sts)
ROWS 6, 8 & 10: P2, k5, p2.

ROWS 7 & 9: K2, p5, k2.
ROW 11: K1, ssk, p3, k2tog, k1. (7 sts)
ROW 12: P2, k3, p2.
ROW 13: K1, ssk, p1, k2tog, k1. (5 sts)
ROWS 14 & 16: Purl.
ROW 15: Knit.
ROW 17: Ssk, k1, k2tog. (3 sts)
ROW 18: P3tog. (1 st)
Fasten off.

Large

Cast on 7 sts.
ROWS 1-5: As for medium petal.
ROWS 6, 8, 10 & 12: P2, k5, p2.
ROWS 7, 9 & 11: K2, p5, k2.
ROW 13: K1, ssk, p3, k2tog, k1. (7 sts)
ROW 14: P2, k3, p2.
ROW 15: K2, p3, k2.
ROWS 16-17: As rows 14–15.
ROW 18: As row 14.
ROW 19: K2, p3tog, k2. (5 sts)
ROW 20: P2, k1, p2.
ROW 21: K2, p1, k2.
ROWS 22 & 24: Purl.
ROW 23: K1, cdd, k1. (3 sts)
ROW 25: Cdd. (1 st)
Fasten off.

Small

Medium

Large

Cocoa Sundrop (page 48) is made using small concave petals.

53 GARTER PETALS |

Yarn: Worsted-weight wool

METHOD

NOTE: Either side of petals may be used as RS.

Small
Cast on 3 sts.
ROWS 1-2: Knit.
ROW 3: Kfb, k1, kfb. (5 sts)
ROWS 4-6: Knit.
ROW 7: K1, cdd, k1. (3 sts)
ROWS 8-10: Knit.
ROW 11: Cdd. (1 st)
Fasten off.

Medium
Cast on 5 sts.
ROW 1: Knit.
ROW 2 AND ALL EVEN ROWS: Knit.
ROW 3: Kfb, k3, kfb. (7 sts)
ROW 5: Kfb, k5, kfb. (9 sts)
ROW 7: Knit.
ROW 9: K3, cdd, k3. (7 sts)
ROW 11: K2, cdd, k2. (5 sts)
ROW 13: K1, cdd, k1. (3 sts)
ROW 15: Cdd. (1 st)
Fasten off.

Large
Cast on 3 sts.
ROWS 1-2: Knit.
ROW 3: Kfb, k1, kfb. (5 sts)
ROW 4: Kfb, k3, kfb. (7 sts)
ROWS 5-12: Knit.
ROW 13: K2, cdd, k2. (5 sts)
ROW 14: Knit.
ROW 15: K1, cdd, k1. (3 sts)
ROW 16: Knit.
ROW 17: Cdd. (1 st)
Fasten off.

Small

Medium

Large

54 VEINED PETALS \/

Yarn: Worsted-weight wool

METHOD

Small
Cast on 3 sts.
ROWS 1-5: As for small concave petal (page 64).
ROW 6 (RS): P2, k2, p1, k2, p2.
ROW 7: K2, p2, k1, p2, k2.
ROWS 8-9: As rows 6-7.
ROW 10: As row 6.
ROW 11: Ssk, p2, k1, p2, k2tog. (7 sts)
ROW 12: P1, ssk, p1, k2tog, p1. (5 sts)
ROW 13: K1, cdd, k1. (3 sts)
ROW 14: Purl.
ROW 15: Cdd. (1 st)
Fasten off.

Long
Cast on 3 sts.
ROW 1 (RS): Knit.
ROW 2: Kfb, p1, kfb. (5 sts)
ROW 3: Knit.
ROW 4: K2, p1, k2.
ROW 5: Knit.
Repeat rows 4-5 five times.
(15 rows in total; length of petal may be varied here)
ROW 16: Ssk, k1, k2tog. (3 sts)
ROW 17: K1, p1, k1.
ROW 18: Cdd. (1 st)
Fasten off.

Small

Long

Yarn: DK wool

Needles: 2 double-pointed needles

METHOD

Small

Using dpn, cast on 3 sts and knit a 1¼in (3cm) long cord. Continue on these sts in rows in the usual way:

ROW 1 (RS): K1, yo, k1, yo, k1. (5 sts)
ROW 2 & ALL WS ROWS: Knit.
ROW 3: K2, yo, k1, yo, k2. (7 sts)
ROW 5: K3, yo, k1 yo, k3. (9 sts)
ROW 7: K4, yo, k1, yo, k4. (11 sts)
ROW 9: K5, yo, k1, yo, k5. (13 sts)
ROW 11: Ssk, k9, k2tog. (11 sts)
ROW 13: Ssk, k7, k2tog. (9 sts)
ROW 15: Ssk, k5, k2tog. (7 sts)
ROW 17: Ssk, k3, k2tog. (5 sts)
ROW 19: Ssk, k1, k2tog. (3 sts)
ROW 21: Sk2po. (1 st)
Fasten off.

Large

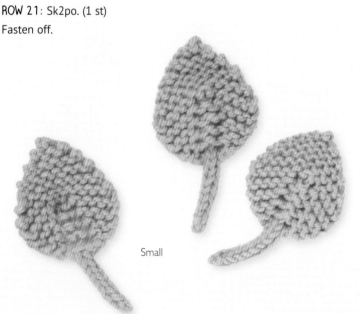

Small

Large

Using dpn, cast on 3 sts and knit a 1¾in (4.5cm) long cord. Continue on these sts in rows in the usual way:

ROW 1 (RS): K1, yo, k1, yo, k1. (5 sts)
ROW 2: K2, p1, k2.
ROW 3: K2, yo, k1, yo, k2. (7 sts)
ROW 4 & ALL WS ROWS: Knit, working center st as p1.
ROW 5: K3, yo, k1, yo, k3. (9 sts)
ROW 7: K4, yo, k1, yo, k4. (11 sts)
ROW 9: K5, yo, k1, yo, k5. (13 sts)
ROW 11: K6, yo, k1, yo, k6. (15 sts)
ROW 13: K7, yo, k1, yo, k7. (17 sts)
ROW 15: Knit.
ROW 16 & ALL FOLL WS ROWS: Knit.
ROW 17: Ssk, k13, k2tog. (15 sts)
ROW 19: Ssk, k11, k2tog. (13 sts)
ROW 21: Ssk, k9, k2tog. (11 sts)
ROW 23: Ssk, k7, k2tog. (9 sts)
ROW 25: Ssk, k5, k2tog. (7 sts)
ROW 27: Ssk, k3, k2tog. (5 sts)
ROW 29: Ssk, k1, k2tog. (3 sts)
ROW 31: Sk2po. (1 st)
Fasten off.

VEINED LEAVES I

Yarn: Worsted-weight wool in green

METHOD

Small

Cast on 1 st.

ROW 1 (RS): (K in front, p in back, k in front) of same st. (3 sts)

ROW 2: K1, p1, k1.

ROW 3: Kfb, k1, kfb. (5 sts)

ROW 4: K2, p1, k2.

ROW 5: Knit.

ROWS 6-7: As rows 4–5.

ROW 8: As row 4.

ROW 9: K1, cdd, k1. (3 sts)

ROW 10: K1, p1, k1.

ROW 11: Cdd. (1 st)

Fasten off.

Medium

Cast on 1 st.

ROW 1 (WS): Knit.

ROW 2: (K in front, p in back, k in front) of same st. (3 sts)

ROW 3: K1, p1, k1.

ROW 4: Kfb, k1, kfb. (5 sts)

ROW 5: K2, p1, k2.

ROW 6: Kfb, k3, kfb. (7 sts)

ROW 7: K3, p1, k3.

ROW 8: Kfb, k5, kfb. (9 sts)

ROW 9: K4, p1, k4.

ROW 10: Knit.

Repeat rows 9–10 twice more.

ROW 15: As row 9.

ROW 16: K3, cdd, k3. (7 sts)

ROW 17: K3, p1, k3.

ROW 18: K2, cdd, k2. (5 sts)

ROW 19: K2, p1, k2.

ROW 20: K1, cdd, k1. (3 sts)

ROW 21: K1, p1, k1.

ROW 22: Cdd. (1 st)

Fasten off.

Large

Cast on 1 st.

ROW 1 (WS): Knit.

ROW 2: (K in front, p in back, k in front) of same st. (3 sts)

ROW 3: K1, p1, k1.

ROW 4: Kfb, k1, kfb. (5 sts)

ROW 5: K2, p1, k2.

ROW 6: Kfb, k3, kfb. (7 sts)

ROW 7: K3, p1, k3.

ROW 8: Kfb, k5, kfb. (9 sts)

ROW 9: K4, p1, k4.

ROW 10: Kfb, k7, kfb. (11 sts)

ROW 11: K5, p1, k5.

ROW 12: Kfb, k9, kfb. (13 sts)

ROW 13: K6, p1, k6.

ROW 14: Knit.

Repeat rows 13–14 three times.

ROW 21: As row 13.

ROW 22: K5, cdd, k5. (11 sts)

ROW 23: K5, p1, k5.

ROW 24: K4, cdd, k4. (9 sts)

ROW 25: K4, p1, k4.

ROW 26: K3, cdd, k3. (7 sts)

ROW 27: K3, p1, k3.

ROW 28: K2, cdd, k2. (5 sts)

ROW 29: K2, p1, k2.

ROW 30: K1, cdd, k1. (3 sts)

ROW 31: K1, p1, k1.

ROW 32: Cdd. (1 st)

Fasten off.

Thin

Cast on 1 st.

ROW 1 (RS): Kfbf. (3 sts)

ROW 2: K1, p1, k1.

ROW 3: Knit.

ROW 4: K1, p1, k1.

ROW 5: K1, m1, k1, m1, k1. (5 sts)

ROW 6: K2, p1, k2.

ROW 7: Knit.

ROW 8: K2, p1, k2.

ROW 9: K2, m1, k1, m1, k2. (7 sts)

ROWS 10, 12, 14 & 16: K3, p1, k3.

ROWS 11, 13 & 15: Knit.

ROW 17: K2, cdd, k2. (5 sts)

ROW 18: K2, p1, k2.

ROW 19: Knit.

ROW 20: K2, p1, k2.

ROW 21: K1, cdd, k1. (3 sts)

ROW 22: K1, p1, k1.

ROW 23: Cdd. (1 st)

Fasten off.

Small

Medium

Large

Thin

JAGGED LEAVES \|//

Yarn: Worsted-weight wool

METHOD

Picot edging

Make a large veined leaf (page 67).

Work right and left edges separately, with four picots along each edge, as follows:

RIGHT EDGE: With RS facing, pick up and knit 1 st from center st at bottom point of leaf, 16 sts along right edge up to top of leaf, and 1 st from bound-off st at top point. (18 sts)

PICOT BIND-OFF (WS): Bind off 2 sts, *slip 1 from right needle onto left needle, cast 2 sts onto left needle using knitted method, bind off 5 sts (the 2 just added, then the next 3); repeat from * 3 times, then bind off remaining sts.

LEFT EDGE: With RS facing, pick up and knit 1 st from side of right-edge picot bind-off row, 1 st from top point of leaf, 16 sts along left edge down to bottom of leaf, 1 st from center st at bottom point, and 1 st from side of right-edge picot bind-off row. (20 sts)

PICOT BIND-OFF (WS): Bind off 5 sts, *slip 1 from right needle onto left needle, cast 2 sts onto left needle using knitted method, bind off 5 sts (the 2 just added, then the next 3); repeat from * 3 times, then bind off remaining sts.

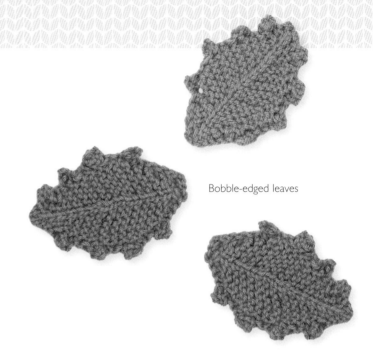

Bobble-edged leaves

Bobble edging

Make a large veined leaf (page 67).

Work right and left edges separately, with four bobbles along each edge, as follows:

RIGHT EDGE: With RS facing, pick up and knit 18 sts as for picot edging.

BOBBLE BIND-OFF (WS): *Bind off 2 sts, (k1, p1, k1) in next st, turn, p3, turn, k3, lift 2nd and 3rd sts on right needle over first st to complete bobble, then bind off this st; repeat from * 3 times, then bind off remaining sts.

LEFT EDGE: With RS facing, pick up and knit 20 sts as for picot edging.

BOBBLE BIND-OFF (WS): Bind off 3 sts, *bind off 2 sts, (k1, p1, k1) in next st, turn, p3, turn, k3, lift 2nd and 3rd sts on right needle over first st to complete bobble, then bind off this st; repeat from * 3 times, then bind off remaining sts.

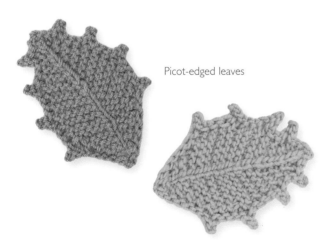

Picot-edged leaves

58 MISTLETOE

Yarn: DK yarn

Needles: 2 double-pointed needles

Extras: 2 pearlized buttons or beads

METHOD

NOTE: If you prefer knitted berries, make them as for the holly berries (page 70).

Leaves

Using pair of needles, cast on 5 sts by thumb method.

ROW 1 (RS): Kfb, k2, kfb, k1. (7 sts)

ROW 2 & ALL WS ROWS: Knit.

ROW 3: Kfb, k4, kfb, k1. (9 sts)

ROWS 5 & 7: Knit.

ROW 9: K1, k2tog, k6. (8 sts)

ROW 11: K1, k2tog, k5. (7 sts)

ROW 13: K1, k2tog, k4. (6 sts)

ROW 15: Knit.

ROW 17: K1, k2tog, k3. (5 sts)

ROW 19: Knit.

ROW 21: K1, k2tog, k2. (4 sts)

ROW 23: Knit.

ROW 25: K1, k2tog, k1. (3 sts)

ROW 27: Knit.

ROW 29: Kfb, k2. (4 sts)

ROW 31: Knit.

ROW 33: Kfb, k3. (5 sts)

ROW 35: Knit.

ROW 37: Kfb, k4. (6 sts)

ROW 39: Kfb, k5. (7 sts)

ROW 41: Kfb, k6. (8 sts)

ROW 43: Kfb, k7. (9 sts)

ROWS 45 & 47: Knit.

ROW 49: K1, k2tog, k3, k2tog, k1. (7 sts)

ROW 51: K1, k2tog, k1, k2tog, k1. (5 sts)

Bind off knitwise.

Stem

Using dpn, cast on 2 sts and knit a 2in (5cm) long cord. Bind off. Attach stem to leaves and sew on beads for berries.

Finishing

Curving the lower edge, press to shape. Attach stem and sew on berries.

59 CHERRIES

Yarn: Fine wool/cotton in red (A) and green (B)

Needles: 2 double-pointed needles

Extras: Batting

METHOD

Cherries (make 2)

Using A, cast on 12 sts by cable method.

ROW 1 (RS): K12.

ROW 2: P10, w&t.

ROW 3: K8, w&t.

ROW 4: P6, w&t.

ROW 5: K4, w&t.

ROW 6: P to end.

Repeat rows 1–6 four times. Bind off.

Stem (make 2)

Using dpn and B, and leaving extra-long ends, cast on 3 sts and knit a 2in (5cm) long cord.

Finishing

Seam each cherry and insert batting before closing the seam. Thread a yarn end from one stem onto a yarn needle and take it through the center of a cherry, pull it tight enough to shape the cherry, then take it back through to the top and fasten off. Join the two stems at the top by knotting the ends and then use them to make a short chain.

Yarn: Tapestry yarn in dark green (A) and scarlet (B)

Needles: 2 pairs, one pair a size smaller than the other; 2 double-pointed needles

METHOD

First leaf section

Using larger pair of needles and A, cast on 20 sts by knitted method.

ROW 1 (RS): K2tog, k16, ssk. (18 sts)

ROW 2 & ALL WS ROWS: Knit.

ROW 3: K2tog, k14, ssk. (16 sts)

ROW 5: K2tog, k12, ssk. (14 sts)

ROW 7: K2tog, k10, ssk. (12 sts)

ROW 9: K2tog, k8, ssk. (10 sts)*

ROW 10: Knit.

Break off yarn but leave sts on needle. Using smaller pair of needles and with RS facing, pick up and k9 sts along first shaped edge, k10 sts from needle, pick up and k9 sts along 2nd shaped edge. (28 sts)

Change to larger pair of needles.

NEXT ROW: [Cast on 3 sts, bind off 7 sts] 5 times.

Bind off remaining 7 sts.

2nd leaf section

Work as first section to *, so ending with a RS row. Break off yarn but leave sts on needle. Using smaller pair of needles and with WS facing, pick up and k8 sts along first shaped edge, k10 sts from needle, pick up and k8 sts along 2nd shaped edge. (26 sts)

Change to larger pair of needles.

NEXT ROW: Kfb, k23, kfb, k1. (28 sts)

NEXT ROW: Bind off 4 sts, [cast on 3 sts, bind off 7 sts] 4 times.

Bind off remaining 7 sts.

Finishing leaf

Place the two sections RS together and, starting at the top of the leaf and using smaller pair of needles, *pick up and k1 in first pair of cast-on sts; repeat from * in next pair of sts, then bind off first st. Continue to bind off both cast-on edges together in this way, then the row-ends of the picot edge. Using dpn, (k1, yo, k1) in remaining st. Continue on these 3 sts to knit a 1⅛in (3cm) long cord, then bind off. Press picot edges only.

Berry

Using B, cast on 2 sts.

ROW 1 (RS): Kfbf, kfb. (5 sts)

ROWS 2 & 4: Purl.

ROW 3: Knit.

ROW 5: Ssk, k1, k2tog. (3 sts)

Break off yarn and draw through remaining sts. Use this end to gather and stitch all edges, while padding the berry with the first end.

61 MAPLE LEAF

Yarn: DK yarn

Needles: 2 double-pointed needles

METHOD

NOTE: Slip stitches purlwise with yarn at back.

Leaf

Cast on 11 sts.

ROW 1 (RS): K2, yo, k3, slip 1, k3, yo, k2. (13 sts)

ROW 2 & ALL WS ROWS: K to center st, p1, k to end.

ROW 3: K2, yo, k4, slip 1, k4, yo, k2. (15 sts)

ROW 5: K2, yo, k5, slip 1, k5, yo, k2. (17 sts)

ROW 7: K2, yo, k6, slip 1, k6, yo, k2. (19 sts)

ROW 9: K2, yo, k7, slip 1, k7, yo, k2. (21 sts)

ROW 11: K2, yo, k8, slip 1, k8, yo, k2. (23 sts)

ROW 13: Cast off 6 sts knitwise, k5 (including st already on needle), slip 1, k11. (17 sts)

ROW 14: Cast off 6 sts, k5, p1, k5. (11 sts)

ROW 15: As row 1.

ROW 17: As row 3.

ROW 19: As row 5.

ROW 21: As row 7.

ROW 23: Bind off 4 sts, k5, slip 1, k9. (15 sts)

ROW 24: Bind off 4 sts, k5, p1, k5. (11 sts)

ROW 25: K3, ssk, slip 1, k2tog, k3. (9 sts)

ROW 26 & ALL WS ROWS: As row 2.

ROW 27: K2, ssk, slip 1, k2tog, k2. (7 sts)

ROW 29: K1, ssk, slip 1, k2tog, k1. (5 sts)

ROW 31: Ssk, slip 1, k2tog. (3 sts)

ROW 33: S2kpo. (1 st)

Fasten off and press leaf to shape.

Stalk

Using dpn, cast on 3 sts and knit a 1⅜in (3.5cm) long cord. Attach to WS of leaf.

62 ELDER LEAF

Yarn: DK yarn

METHOD

Main stem and top leaf

Make a 30-st chain, ending with 1 st on left needle.

*ROW 1 (RS): (K1, [yo, k1] 4 times) in st. (9 sts)

ROWS 2-4: Knit.

ROW 5: K2tog, k5, skpo. (7 sts)

ROWS 6, 8 & 10: Knit.

ROW 7: K2tog, k3, skpo. (5 sts)

ROW 9: K2tog, k1, skpo. (3 sts)

ROW 11: Knit.

ROW 12: K3tog. (1 st)

Fasten off.

Side leaves (make 4)

Make a 4-st chain, ending with 1 st on left needle. Work as top leaf from *. Press, then attach shorter stalks to main stem.

63 ELM LEAF V

Yarn: Sport-weight yarn

Extras: 2 double-pointed needles

METHOD

NOTE: Slip stitches purlwise with yarn at back. The leaf is worked from the top downward.

Leaf

Cast on 9 sts.

ROW 1 (RS): [K1, yo] twice, ssk, slip 1, k2tog, [yo, k1] twice. (11 sts)

ROW 2 & ALL WS ROWS: K1, p to last st, k1.

ROW 3: [K1, yo] twice, k1, ssk, slip 1, k2tog, k1, [yo, k1] twice. (13 sts)

ROW 5: [K1, yo] twice, k2, ssk, slip 1, k2tog, k2, [yo, k1] twice. (15 sts)

ROW 7: [K1, yo] twice, k3, ssk, slip 1, k2tog, k3, [yo, k1] twice. (17 sts)

ROW 9: [K1, yo] twice, k4, ssk, slip 1, k2tog, k4, [yo, k1] twice. (19 sts)

ROW 11: K6, sk2po, slip 1, k2sso, k6. (15 sts)

ROW 13: K4, sk2po, slip 1, k2sso, k4. (11 sts)

ROW 15: K2, sk2po, slip 1, k2sso, k2. (7 sts)

ROW 17: Sk2po, slip 1, k2sso. (3 sts)

ROW 18: Purl.

Stalk

Slip remaining 3 sts onto a dpn and knit a 1in (2.5cm) long cord. Bind off.

---

64 WHITEBEAM LEAF I

Yarn: DK yarn

METHOD

Stalk

Make a 10-st chain, ending with 1 st on left needle.

Leaf

ROW 1 (RS): (K1, yo, k1) in st. (3 sts)

ROW 2: P3.

ROW 3: K1, m1R, k1, m1L, k1. (5 sts)

ROW 4 & ALL WS ROWS: K1, p to last st, k1.

ROW 5: K2, m1R, k1, m1L, k2. (7 sts)

ROW 7: K3, m1R, k1, m1L, k3. (9 sts)

ROW 9: K4, m1R, k1, m1L, k4. (11 sts)

ROW 11: K5, m1R, k1, m1L, k5. (13 sts)

ROWS 13 & 15: Knit.

ROW 17: K5, s2kpo, k5. (11 sts)

ROW 19: K4, s2kpo, k4. (9 sts)

ROW 21: K3, s2kpo, k3. (7 sts)

ROW 23: K2, s2kpo, k2. (5 sts)

ROWS 24 & 26: Purl.

ROW 25: K1, s2kpo, k1. (3 sts)

ROW 27: S2kpo. (1 st)

Fasten off.

WS facing, pin to shape and press.

65 BEECH LEAF

Yarn: DK yarn

METHOD

Stem
Make an 8-st chain, ending with 1 st on left needle.

Leaf
ROW 1 (RS): (K1, yo, k1) in st. (3 sts)
ROW 2: Purl.
ROW 3: K1, [yo, k1] twice. (5 sts)
ROW 4: P1, [k1, p1] twice.
ROW 5: K1, p1, yo, k1, yo, p1, k1. (7 sts)
ROW 6: P1, k1, p3, k1, p1.

ROW 7: K1, p1, k1, yo, k1, yo, k1, p1, k1. (9 sts)
ROW 8: P1, [k1, p1] 4 times.
ROW 9: [K1, p1] twice, yo, k1, yo, [p1, k1] twice. (11 sts)
ROW 10: [P1, k1] twice, p3, [k1, p1] twice.
ROW 11: [K1, p1] twice, k1, yo, k1, yo, k1, [p1, k1] twice. (13 sts)
ROW 12: P1, [k1, p1] 6 times.
ROWS 13-14 & ALL FOLL WS ROWS: Rib as set.
ROW 15: Skpo, rib 9, k2tog. (11 sts)
ROW 17: Skpo, rib 7, k2tog. (9 sts)
ROW 19: Skpo, rib 5, k2tog. (7 sts)

ROW 21: Skpo, rib 3, k2tog. (5 sts)
ROW 23: Skpo, k1, k2tog. (3 sts)
ROW 25: S2kpo.
Fasten off.

66 POPLAR LEAF

Yarn: DK yarn

METHOD
NOTE: Slip stitches purlwise with yarn at back.

Stem
Cast on 10 sts by thumb method. Bind off 9 sts knitwise. Do not turn; drop left needle to leave 1 st on right needle.

Leaf
ROW 1 (WS): Yo, k1b in nearest st of cast-on row. (3 sts)

Turn and resume with 2 needles.
ROW 2: K1, p1, k1.
ROW 3: K1, m1, slip 1, m1, k1. (5 sts)
ROW 4 & ALL RS ROWS: K to center st, p1, k to end.
ROW 5: K2, m1, slip 1, m1, k2. (7 sts)
ROW 7: K3, m1, slip 1, m1, k3. (9 sts)
ROW 9: K4, m1, slip 1, m1, k4. (11 sts)
ROW 11: K5, m1, slip 1, m1, k5. (13 sts)
ROWS 13 & 15: Knit.
ROW 17: K5, s2kpo, k5. (11 sts)
ROW 19: K4, s2kpo, k4. (9 sts)
ROW 21: K3, s2kpo, k3. (7 sts)
ROW 23: K2, s2kpo, k2. (5 sts)

ROW 25: K1, s2kpo, k1. (3 sts)
ROW 27: S2kpo. (1 st)
Fasten off.
WS facing, pin to shape and press.

LOGANBERRY LEAF

Yarn: DK yarn

Needles: 2 double-pointed needles

METHOD

Small leaf (make 2)

Using dpn, cast on 3 sts and knit a ⅝in (1.5cm) long cord. Do not bind off; turn and work k1, p1, k1.

Change to pair of needles.

ROW 1 (RS): K1, m1, k1, m1, k1. (5 sts)

ROWS 2, 4, 6, 8, 10 & 12: K to center st, p1, k to end.

ROW 3: K2, m1, k1, m1, k2. (7 sts)

ROW 5: K3, m1, k1, m1, k3. (9 sts)

ROW 7: K4, m1, k1, m1, k4. (11 sts)

ROW 9: K5, m1, k1, m1, k5. (13 sts)

ROW 11: K6, m1, k1, m1, k6. (15 sts)

ROWS 13-18: Knit.

ROW 19: K1, ssk, k to last 3 sts, k2tog, k1. (13 sts)

ROWS 20-22: Knit.

ROWS 23, 25, 27 & 29: K1, ssk, k to last 3 sts, k2tog, k1.

ROWS 24, 26, 28, 30 & 32: Knit.

ROW 31: K1, sk2po, k1. (3 sts)

ROW 33: Sk2po. (1 st)

Fasten off.

Large leaf

Using dpn, cast on 3 sts and knit a 1¾in (4.5cm) long cord. Do not bind off; turn and work k1, p1, k1.

Change to pair of needles.

ROW 1 (RS): K1, m1, k1, m1, k1. (5 sts)

ROWS 2, 4, 6, 8, 10, 12 & 14: K to center st, p1, k to end.

ROW 3: K2, m1, k1, m1, k2. (7 sts)

ROW 5: K3, m1, k1, m1, k3. (9 sts)

ROW 7: K4, m1, k1, m1, k4. (11 sts)

ROW 9: K5, m1, k1, m1, k5. (13 sts)

ROW 11: K6, m1, k1, m1, k6. (15 sts)

ROW 13: K7, m1, k1, m1, k7. (17 sts)

ROWS 15-24: Knit.

ROW 25: K1, ssk, k to last 3 sts, k2tog, k1. (15 sts)

ROWS 26-28: Knit.

ROWS 29, 31, 33, 35 & 37: K1, ssk, k to last 3 sts, k2tog, k1.

ROWS 30, 32, 34, 36, 38 & 40: Knit.

ROW 39: K1, sk2po, k1. (3 sts)

ROW 41: Sk2po. (1 st)

Fasten off.

Finishing

Arrange stalks of small leaves at an angle about halfway down stalk of large leaf and sew in place.

68 LOGANBERRY \/

Yarn: DK yarn in crimson (A) and green (B)

Extras: Batting; 72 red beads with holes large enough to take yarn, plus a few extra

METHOD

NOTE: Use needles smaller than usual for the yarn to make a firmer fabric. Thread beads onto yarn before casting on.

SPECIFIC ABBREVIATION

b1 = bead 1: bring yarn to front, slip next stitch purlwise, slide bead along yarn so that it sits snugly against work, take yarn to back ready to knit next stitch.

Berry (make 1 back and 1 front)

Using A, cast on 3 sts.
ROW 1 (WS): Kfb, p1, kfb. (5 sts)
ROW 2: [K1, b1] twice, k1.
ROW 3: Kfb, p3, kfb. (7 sts)
ROWS 4, 6 & 8: [K1, b1] to last st, k1.
ROW 5: Kfb, p5, kfb. (9 sts)
ROW 7: Kfb, p7, kfb. (11 sts)
ROWS 9, 11, 13, 15 & 17: K1, p9, k1.
ROWS 10 & 14: K2, [b1, k1] to last st, k1.
ROWS 12 & 16: [K1, b1] to last st, k1.
ROW 18: Ssk, [b1, k1] to last 3 sts, b1, k2tog. (9 sts)
ROW 19: K1, p7, k1. Bind off.

Calyx

Using B, cast on 8 sts.
ROW 1 (WS): Bind off 5 sts, k2. (3 sts)
ROW 2: K3, turn, cast on 5 sts. (8 sts)
Repeat rows 1–2 four times.
Bind off.

Finishing

Sew back and front together, stuffing firmly before closing seam. Sew a few beads onto seam. With RS outward, roll calyx and secure cast-on and bound-off edges at straight edge, then sew to top of berry.

69 BLACKBERRY \/

Yarn: Tapestry wool in dark purple (A) and green (B)

Extras: 54 black beads with holes large enough to take yarn; batting

METHOD

Berry (make 1 back and 1 front)

Work as for loganberry to end of row 11 (see above).
ROW 12: [K1, b1] to last st, k1.
ROW 13: K1, p9, k1.
ROW 14: Ssk, [b1, k1] 3 times, b1, k2tog. (9 sts)
ROW 15: K1, p7, k1.
Bind off.

Calyx

Using B, cast on 6 sts.
ROW 1 (RS): Bind off 3 sts, k2. (3 sts)
ROW 2: K3, turn, cast on 3 sts by cable method. (6 sts)

Repeat rows 1–2 three times.
Work row 1 again, binding off all sts at the same time.

Finishing

Finish as for Loganberry.

70 LEMON \|/

Yarn: Fine cotton

Needles: 4 double-pointed needles

Extras: Batting

METHOD

Cast on 3 sts.

ROW 1 (RS): [Kfb] twice, k1.
(5 sts)

ROW 2: Purl.

ROW 3: K1, [m1, k1] 4 times.
(9 sts)

Slip 3 sts onto each of 3 dpn and continue in rounds.

ROUND 1: Knit.

ROUND 2: *K1, [m1, k1] twice; repeat from * twice. (15 sts)

ROUND 3: Knit.

ROUND 4: *K1, [m1, k1] 4 times; repeat from * twice. (27 sts)

ROUNDS 5-7: Knit.

ROUND 8: *K2, m1, k5, m1, k2; repeat from * twice. (33 sts)

ROUNDS 9-11: Knit.

ROUND 12: *K3, m1, k5, m1, k3; repeat from * twice. (39 sts)

ROUNDS 13-20: Knit.

ROUND 21: *K2, k2tog, k5, k2tog, k2; repeat from * twice. (33 sts)

ROUNDS 22-24: Knit.

ROUND 25: *K2, k2tog, k3, k2tog, k2; repeat from * twice. (27 sts)

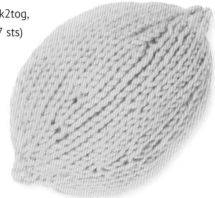

71 LEMON SLICE \|/

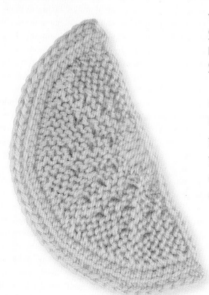

Yarn: DK yarn in lemon (A) and cream (B)

Extras: Crochet hook; contrasting color yarn

METHOD

NOTE: Slip stitches knitwise with yarn at back. Do not break off yarn at each color change, but carry yarn not in use up side of work.

Using crochet hook and spare yarn, make 12ch. Fasten off. Using A, pick up and k10 sts in the back loops of the chain and then knit 1 row.

*Continue in A.

ROW 1: Knit.

ROW 2: Slip 1, k3, turn, k to end.

ROW 3: Slip 1, k5, turn, k to end.

ROW 4: Slip 1, k7, turn, k to end.

ROW 5: Slip 1, k5, turn, k to end.

ROW 6: Slip 1, k3, turn, k to end.

ROW 7: Slip 1, k to end.**

Change to B.

ROW 8 (RS): Knit.

ROW 9: Slip 1, k to end.

Repeat from * three times, then from * to ** once.

Break off A.

With RS facing, using crochet hook and B, work across sts on needle in crochet, working 1sc in each st as you slip it off the needle, 2sc in corner, 1sc in each garter ridge around large curve, 2sc in corner. Remove starting chain worked in spare yarn, slipping each st carefully onto knitting needle, and work 1sc in each st. Continuing across small

ROUNDS 26-28: Knit.
ROUND 29: *K1, [k2tog] 4 times; repeat from * twice. (15 sts)
ROUND 30: Knit.
ROUND 31: *K1, [k2tog] twice; repeat from * twice. (9 sts)
ROUND 32: Knit.
Insert batting.
ROUND 33: *K1, k2tog; repeat from * twice. (6 sts)

ROUND 34: [K2tog] 3 times. (3 sts)
Break off yarn and pass through remaining 3 sts. Close row-ends at the beginning.

curve, work 1sc, 1hdc, [2tr tog] twice, 1hdc, 1sc in curve. Join by stitching loop to first sc. Fasten off.
With RS facing and large curve at top, rejoin B in right-hand corner of curve. Work 1sc in each sc along large curve and 2sc in each sc where A wedges meet.
With RS facing and large curve at top, join A in first sc of last row. Work 1sc in back loop of each sc along large curve. Fasten off.

Yarn: Fine cotton

Needles: 2 double-pointed needles

METHOD

NOTE: Slip stitches purlwise with yarn at front.

Stalk

Using dpn, cast on 3 sts and knit a 1in (2.5cm) long cord.

Leaf

Now work on these 3 sts in rows.

ROW 1 (RS): Cast on 6 sts by cable method, k to last st, p1. (9 sts)
ROW 2: Cast on 6 sts as before, k to end. (15 sts)
ROW 3: Kfb, k4, ssk, slip 1, k2tog, k3, kfb, k1.
ROW 4: Knit.
Repeat rows 3–4 three times.
ROW 11: K1, ssk, k2, ssk, slip 1, k2tog, k2, k2tog, k1. (11 sts)

ROW 12 & ALL WS ROWS: Knit.
ROW 13: K5, slip 1, k5.
ROW 15: K1, [ssk] twice, slip 1, [k2tog] twice, k1. (7 sts)
ROW 17: K3, slip 1, k3.
ROW 19: K1, ssk, slip 1, k2tog, k1. (5 sts)
ROW 21: K1, sk2po, k1. (3 sts)
ROW 23: Sk2po. (1 st)
Bind off.

73 OAK LEAF \|/

Yarn: DK wool in olive green (A), ocher (B), and lemon (D)

Needles: 2 double-pointed needles

METHOD

NOTE: The instruction after a bind-off includes the stitch already on the right needle. Slip stitches purlwise with yarn at front.

Using A and dpn, cast on 3 sts and knit a 1in (2.5cm) long cord. Now work on these 3 sts in rows.

ROW 1 (WS): Cast on 5 sts by cable method, k7, p1. (8 sts)

ROW 2: Cast on 5 sts as before, k6, slip 1, k6. (13 sts)

ROW 3: Knit.

ROW 4: K6, slip 1, k6.

ROWS 5-6: As rows 3–4.

ROW 7: Bind off 2 sts, k11. (11 sts)

ROW 8: Bind off 2 sts, k4, slip 1, k4. (9 sts)

ROWS 9-10: Knit.

ROW 11: Cast on 2 sts, k11. (11 sts)

ROW 12: Cast on 2 sts, k6, slip 1, k6. (13 sts)

ROW 13: Knit.

Change to B.

ROW 14: Knit.

ROW 15: Bind off 3 sts, k10. (10 sts)

ROW 16: Bind off 3 sts, k3, slip 1, k3. (7 sts)

ROWS 17-18: Knit.

ROW 19: Cast on 2 sts, k9. (9 sts)

ROW 20: Cast on 2 sts, k5, slip 1, k5. (11 sts)

ROW 21: Knit.

Change to C.

ROW 22: Knit.

ROW 23: Bind off 3 sts, k8. (8 sts)

ROW 24: Bind off 3 sts, k2, slip 1, k2. (5 sts)

ROWS 25-26: Knit.

ROW 27: Ssk, slip 1, k2tog. (3 sts)

Bind off.

74 ACORN |

Yarn: DK wool in brown (A), beige (B), and green (C)

Needles: 2 double-pointed needles

Extras: Batting

METHOD

Acorn

Using A, cast on 6 sts.

ROW 1 (RS): [Kfb] 6 times. (12 sts)

ROWS 2 & 4: Knit.

ROW 3: [Kfb] 12 times. (24 sts)

ROW 5: [K2tog] 12 times. (12 sts)

ROW 6: Knit.

Change to B.

Beginning with a k row, work 6 rows st-st.

ROW 13: [K2tog] 6 times. (6 sts)

ROW 14: Purl.

ROW 15: [K2tog] 3 times. (3 sts)

Break off yarn and pass through remaining 3 sts.

Stem

Using C and dpn, cast on 3 sts and knit a 2in (5cm) long cord.

Finishing

Seam the acorn from the top, inserting batting and the end of the stem before closing the seam.

75 FLY AGARIC \\/

Yarn: DK yarn in red (A) and white (B)
Extras: Batting

METHOD

NOTE: In nature this mushroom is poisonous and children should be told not to touch it.

Cap

Using A, cast on 3 sts by knitted method.
ROW 1 (RS): [K1, yo] twice, k1. (5 sts)
ROW 2: [P1, p1tbl] twice, p1.
ROW 3: [K1, yo] 4 times, k1. (9 sts)
ROWS 4, 6 & 8: [P1, p1tbl] to last st, p1.

ROW 5: [K1, yo] 8 times, k1. (17 sts)
ROW 7: [K1, yo] 16 times, k1. (33 sts)
ROW 9: [K3, yo] 10 times, k3. (43 sts)
ROW 10: Purl, working each yo as p1tbl.
ROW 11: Knit.
ROW 12: Purl.*
Change to B.
ROWS 13-14: Knit.
**ROW 15: [K1, p2] to last st, k1.
ROW 16: [P1, k2] to last st, p1.
ROW 17: [K1, p2tog] to last st, k1. (29 sts)
ROW 18: [P1, k1] to last st, p1.

ROW 19: [Sk2po, p1] 7 times, k1. (15 sts)
ROW 20: As row 18.
ROW 21: [Skpo] 7 times, k1. (8 sts)

Stalk

Beginning with a p row, work 9 rows st-st.
ROW 31: [K2, yo] 3 times, k2. (11 sts)
ROW 32: As row 10.
ROW 33: Knit.
ROW 34: Purl.
ROW 35: Work k1, [k2tog] 5 times, binding off firmly at the same time.

Finishing

Gather base and, taking in half a stitch from each edge, join side seam using mattress stitch, stuffing as you go. Split yarn B in half and embroider French knots onto top of cap.

76 FIELD MUSHROOM \\/

Yarn: Sport-weight yarn in beige (A) and dark brown (B)

METHOD

Work as for Fly Agaric to * (see above).
ROWS 13-14: Knit.
Change to B.
ROW 15: Knit.
ROW 16: [P1, k2] to last st, p1.

Continue as Fly Agaric from ** to end, using A for stalk and noting that row numbering for this mushroom will become 17-37. Seam and stuff as for Fly Agaric, but do not add French knots.

Yarn: DK wool or tapestry wool in orange (A) and green (B)

Needles: 2 double-pointed needles

Extras: Batting; raffia (optional)

METHOD

NOTE: The carrot is worked from the top downward.

Carrot

Using A, cast on 4 sts.

ROW 1 (RS): [Kfbf] 4 times. (12 sts)

ROW 2 & ALL WS ROWS: Purl.

ROW 3: [Kfb, k1] 6 times. (18 sts)

Beginning with a p row, work 3 rows st-st.

ROW 7: [K1, k2tog] 6 times. (12 sts)

Work 3 rows st-st.

ROW 11: [K2tog, k1] 4 times. (8 sts)

Work 5 rows st-st.

ROW 17: [K2tog] 4 times. (4 sts)

Work 5 rows st-st.

ROW 23: [K2tog] twice. (2 sts)

With RS facing, slip these 2 sts onto a dpn and knit a cord for 4 rounds. Take yarn across back and k2tog. Fasten off, leaving an end for the root and seaming.

Tops (make 5 per carrot)

Using B, make a 10-st chain. Fasten off.

Finishing

Divide end of yarn A at root of carrot to leave one strand for root. Using remaining strands of yarn A, seam the carrot, stuffing as you go. Knot ends of tops and insert before closing seam. Tie the bunch of carrots together with raffia.

Yarn: DK wool in white (A), pale green (B), and mauve (C)

Needles: 4 double-pointed needles

Extras: Batting

METHOD

Bottom of stalk

Using A, cast on 9 sts. Slip 3 sts onto each of 3 dpn and continue in rounds of knit for 1in (2.5cm), ending between needles. Do not break off yarn A.

First bract

Change to B.
K3 sts on next needle, turn, p3, turn, s2kpo. (1 st)
Fasten off.

Remaining stalk and bracts

Resume A and, working into A sts behind and beneath first row of B sts, pick up and k3 sts. Continue stalk on all 9 sts, working bracts on each needle in turn and at approximately 1in (2.5cm) intervals until stalk measures 5in (13cm). Break off A and continue in B.

Tip of asparagus

*(K1, m1, k1, m1, k1) in next 3 sts, turn.
Continue on these 5 sts: p5, turn, k5, turn, p5, turn.
NEXT ROW (RS): K2tog, k1, ssk. (3 sts)
NEXT ROW: P3.
NEXT ROW: S2kpo. (1 st)
Fasten off.
Repeat from * twice.
Using B, pick up and k3 sts from behind each bract as before. Continue in rounds on these 9 sts.
ROUNDS 1-2: Knit.
ROUND 3: [(K1, m1, k1, m1, k1) in next 3 sts] 3 times. (15 sts)
ROUNDS 4-6: Knit.
Change to C.

ROUND 7: [K2tog, k1, ssk] 3 times. (9 sts)
ROUND 8: Knit.
Fill tip with batting and yarn ends.
ROUND 9: [S2kpo] 3 times. (3 sts)
Break off yarn and pass through remaining 3 sts.

Finishing

Catch down tips of bracts using ends. Use a pencil to push batting into stalk. Close base of stalk by weaving end across opening.

Yarn: Worsted-weight cotton in lemon yellow (A); worsted-weight wool in black (B) and blue (C)

Extras: 2 black beads; black sewing thread; fabric glue (optional)

METHOD

Left wing

Using A, cast on 9 sts.

ROW 1 (WS): Knit.

ROW 2: Kfb, k7, kfb. (11 sts)

ROWS 3, 5, 7, 9 & 11: Knit.

ROW 4: K2tog, place marker (decreases for wing shaping will be worked on marker side), k9. (10 sts)

ROW 6: K2tog, k8. (9 sts)

ROW 8: K2tog, k7. (8 sts)

ROW 10: K2tog, k6. (7 sts)

ROW 12: K2tog, k3, turn leaving 2 sts unworked.

ROW 13: Slip 1, k3 to end.

ROW 14: K2tog, k4. (5 sts)

ROWS 15, 17 & 19: Knit.

ROW 16: K2tog, k3. (4 sts)

ROW 18: K2tog, k2. (3 sts)

ROW 20: K2tog, k1. (2 sts)

ROW 21: Knit.

Bind off.

Right wing

Using A, cast on 9 sts.

ROW 1 (WS): Knit.

ROW 2: Kfb, k7, kfb. (11 sts)

ROWS 3, 5, 7, 9 & 11: Knit.

ROW 4: K9, place marker (decreases for wing shaping will be worked on marker side), k2tog. (10 sts)

ROW 6: K8, ssk. (9 sts)

ROW 8: K7, ssk. (8 sts)

ROW 10: K6, ssk. (7 sts)

ROW 12: K5, ssk. (6 sts)

ROW 13: K4, turn leaving 2 sts unworked.

ROW 14: Slip 1, k1, ssk.

ROW 15: Knit. (5 sts)

ROW 16: K3, ssk. (4 sts)

ROW 17: Knit.

ROW 18: K2, ssk. (3 sts)

ROW 19: Knit.

ROW 20: K1, ssk. (2 sts)

ROW 21: Knit.

Bind off.

Right-wing edging

Using B and with RS facing, pick up and knit 11 sts along top (cast-on) edge of wing. Bind off knitwise. Using B and with RS facing, pick up and knit 2 sts from bound-off sts at bottom of wing, 11 sts up right edge, and 1 st from side of top edging. (14 sts)

ROW 1 (WS): K14.
ROW 2: K3, turn.
ROW 3: Slip 1, k2.
ROW 4: To make swallowtail, cast 4 sts onto left needle using knitted method, bind off 4 sts (1 st on right needle); k13 to end.
Bind off knitwise.

Left-wing edging

Using B and with RS facing, pick up and knit 11 sts along top (cast-on) edge of wing. Bind off knitwise.
Using B and with RS facing, pick up and knit 1 st from left side of top edging, 11 sts down left edge, and 2 sts from bound-off sts at bottom of wing. (14 sts)

ROW 1 (WS): K3, turn.
ROW 2: Slip 1, k2.
ROW 3: K14 to end.
ROW 4: K14; to make swallowtail, cast 4 sts onto left needle using knitted method, bind off 4 sts (1 st on right needle).
Bind off knitwise to end.

Body

Using B, cast on 3 sts.
ROW 1 (RS): Knit.
ROW 2 & ALL WS ROWS: Purl.
ROW 3: Kfb, k1, kfb. (5 sts)
ROW 5: Kfb, k3, kfb. (7 sts)
ROW 7: Knit.
ROW 9: Kfb, k5, kfb. (9 sts)
ROW 11: Knit.
Continue in st-st until body measures same length as inner (unfinished) edges of wings (including swallowtails).
Shape head as follows:
NEXT ROW: K2tog, k5, ssk. (7 sts)
NEXT ROW: Purl.
NEXT ROW: K2tog, k3, ssk. (5 sts)
NEXT ROW: P2tog, p1, p2tog. (3 sts)
NEXT ROW: Knit.
Break off yarn and pass through remaining 3 sts.

Finishing

Using B, fold body in half lengthwise and sew seam, stuffing body lightly with scraps of yarn as you do so. Sew wings on either side of body. Using double strand of A, work running stitch along sides of wings, through the edging. Work two long straight stitches at either side of head. Using double strand of B, work long straight stitches at upper edge of each wing, decreasing in length toward outer edge of wings. Using double strand of C, work random straight stitches at lower edge of each wing. Using sewing thread, sew a bead at each side of head for eyes. Using single strand of B, add antennae at top of head, above the eyes. Trim antennae to about 1in (2.5cm) and stiffen with fabric glue if desired.

Yarn: DK yarn in buff (A), rust (B), blue (C), yellow (D), and black (E)

Needles: 3 knitting needles

METHOD

Right lower wing

Using A, cast on 1 st.

ROW 1 (RS): (K1, yo, kfb) in same st. (4 sts)

ROW 2: Purl.

ROW 3: [Kfb, k1] twice. (6 sts)

ROW 4: Pfb, p3, pfb, p1. (8 sts)

ROW 5: K2, k2tog, [yo] 3 times, ssk, k2. (9 sts)

ROW 6: P3, (k1, p1, k1) in triple yo, p3.*

ROW 7: Ssk, k7. (8 sts)

ROW 8: P6, ssp. (7 sts)

ROW 9: Ssk, k5. (6 sts)

ROW 10: P4, ssp. (5 sts)

Bind off knitwise.

Left lower wing

Using A, work as right lower wing to *.

ROW 7: K7, k2tog. (8 sts)

ROW 8: P2tog, p6. (7 sts)

ROW 9: K5, k2tog. (6 sts)

ROW 10: P2tog, p4. (5 sts)

Bind off knitwise.

Right upper wing

Using B, work as right lower wing to *.

ROW 7: Knit.

ROW 8: Purl.

ROW 9: K7, k2tog. (8 sts)

ROWS 10 & 12: Purl.

ROW 11: K6, k2tog. (7 sts)

Change to A.

ROW 13: K5, k2tog. (6 sts)

ROW 14: Ssp, p4. (5 sts)

ROW 15: K5; along straight row-ends of right lower wing with RS facing, pick up and k6 sts. (11 sts)

Leave sts on spare needle.

Left upper wing

Using B, work as right lower wing to *.

ROW 7: Knit.

ROW 8: Purl.

ROW 9: Ssk, k7. (8 sts)

ROWS 10 & 12: Purl.

ROW 11: Ssk, k6. (7 sts)

Change to A.

ROW 13: Ssk, k5. (6 sts)

ROW 14: P4, ssp. (5 sts)

Break off yarn.

With RS facing, pick up and k6 sts along straight row-ends of left lower wing, then k5 sts of left upper wing. (11 sts) Do not break off yarn. With RS together, place both sets of sts on parallel needles and, using 3rd needle, bind them off together knitwise.

Body

Using A, cast on 10 sts.

ROW 1 (RS): (K1, yo, k1) in first st, turn, k3, turn, slip 2nd and 3rd sts over first st, knit first st tbl. Bind off knitwise.

Finishing

Press wings to shape. Fasten off ends, working a few sts over first cast-on st of each wing. Using C for lower wings and D for upper wings, work a ring of running stitch around eyelets, then overcast these edges. Outline overcast sts with a ring of backstitch in E. Catch down edges of lower wings underneath upper wings. Sew body in place. Using single strand of A, add antennae at top of head.

Yarn: DK yarn in brown (A) and orange (B)

Needles: 2 pairs, one pair a size smaller than the other

METHOD

SPECIFIC ABBREVIATION

inc2 = increase 2: (k1tbl, k1) in next st, insert left needle behind vertical strand between the 2 sts just made and k this tbl.

Wings

Using larger needles and A, cast on 3 sts.

ROW 1 (RS): [Kfb] twice, k1. (5 sts)

ROW 2: [Pfb] 4 times, p1. (9 sts)

ROW 3: [Kfb] 8 times, k1. (17 sts)

On next and every rib row, work all k sts on RS and all p sts on WS through back of loop.

ROW 4 (WS): K1, [p1, k1] 8 times.

ROW 5: P1, [k1, pfb] 7 times, k1, p1. (24 sts)

Change to B.

ROW 6: K1, [p1, k2] 7 times, p1, k1.

ROW 7: P1, [k1, p1, m1, p1, k1, p2] 3 times, k1, p1, m1, p1, k1, p1. (28 sts)

ROW 8: [K1, p1] 3 times, *k2, [p1, k1] twice, p1; repeat from * twice, k1.

ROWS 9-10: K all k sts and p all p sts as they appear.

ROW 11: P1, [k1, p1, inc2, p1, k1, p2] 3 times, k1, p1, inc2, p1, k1, p1. (36 sts)

ROW 12: [K1, p1] 4 times, k2, *[p1, k1] 3 times, p1, k2; repeat from * once, [p1, k1] 4 times.

ROWS 13-14: As rows 9–10.

First wing tip

**NEXT ROW (RS): P1, k1, [pfb, k1] 3 times, p1, turn.

Continue on these 12 sts.

NEXT ROW: K1, p1, [k2, p1] 3 times, k1.

NEXT ROW: K2tog, [p2, k1] twice, p2, ssk. (10 sts)

Fasten off and leave sts on spare yarn.***

2nd wing tip

With RS facing, rejoin B to first of remaining sts. Work as first wing tip from ** to ***.

3rd and 4th wing tips

As 2nd wing tip.

Binding off wing tips

With WS facing, slip sts of first wing tip onto needle. Using smaller needles and A, and working all bound-off sts knitwise, bind off 1 st, *slip st onto left needle, cast on 1 st, bind off 3 sts; repeat from * to end. Work remaining wing tips to match.

Wing edging

With RS facing, using smaller needles and A, pick up and k12 sts along side edge of first wing. Bind off knitwise. Edge 4th wing to match.

Body

Using larger needles and A, cast on 2 sts.

ROW 1 (RS): Knit.

ROWS 2 & 4: Purl.

ROW 3: K1, m1, k1. (3 sts)

ROW 5: K1, [m1, k1] twice. (5 sts)

St-st 3 rows.

ROW 9: K1, m1, k3, m1, k1. (7 sts)

St-st 5 rows.

ROW 15: K1, ssk, k1, k2tog, k1. (5 sts)

ROWS 16 & 18: Purl.

ROW 17: K1, s2kpo, k1. (3 sts)

ROW 19: S2kpo. (1 st)

Fasten off.

Finishing

Gather center top of wings. Using A, neaten corners around wing tips. Using single strand of A, make a spot by working 2 small stitches between each rib near the bound-off edge. Seam body and stitch in place. Using A, add antennae at top of head.

LARGE BLUE \/

Yarn: DK yarn in pale blue (A) and deep blue (B)

Needles: 3 knitting needles

METHOD

Right lower wing

Using A, cast on 4 sts.

ROW 1 (RS): K2, kfb, k1. (5 sts)

ROW 2 & ALL WS ROWS: Knit.

ROW 3: Kfb, k2, kfb, k1. (7 sts)

ROW 5: K5, kfb, k1. (8 sts)

ROW 7: K6, kfb, k1. (9 sts)

ROW 8: Knit.

Break off yarn and leave sts on spare needle.

Left lower wing

Using A, cast on 4 sts.

ROW 1 (RS): Kfb, k3. (5 sts)

ROW 2 & ALL WS ROWS: Knit.

ROW 3: Kfb, k2, kfb, k1. (7 sts)

ROW 5: Kfb, k6. (8 sts)

ROW 7: Kfb, k7. (9 sts)

ROW 8: Knit.

Break off yarn and, with both RS facing,
slip sts of right lower wing onto left needle.
(18 sts)

ROW 9: Knit.

ROW 11: K1, k2tog, k to last 3 sts, k2tog, k1.
(16 sts)

ROW 13: As row 11. (14 sts)

ROW 15: K1, k2tog, k2, [k2tog] twice, k2,
k2tog, k1. (10 sts)

ROW 17: K1, [k2tog] 4 times, k1. (6 sts)

ROW 18: Knit.

Break off yarn and leave sts on spare needle.

Right upper wing

Using A, cast on 6 sts.

ROW 1 (RS): Kfb, k3, kfb, k1. (8 sts)

ROW 2: Kfb, k7. (9 sts)

ROW 3: Kfb, k6, kfb, k1. (11 sts)

ROW 4: Kfb, k10. (12 sts)

Break off yarn and leave sts on spare needle.

Left upper wing

Using A, cast on 6 sts.

ROW 1 (RS): Kfb, k3, kfb, k1. (8 sts)

ROW 2: K6, kfb, k1. (9 sts)

ROW 3: Kfb, k6, kfb, k1. (11 sts)

ROW 4: K9, kfb, k1. (12 sts)

Break off yarn and leave sts on spare needle.

ROW 5 (JOINING ROW): With all RS facing,
across sts of right upper wing work kfb, k11;
across sts of lower wings work k1, [k2tog]
twice, k1; across sts of left upper wing work
k10, kfb, k1. (30 sts)

ROW 6: Knit.

ROW 7: Kfb, k12, [k2tog] twice, k11, kfb, k1.

ROW 8: Knit.

ROW 9: K13, [k2tog] twice, k13. (28 sts)

ROW 10: Knit.

ROW 11: K1, k2tog, k9, [k2tog] twice, k9,
k2tog, k1. (24 sts)

ROW 12: Bind off knitwise, working k1,
k2tog, k18, k2tog, k1 across the row.

Body

Using B, cast on 1 st.

ROW 1 (RS): (K1, yo, k1) in same st. (3 sts)

ROW 2: P1, p1tbl, p1.

ROW 3: K1, [yo, k1] twice. (5 sts)

ROW 4: P1, [p1tbl, p1] twice.

ROW 5: Knit.

ROW 6: Purl.

ROWS 7-8: As rows 5–6.

ROW 9: K2tog, k1, skpo. (3 sts)

ROW 10: Purl.

ROWS 11-12: As rows 5–6.

ROW 13: S2kpo. (1 st)

Fasten off.

Finishing

Press to shape. Lightly gather center of
butterfly vertically to measure slightly less
than length of body. Attach body. Pinch
upper and lower wings together, with upper
over lower, and hold with a few sts on WS.
Using B, add antennae at top of head.

Yarn: Sport-weight yarn in mid-blue (A) and deep blue (B)

Needles: 3 knitting needles

METHOD

Lower wings (make 2)

Using A, cast on 12 sts.

ROW 1 (RS): K2, [p2, k1] 3 times, k1.

ROW 2: K1, [p1, k2] 3 times, p1, k1.

ROW 3: K2, [p2tog, k1] 3 times, k1. (9 sts)

ROW 4: K1, [p1, k1] 4 times.

ROW 5: K1, sk2po, p1, sk2po, k1. (5 sts)

ROW 6: K1, [p1, k1] twice.

ROW 7: K1, sk2po, k1. (3 sts)

Break off yarn and leave sts on spare needle.

Upper wings (make 2)

Using A, cast on 12 sts.

ROW 1 (RS): K2, [p2, k1] 3 times, k1.

ROW 2: K1, [p1, k2] 3 times, p1, k1.

ROWS 3-4: As rows 1–2.

ROW 5: K2, [p2tog, k1] 3 times, k1. (9 sts)

ROW 6: K1, [p1, k1] 4 times.

ROW 7: K2, [p1, k1] 3 times, k1.

ROW 8: As row 6.

ROW 9: K1, sk2po, p1, sk2po, k1. (5 sts)

ROW 10: K1, [p1, k1] twice.

ROW 11: K1, sk2po, k1. (3 sts)

Break off yarn and leave sts on spare needle.

Body

Using B, cast on 6 sts by cable method. Bind off knitwise.

Finishing

With RS together, line up pair of upper wings and pair of lower wings on 2 needles, then use 3rd needle to bind them off together knitwise. Press wings lightly. With yarn ends to the top, stitch body to wings, then use ends to add antennae at top of head.

ADONIS BLUE

Yarn: DK wool in pale blue (A) and deep blue (B)

Needles: 2 double-pointed needles

METHOD

NOTE: Slip stitches purlwise.

Right upper wing

Using A, cast on 4 sts.

ROW 1 (RS): [Kfb] 3 times, k1. (7 sts)

ROW 2: P1tbl, [k1, p1tbl] 3 times.

ROW 3: K1tbl, [p1, k1tbl] 3 times.

Repeat rows 2–3 (rib) three times.*

ROW 10 (WS): Rib 5, turn, slip 1, rib to end.

ROW 11: Rib 3, turn, slip 1, rib to end.

**Break off yarn. Slip sts onto other needle.
With RS facing and B, and working in back
strand only of sts at row-ends, pick up and
k1 st from shorter side edge, k7 sts from
needle, pick up and k3 sts from longer side
edge (if necessary, pick up side edge sts on
separate needle, then slip them onto
working needle). (11 sts)

Slipping first st, bind off loosely knitwise.

Right lower wing

With RS facing and A, and working in back
strand only and starting at row 1, pick up
and k5 sts along first half of shorter edge
of upper wing.

ROW 1: Pfkb, p1tbl, k1, pfkb, p1tbl. (7 sts)

ROW 2: K1tbl, [p1, k1tbl] 3 times.

ROW 3: P1tbl, [k1, p1tbl] 3 times.

Repeat rows 2–3 once.

ROW 6 (RS): Rib 5, turn, slip 1, rib 2, turn,
slip 1, rib to end.

Break off yarn. Slip sts onto other needle.
With RS facing and B, and working in back
strand only at row-ends, pick up and k2 sts
from side edge, k7 sts from needle, pick up
and k2 sts from 2nd side edge. (11 sts)

Slipping first st, bind off loosely knitwise.

Left upper wing

Work as right upper wing to *, then work
row 2 again.

ROW 11 (RS): Rib 5, turn, slip 1, rib to end.

ROW 12: Rib 3, turn, slip 1, rib to end.

Continue as right upper wing from **, picking
up 3 sts from longer side edge and 1 st from
shorter edge.

Left lower wing

Work to match right lower wing, picking
up sts along 2nd half of shorter edge of
upper wing.

Body

Using B and dpn, cast on 2 sts.

[Kfb] twice, turn, [p2tog] twice, turn.
Working on these 2 sts, knit a 1¼in (3cm)
long cord. Skpo and fasten off.

Finishing

Press to shape. Join pairs of wings in center
and attach body. Using single strand of B,
add antennae at top of head.

Yarn: Sport-weight yarn in dark gray (A) and pale gray (B)

Needles: 2 pairs, one pair a size small than the other; 2 double-pointed needles in the smaller size

Extras: Batting; 2 pins with black heads

METHOD

Horns (make 2)

Using A and dpn, cast on 2 sts and knit a cord for 3 rounds. Leave sts on spare needle.

Body

Using larger needles and A, cast on 3 sts.

ROW 1 (RS): [Kfb] twice, k1. (5 sts)

ROWS 2, 4, 6, 8 & 10: Purl.

ROW 3: K1, [m1, k1] 4 times. (9 sts)

ROW 5: K4, k2 sts of first horn, bring horn to RS, k1, k2 sts of 2nd horn, bring horn to RS, k4. (13 sts)

ROW 7: K5, m1, k3, m1, k5. (15 sts)

ROW 9: K5, [m1, k5] twice. (17 sts)

ROW 11: K1, [p1, k1] 8 times.

ROW 12: P1, [k1, p1] 8 times.

Repeat rows 11–12 three times.

ROW 19: Ssk, rib to last 2 sts, k2tog. (15 sts)

ROW 20: P1, rib to last st, p1.

ROW 21: K1, rib to last st, k1.

ROW 22: As row 20.

Repeat rows 19–22 four times, then rows 19–20 once again. (5 sts)

ROW 41: K1, s2kpo, k1. (3 sts)

Bind off purlwise.

Frill

With RS facing, using smaller needles and A, and starting at center of cast-on edge, pick up and k33 sts along side edge, ending at center of bound-off edge.

Change to B.

NEXT ROW: Purl.

NEXT ROW: K1, [m1, k1] 32 times. (65 sts)

NEXT ROW: Purl.

Bind off knitwise.

Starting at bound-off edge, work 2nd frill to match.

Underside

Using larger needles and A, cast on 2 sts.

ROW 1 (RS): Kfb, k1. (3 sts)

ROW 2 & ALL WS ROWS: Purl.

ROW 3: K1, [m1, k1] twice. (5 sts)

ROW 5: K1, m1, k3, m1, k1. (7 sts)

ROW 7: K1, m1, k5, m1, k1. (9 sts)

Beginning with a p row, work 13 rows st-st.

ROW 21: Ssk, k to last 2 sts, k2tog. (7 sts)

Work 7 rows st-st.

ROW 29: As row 21. (5 sts)

Work 7 rows st-st.

ROW 37: As row 21. (3 sts)

Work 3 rows st-st.

ROW 41: S2kpo. (1 st)

Fasten off.

Finishing

Lightly press ribs widthwise. Join ends of frill. Join underside along picked-up edge of frill, stuffing as you go. Insert a pin in each horn.

86 SMOOTH CATERPILLAR \/

Yarn: Sport-weight yarn in green (A) and lime green (B)

Needles: 2 pairs, one pair a size smaller than the other

Extras: 2 sequins

METHOD
Upper body
Using larger needles and A, cast on 5 sts.

ROW 1 (RS): Pfb, p2, pfb, p1. (7 sts)

ROWS 2 & 4: Knit.

ROW 3: Pfb, p4, pfb, p1. (9 sts)

ROWS 5: Knit.

ROW 6: Purl.

ROW 7: Purl.

ROW 8: Knit.

ROW 9: Purl.

ROW 10: Knit.

Repeat rows 5–10 three times, then rows 5–6 once again.

ROW 31: P1, p2tog, p3, p2tog, p1. (7 sts)

ROW 32: Knit.

ROW 33: P1, [p2tog, p1] twice. (5 sts)

Bind off knitwise.

Legs and underside
Using smaller needles and B, with RS facing, along one side pick up and k3 sts from shaped edge, [1 st from st-st, 3 sts from reverse st-st] 4 times, 1 st from st-st, 3 sts along remaining shaped edge. (23 sts)

P 1 row. K 1 row.

NEXT ROW: P1, [yo, p2tog] 11 times.

K 1 row. P 1 row.

NEXT ROW: [Insert right needle into st on left needle, then in corresponding B loop of pick-up row, k both sts tog] 23 times. Bind off purlwise.

Work 2nd side to match.

Finishing
Seam bound-off edges on underside. Stuff by threading several strands of A onto yarn needle and taking them through body. Neaten each end of caterpillar. Sew on sequins for eyes.

87 STRIPED CATERPILLAR |

Yarn: DK cotton in lime green (A) and black (B)

Extras: Yellow tapestry wool; batting; 18 black beads; 2 green sequins

METHOD
Using A, cast on 5 sts.

ROW 1 (WS): Purl.

ROW 2: [Kfb] 5 times. (10 sts)

ROW 3: Purl.

ROW 4: K2, [m1, k1] 8 times. (18 sts)

ROW 5: Purl.

ROWS 6-7: Using B, work 2 rows st-st.

ROWS 8-11: Using A, work 4 rows st-st.

Repeat rows 6–11 six times, then rows 6–9 once again.

NEXT ROW (RS): [K1, k2tog] 6 times. (12 sts)

Work 1 row st-st in A, 2 rows in B, and 4 rows in A.

Thread yarn through sts and draw up for tail.

Finishing
Using tapestry wool, make three French knots in center of each black stripe. Join row-ends and fill with batting. Gather cast-on sts to close head. Using B, make a loop to draw up the body in each green section except the head and tail. Stitch a pair of beads on the underside of each B stripe. Sew on sequins for eyes.

Yarn: For small caterpillar: fringed yarn in black (A) and copper (B); for large caterpillar: fringed yarn in black used double (A), and in copper and orange used together (B)

Optional: 18-gauge (1mm) galvanized steel wire or jewelry wire; wire clippers; round-nose pliers; smooth black yarn

METHOD

NOTE: The small caterpillar is worked using a single strand of yarn throughout, in the usual way. The large caterpillar is worked using two strands of yarn together throughout—two strands of black for A, and one strand each of copper and orange for B—and correspondingly larger needles.

Both woolly bear caterpillars

Using A, cast on 5 sts.
ROW 1 (RS): Knit.
ROW 2: Purl.
ROW 3: [Kfb] 5 times. (10 sts)
ROW 4: Purl.
ROW 5: Knit.
ROW 6: Purl.
Break off A and join B.
ROWS 7, 9, 11, 13 & 15: Knit.
ROWS 8, 10, 12, 14 & 16: Purl.
Break off B and rejoin A.

ROWS 17, 19, 21 & 23: Knit.
ROWS 18, 20, 22 & 24: Purl.
ROW 25: [K2tog] 5 times. (5 sts)
Break off yarn, leaving 6in (15cm) tail. Thread tail into a yarn needle and pass through remaining 5 sts. Tighten to close end of caterpillar and secure with a couple of backstitches.

Finishing

Do not trim off the yarn tails (just leave them inside the caterpillar). If you wish to make the caterpillars bendable, cut a piece of wire a little longer than caterpillar. Using pliers, wrap each end of the wire back on itself for about 1/8in (3mm) to make a rounded end. Fold body in half lengthwise, enclosing the wire and yarn tails inside, and sew seam using smooth black yarn. No stuffing is necessary because the yarn is fluffy enough to fill out the shape of the caterpillar.

Yarn: Worsted-weight wool in brown tweed (A) and amber (B)

Extras: 28-gauge (0.3mm) galvanized steel wire or jewelry wire for wings; 2 brown wooden beads; brown sewing thread; 4 black bobby pins; wire clippers; round-nose pliers; glue suitable for use with metal

METHOD

Body

Using A, cast on 3 sts.

ROW 1 (RS): Knit.

ROW 2: Purl.

ROW 3: [Kfb] 3 times. (6 sts)

ROW 4: Purl.

ROW 5: Kfb, k4, kfb. (8 sts)

ROW 6: Purl.

Without breaking off A, join B.

ROW 7: Using B, kfb, k6, kfb. (10 sts)

ROW 8: Using B, purl.

ROW 9: Using A, kfb, k8, kfb. (12 sts)

ROW 10: Using A, purl.

ROW 11: Using B, knit.

ROW 12: Using B, purl.

ROW 13: Using A, knit.

ROW 14: Using A, [p2tog] 6 times. (6 sts)

ROW 15: Using A, knit.

ROW 16: Using A, purl.

Break off A and continue in B.

ROW 17: [Kfb] 6 times. (12 sts)

ROW 18: Purl.

ROW 19: Knit.

ROW 20: Purl.

ROWS 21-22: As rows 19–20.

ROW 23: [K2tog] 6 times. (6 sts)

Break off B and rejoin A.

ROW 24: Purl.

ROW 25: [Kfb] 6 times. (12 sts)

ROW 26 (WS): Knit.

ROW 27: Purl.

ROW 28: Knit.

ROW 29: Purl.

ROW 30: [K2tog] 6 times. (6 sts)

Break off yarn, leaving 8in (20cm) tail. Thread tail into a yarn needle and pass through remaining 6 sts. Tighten to close top of head.

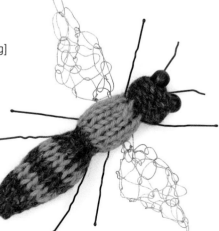

Wings (make 2)

Using wire, cast on 2 sts.

ROWS 1-2: Knit.

ROW 3: K1, lift strand lying before next st and knit into it, k1. (3 sts)

ROW 4: Knit.

ROW 5: K1, k2tog. (2 sts)

ROW 6: K2tog. (1 st)

Cut wire, leaving 10in (25cm) tail. Pass through remaining stitch and weave along side edge to cast-on edge. Bend to resemble a bee wing.

Finishing

Fold body in half lengthwise and sew seam, stuffing body with scraps of yarn A (or similar color) as you do so. Using A, work running stitch around waist (row 15) and neck (row 24) decreases, then gather tightly and secure.

Using sewing thread, sew on beads for eyes at top of head. Use pliers to bend bobby pins into the shape of three pairs of legs and a pair of antennae, trimming with wire clippers. Thread legs through bee's body and antennae through head between eyes. To steady them, apply a small amount of glue to the points that join the knitted piece. Attach a wing at each side of body by threading the tails of wire securely through body. To neaten ends of wire and avoid sharp points, cut away the excess wire, then wind the tip back on itself for about $1/8$in (3mm) and squeeze with pliers. Push the wire ends into the body.

Yarn: DK cotton in brown (A) and yellow (B)

Extras: Batting; pale yellow organza ribbon; hairspray; black plastic from frozen food container; 2 black beads; thick black sewing thread

METHOD

Using A, cast on 4 sts.

ROW 1 (RS): Knit.

ROW 2: [Pfb] 4 times. (8 sts)

ROW 3: Knit.

ROW 4: P1, m1p, p6, m1p, p1. (10 sts)

ROW 5: K1, m1, k8, m1, k1. (12 sts)

ROW 6: Purl.

ROW 7: K1, m1, k10, m1, k1. (14 sts)

Beginning with a p row, work 2 rows st-st in B,

2 rows in A, and 2 rows in B.

Break off B and work 10 rows st-st in A.

Break off yarn and pass through remaining 14 sts.

This gathered end forms the head.

Finishing

Starting at head, join row-ends, stuffing with batting as you go. Bind with A to form neck. Spray ribbon with hairspray to prevent fraying, then cut wings using template. Thread them through body just above neck. Using template, cut legs from plastic and stitch to underside of body. Sew on beads for eyes and add antennae of thick black thread, stiffened with hairspray.

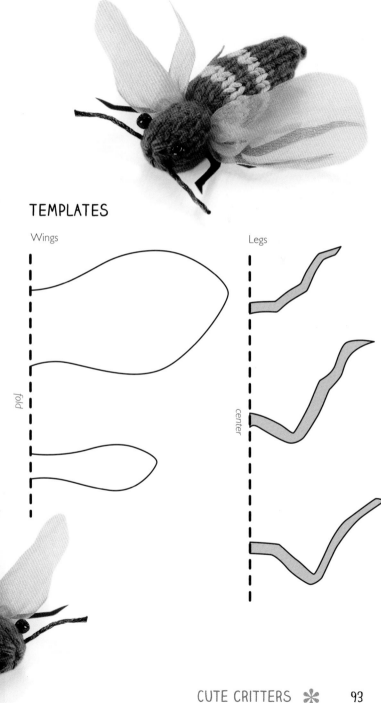

TEMPLATES

Wings

fold

Legs

center

91 BUMBLE BEE

Yarn: Sport-weight brushed yarn in orange (A) and black (B)

Extras: Batting; pale gray organza ribbon; hairspray; felt-tipped pen with fine point; black leather thonging; black sewing thread; 3 black beads; 3 bobby pins

METHOD
Using A, cast on 6 sts.
ROW 1 (RS): [Kfb] 6 times. (12 sts)
ROW 2: [Pfb, p1] 6 times. (18 sts)
ROW 3: Knit.
ROW 4: Purl.
Beginning with a k row, continue in st-st for 2 rows in B, 4 rows in A, 10 rows in B, and 4 rows in A.
Break off A and continue in B.
NEXT ROW: Knit.
NEXT ROW: [P2tog] 9 times. (9 sts)
NEXT ROW: Knit.
Thread yarn through remaining 9 sts, draw up, and fasten off.

Finishing
Gathering cast-on sts, join row-ends and fill with batting before completing seam. Pull a loop tight around body to make neck. Spray ribbon with hairspray to prevent fraying. Using template, cut wings from ribbon and mark veins with felt-tipped pen. Thread wings through the body just above neck. Pull leather thonging through head for antennae. Add whiskers of black thread, stiffened with hairspray. Sew on beads for eyes and mouth. Push bent bobby pins crosswise through body for legs.

92 FLY

Yarn: Sport-weight metallic yarn in black and green used together

Extras: Batting; pale gray organza ribbon; hairspray; felt-tipped pen with fine point; 2 yellow glass beads; 4 black bobby pins

METHOD
Using 1 strand of each yarn together, cast on 4 sts.
ROW 1 (RS): [Kfb, k1] twice. (6 sts)
ROW 2: Purl.
ROW 3: K1, m1, k to last st, m1, k1. (8 sts)
ROW 4: Purl.
ROW 5: As row 3. (10 sts)
ROW 6: Purl.
ROW 7: As row 3. (12 sts)
ROW 8: Purl.
ROW 9: [K1, m1, k2, m1] 3 times, k1, m1, k2. (19 sts)
Work 8 rows st-st.
ROW 18: P1, [p2tog] 8 times, p2. (11 sts)
Work 4 rows st-st, then thread yarn through sts, draw up, and fasten off.

Finishing
Starting at cast-on edge (tail), join row-ends and add batting before closing at underside of head. Gather tight bands of yarn around body to define head and tail. Spray ribbon with hairspray to prevent fraying, then cut out wings using template. Mark veins with felt-tipped pen and thread wings through body. Sew on beads for eyes and push bobby pins from front to back through body for legs.

TEMPLATE

TEMPLATE

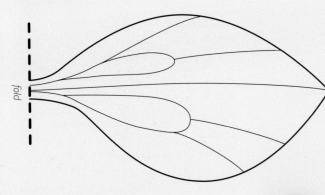

Yarn: DK wool in red (A) and black (B)

Extras: Batting

METHOD

Upper body

Using A, cast on 3 sts.

ROW 1 (RS): [Kfb] twice, k1. (5 sts)

ROW 2 & ALL WS ROWS: Purl.*

ROW 3: Kfb, [k1, m1] twice, kfb, k1. (9 sts)

ROW 5: Kfb, k3, m1, k1, m1, k2, kfb, k1. (13 sts)

ROW 7: Knit.

ROW 9: [K1, ssk] twice, k1, [k2tog, k1] twice. (9 sts)

ROW 11: K1, s2kpo, k1, k2tog, slip st just made onto left needle, pass next st over it, slip st back onto right needle, k1. (5 sts)

Change to B.

ROW 12: Purl.

ROW 13: K1, s2kpo, k1. (3 sts)

ROW 14: Slip 1, p2tog, psso.

Fasten off.

Underside

Using B, work as upper body to *.

ROW 3: Kfb, k2, kfb, k1. (7 sts)

ROWS 5 & 7: Knit.

ROW 9: K1, ssk, k1, k2tog, k1. (5 sts)

ROW 11: K1, s2kpo, k1. (3 sts)

ROW 12: Slip 1, p2tog, psso. (1 st)

Fasten off.

Finishing

Using B, duplicate stitch 5 spots onto upper body. With WS and cast-on edges together, use A to join upper body to underside, inserting batting before closing at head. If any A stitches show on underside, cover them when fastening off B.

BLUE TIT

Yarn: Sport-weight yarn in white (A), blue (B), black (C), olive (D), and yellow (E)

Needles: 4 double-pointed needles

Extras: Batting; 2 black beads; soft wire for jewelry making; small pliers (optional)

METHOD

NOTE: This bird should not be used as a toy, but it could be made without legs and with French knots for eyes to make it safe for young children.

Head

Using A and 2 dpn, cast on 2 sts.
ROW 1 (RS): K1, m1, k1. (3 sts)
ROW 2: Purl.
ROW 3: K1, [m1, k1] twice. (5 sts)
Break off A and join B.
ROW 4 & ALL WS ROWS: Purl.
ROW 5: K1, [m1, k1] 4 times. (9 sts)
ROW 7: K1, m1, k7, m1, k1. (11 sts)

ROW 9: K9, w&t, p7, w&t, k6, w&t, p5, w&t, k to end.
ROW 11: K1, k2tog, k5, ssk, k1. (9 sts)
ROW 13: K1, k2tog, s2kpo, ssk, k1. (5 sts)
ROW 14: Purl.
Break off B.
ROW 15: With RS facing and starting at cast-on edge, using first dpn and A, pick up and k3 sts from A row-ends and 9 sts from B row-ends, with 2nd dpn work (k2tog, k1, ssk) across 5 sts, with 3rd dpn pick up and k9 sts from B row-ends and 3 sts from A row-ends. (27 sts)
Now turn and work in rows with 4 dpn:
ROW 1 (WS): Purl. Break off A.
ROW 2: Using C, knit. Break off C.
ROW 3: Slip first 2 sts of row onto spare yarn. Using separate lengths of yarn, join A and p9 sts, using C p5 sts, using A p9 sts, slip last 2 sts onto spare yarn.
Turn and continue with 23 sts on needles, crossing yarns at each color change on next 6 rows.
ROW 4: K9A, (k1, m1, k3, m1, k1) using B, k9A. (25 sts)
ROW 5: P9A, p7C, p9A.
ROW 6: K9A, k7C, k9A.
ROW 7: P8A, p9C, p8A.
ROW 8: K7A, k11C, k7A.
ROW 9: P6A, p13C, p6A.
Break off A and C. Continue in D.

Back

ROW 10: K8, m1, [k3, m1] 3 times, k8. (29 sts)
ROW 11 & ALL WS ROWS: Purl.

ROW 12: Knit.
ROW 14: [K2tog] twice, k7, [m1, k7] twice, [ssk] twice. (27 sts)
ROW 16: [K2tog] twice, k6, m1, k7, m1, k6, [ssk] twice. (25 sts)
ROW 18: [K2tog] twice, k5, m1, k7, m1, k5, [ssk] twice. (23 sts)
Continue to decrease and increase in this way on RS rows, working 1 st less beside each double decrease, until row 26 has been completed and 15 sts remain.
ROW 28: [K2tog] twice, m1, k7, m1, [ssk] twice. (13 sts)
ROW 30: [K2tog] twice, k5, [ssk] twice. (9 sts)
ROW 32: K2tog, k5, ssk. (7 sts)
Break off D and continue in B.

Back of tail

NEXT ROW: Purl.
RIB ROW 1 (RS): K2, [p1, k1] twice, k1.
RIB ROW 2: K1, [p1, k1] 3 times.
Repeat rib rows 1–2 three times, then rib row 1 again. Bind off knitwise.

Front

With RS facing, slip remaining 4 sts of head onto needle and rejoin C to work bib.
ROW 1: [K2tog] twice. (2 sts)
ROW 2 & ALL WS ROWS: Purl.
ROW 3: K1, m1, k1. (3 sts)
ROW 5: K1, [m1, k1] twice. (5 sts)
ROW 7: K1, m1, k3, m1, k1. (7 sts)
Break off C and continue in E.
Beginning with a p row, work 3 rows st-st.
ROW 11: K1, [m1, k1] 6 times. (13 sts)
ROW 13: K1, m1, k to last st, m1, k1. (15 sts)

ROW 15: As row 13. (17 sts)

ROW 17: K to last 2 sts, w&t, p to last 2 sts, w&t, k to last 3 sts, w&t, p to last 3 sts, w&t, k to end.

ROW 19: As row 13. (19 sts)

ROW 21: As row 17.

ROW 23: As row 13. (21 sts)

ROW 25: As row 17.

ROW 27: Ssk, k3, ssk, k7, k2tog, k3, k2tog. (17 sts)

ROW 29: Ssk, k2, ssk, k5, k2tog, k2, k2tog. (13 sts)

ROW 31: Ssk, k1, ssk, s2kpo, k2tog, k1, k2tog. (7 sts)

Break off E and continue in B.

Front of tail

Work as back of tail.

Wing tips

With RS facing and D, starting at first decrease along edge of left back, pick up and k19 sts. Change to B.

ROW 1: Purl.

ROW 2 (RS): K2, [p1, k1] 7 times, w&t, rib 13, w&t, rib 11, w&t, rib 9, w&t, rib to end. Bind off knitwise.

Work 2nd wing tip to match.

Beak

Using C, cast on 5 sts.

ROW 1 (RS): K1, s2kpo, k1. (3 sts)

Draw yarn through remaining 3 sts and pull tight.

Finishing

Starting with head, turn to WS to carefully fasten off ends. On RS, join edges of C rows of bib to A row-ends and neaten A sts around cast-on group above. Stuff head, then joining cast-on edge into a ring, sew beak to top of bib. Neaten ends of wing tips and, starting at head, join back and front, stuffing as you stitch. Close body at tail end and on RS join both tail pieces by backstitching through both layers just inside the edge sts. Sew on beads for eyes. Cut a length of wire—approximately 18in (45cm)—and using fingers or pliers, leave an end to form an upright in the bird's body and then bend the wire to form 4 toes (diagram 1). Take the wire along the leg, making a 90-degree bend where the top of the leg is to be. Insert the long remaining length of wire through the body to exit where the 2nd leg is to be and, at the same time, bury the first upright in the body above the first leg. Bend the long end into a leg to match the first and trim the excess to make a 2nd upright to go inside the body (diagram 2). Using C, bind the legs and feet, without covering the claws. At the top of the legs, bind further with E.

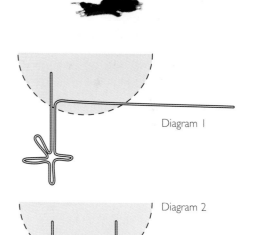

Diagram 1

Diagram 2

Yarn: Worsted-weight wool in reddish orange (A), gray (B), brown (C), and gold (D)

Needles: 4 double-pointed needles

Extras: 2 stitch holders; 2 black beads; black sewing thread; ecru embroidery thread; batting (optional)

METHOD

Belly

Using A and pair of needles, cast on 7 sts.
ROW 1 (RS): Knit.
ROW 2 & ALL WS ROWS: Purl.
ROW 3: K1, m1, k5, m1, k1. (9 sts)
ROW 5: [K1, m1] twice, k5, [m1, k1] twice. (13 sts)
ROW 7: [K1, m1] 3 times, k7, [m1, k1] 3 times. (19 sts)
ROW 9: K1, m1, k to last st, m1, k1. (21 sts)
ROW 11: Knit.
ROW 13: K1, m1, k to last st, m1, k1. (23 sts)
ROW 15: Knit.
ROW 17: K1, m1, k to last st, m1, k1. (25 sts)
ROW 19: Knit.
ROW 21: K23 to last 2 sts, w&t, p21 to last 2 sts, w&t, k20 to last 3 sts, w&t, p19 to last 3 sts, w&t, k22 to end.

ROW 23: Knit all sts.
ROW 25: As row 21.
ROW 27: K17 to last 8 sts, k2tog, w&t, slip first st, p9 to last 8 sts, p2tog, w&t, slip first st, k9 to last 7 sts, k2tog, w&t, slip first st, p9 to last 7 sts, p2tog, w&t, slip first st, k9 to last 6 sts, k2tog, w&t, slip first st, p9 to last 6 sts, p2tog, p to end. (19 sts)
ROW 28 (RS): K2tog, k to last 2 sts, k2tog. (17 sts)
ROW 30: K2tog, k1, k2tog, k to last 5 sts, k2tog, k1, k2tog. (13 sts)
ROW 32: K2tog, k1, k2tog, k3, k2tog, k1, k2tog. (9 sts)
ROW 33: Purl.
Break off yarn and slip remaining 9 sts onto stitch holder.

Tail and back

Using B and pair of needles, cast on 19 sts.
ROW 1 (RS): K2, p3, k9, p3, k2.
ROWS 2, 4, 6, 8, 10 & 12: K all k sts and p all p sts as they appear.
ROW 3: K2, p3, k3, cdd, k3, p3, k2. (17 sts)
ROW 5: K2, p3, k2, cdd, k2, p3, k2. (15 sts)
ROW 7: K2, p3, k1, cdd, k1, p3, k2. (13 sts)
ROW 9: K2, p1, p2tog, k3, p2tog, p1, k2. (11 sts)
ROW 11: K2, p2, k3, p2, k2.
ROW 13: Ssk, p2tog, k3, p2tog, k2tog. (7 sts)
ROW 14: Purl. Place marker on this WS row.
ROW 15: Knit.
ROW 16 & ALL FOLL WS ROWS: Purl.
ROW 17: K1, m1, k5, m1, k1. (9 sts)
ROW 19: Knit.
ROW 21: K1, m1, k7, m1, k1. (11 sts)

ROW 23: Knit.
ROW 25: K1, m1, k9, m1, k1. (13 sts)
ROW 27: K1, m1, k11, m1, k1. (15 sts)
ROW 29: K1, m1, k13, m1, k1. (17 sts)
ROW 31: K1, m1, k15, m1, k1. (19 sts)
ROW 33: K1, m1, k17, m1, k1. (21 sts)
ROWS 35, 37 & 39: Knit.
ROW 40: Purl.
Shape right side of neck as follows:
ROW 41: K7, slip remaining 14 sts onto 2nd stitch holder.
Continue on first 7 sts only as follows:
ROWS 42, 44, 46 & 48: Purl.
ROW 43: K5, k2tog. (6 sts)
ROW 45: K2tog, k2, k2tog. (4 sts)
ROW 47: [K2tog] twice. (2 sts)
ROW 49: K2tog. (1 st)
Fasten off.
Shape left side of neck as follows:
Slip last 7 sts from 2nd stitch holder onto left needle, leaving center 7 sts on holder.
ROW 41: K7.
ROWS 42 & 44: Purl.
ROW 43: K2tog, k5. (6 sts)
ROWS 45-49: As for right side of neck.
Fasten off.

Assembling body

Using B, sew the two pieces together, attaching belly at each end of marked row just above tail section (leave cast-on edge of belly unattached to allow for stuffing later). Ease the side edges so that last row of belly meets top of neck shaping.

Head

Using C, begin at upper body section as follows: using first dpn, pick up and k5 sts from right side of neck, k7 sts from 2nd stitch holder; using 2nd dpn, pick up and k5 sts from left side of neck; using 3rd dpn, knit across belly sts from first stitch holder, working 2 sts together at center to make 8 sts from 9 sts on holder. (25 sts)

ROUNDS 1-5: Knit.

ROUND 6: K4, k2tog, k5, k2tog, k to end. (23 sts)

Break off C. Slip last 4 sts of round 6 onto first dpn, then first 3 sts of round 6; slip next 9 sts onto 2nd dpn; slip remaining 7 sts onto 3rd dpn. (23 sts)

Rejoin C between first and 3rd dpn and work in rows, beginning and ending each row at center front of neck as follows:

ROW 1 (RS): Knit to end.

ROW 2: Purl to end.

Begin short-row shaping for top of head as follows:

K22 to last st, turn.
P21 to last st, turn.
K20 to last 2 sts, turn.
P19 to last 2 sts, turn.
K18 to last 3 sts, turn.
P17 to last 3 sts, turn.

Continue in this way for 8 more rows, until 7 sts remain unworked at each end, ending with a p row.

Now join center sts on 2nd dpn to unworked sts on first and 3rd dpn, beginning with sts on 2nd dpn where you just left off as follows:

ROW 1 (RS): Slip 1, k7, slip 1 st from next dpn onto center dpn, k2tog, turn.

ROW 2: Slip 1, p7, slip 1 st from next dpn onto center dpn, p2tog, turn.

Repeat rows 1–2 six times, ending with a WS row. (9 sts remain on center dpn)

Break off C and join D for beak.

Beak

ROW 1 (RS): Knit. (9 sts)

ROW 2: Purl.

ROW 3: K1, k2tog, k3, k2tog, k1. (7 sts)

ROW 4: Purl.

ROW 5: K2, cdd, k2. (5 sts)

ROW 6: P2tog, p1, p2tog. (3 sts)

ROW 7: Cdd. (1 st)

Fasten off, leaving 6in (15cm) tail for seaming beak.

Wings (make 2)

Using B and pair of needles, cast on 2 sts.

ROW 1 (RS): Knit.

ROW 2: Purl.

ROW 3: Kfb, m1, kfb. (5 sts)

ROW 4: P1, k1, p1, k1, p1.

ROW 5: K1, m1, p1, k1, p1, m1, k1. (7 sts)

ROW 6: P2, k1, p1, k1, p2.

ROW 7: K1, m1, [k1, p1] twice, k1, m1, k1. (9 sts)

ROWS 8, 10 & 12: [P1, k1] 4 times, p1.

ROWS 9 & 11: [K1, p1] 4 times, k1.

ROW 13: K1, m1, [p1, k1] 3 times, p1, m1, k1. (11 sts)

ROWS 14, 16, 18 & 20: [K1, p1] 5 times, k1.

ROWS 15, 17 & 19: [P1, k1] 5 times, p1.

ROW 21: K2tog, [p1, k1] 3 times, p1, k2tog. (9 sts)

ROW 22: K2tog, [p1, k1] twice, p1, k2tog. (7 sts)

ROW 23: K2tog, p1, k1, p1, k2tog. (5 sts)

Bind off in k and p as set.

Finishing

Using tails of yarn, sew top of wings to body. Stuff robin with scraps of yarn B or batting, working batting in from lower opening at tail and upper opening at head. Any holes at top of head where short rows were worked may be closed by stitching firmly with yarn C. Join neck and beak seam. Close tail opening. Using sewing thread, sew a bead at each side of head for eyes. Using embroidery thread, stitch a few small lines above and below each bead to form small crescent shapes.

Yarn: Sport-weight yarn in pink (A) and white (B)

Needles: 4 double-pointed needles

Extras: Batting; 2 red beads

METHOD

Using A and pair of needles, cast on 2 sts.

ROW 1 (RS): Kfb, k1. (3 sts)

ROWS 2 & 4: Purl.

ROW 3: K1, [m1, k1] twice. (5 sts)

ROW 5: Knit.

ROW 6: Purl. Change to B.

ROW 7: K1, [m1, k1] 4 times. (9 sts)

ROW 8: Purl.

ROW 9: K2, m1, [k1, m1] 5 times, k2. (15 sts)

ROW 10: P1, m1p, p to last st, m1p, p1.
(17 sts)

ROW 11: K1, m1, k14, w&t, p13, w&t, k11,
w&t, p9, w&t, k7, w&t, p5, w&t, k10, m1, k1.
(19 sts)

ROW 12: As row 10. (21 sts)

ROW 13: K1, m1, k1, [ssk] 4 times, k1, [k2tog]
4 times, k1, m1, k1. (15 sts)

Change to dpn, putting 5 sts on each of
3 needles and marking beginning of
each round.

ROUND 1 (RS): Knit.

ROUND 2: [K1, m1] 3 times, k2, ssk, k1, k2tog,
k2, [m1, k1] 3 times. (19 sts)

ROUNDS 3-4: Knit.

ROUND 5: K1, m1, [k2, m1] 3 times, k5,
[m1, k2] 3 times, m1, k1. (27 sts)

ROUNDS 6-8: Knit.

ROUND 9: K1, m1, [k2, m1] 3 times, k13,
[m1, k2] 3 times, m1, k1. (35 sts)

ROUNDS 10-12: Knit.

ROUND 13: K1, m1, [k2, m1] 5 times, k13,
[m1, k2] 5 times, m1, k1. (47 sts)

ROUNDS 14-21: Knit.

ROUND 22: K7, ssk, [k2, ssk] twice, k13,
[k2tog, k2] twice, k2tog, k7. (41 sts)

ROUNDS 23-24: Knit.

ROUND 25: K7, ssk, [k1, ssk] twice, k11,
[k2tog, k1] twice, k2tog, k7. (35 sts)

ROUNDS 26-27: Knit.

ROUND 28: K7, [ssk] 3 times, k9, [k2tog]
3 times, k7. (29 sts)

ROUNDS 29-30: Knit.

ROUND 31: K5, [ssk] 3 times, k7, [k2tog]
3 times, k5. (23 sts)

ROUNDS 32-33: Knit.

ROUND 34: K1, [ssk] 4 times, k5, [k2tog]
4 times, k1. (15 sts)

Close underside of head and beak. Insert
batting, lightly filling head but shaping
body firmly.

ROUND 35: K1, [p1, k1] 6 times, p2tog.
(14 sts)

ROUND 36: [K1, p1] to end.

ROUND 37: [K1, pfb] 7 times. (21 sts)

ROUND 38: [K1, p2] to end.

ROUND 39: [K1, p1, m1, p1] 7 times. (28 sts)

ROUNDS 40-42: As round 36.

ROUND 43: [K1, pfb] 14 times. (42 sts)

ROUNDS 44-48: As round 38.

PICOT BIND-OFF: *Cast on 2 sts by knitted
method, bind off 3 sts, slip remaining st from
right needle to left needle; repeat from * to
last st. Fasten off.

Wings (make 2)

Using B and pair of needles, cast on 37 sts.

ROW 1 (RS): P1, [k1, p1] to end.

ROW 2: K1, [p1, k1] to end.

ROW 3: Rib 35, w&t, rib 33, w&t, rib 31, w&t, rib 29, w&t, rib 27, w&t, rib 25, w&t, rib to end.

ROW 4: As row 2.

Picot bind-off as before.

Finishing

Fold wings in half and join along inside of picot bind-off. Flatten tail and join in the same way. Position wings along line of shaping on each side of back. Overcast along top edge of wing, working into each purl st of rib, then sew underside to match, catching down the end of the wing. Sew on beads for eyes.

Yarn: DK yarn for larger egg; sport-weight yarn for smaller egg (an elastic yarn such as pure wool is essential)

Needles: 4 double-pointed needles, two sizes smaller than usual for the yarn

Extras: Egg molds (from craft stores)

METHOD

Cast 3 sts onto 1 dpn.

FOUNDATION ROW (RS): [Kfb] 3 times. (6 sts)

Without twisting, put 2 sts onto each of 3 dpn. With RS facing and using 4 dpn, continue in rounds of knit. Use contrast yarn to mark the end of each round.

ROUND 1: [Kfb] 6 times. (12 sts)

ROUND 2 & ALTERNATE ROUNDS: Knit.

ROUND 3: [K2, m1] 6 times. (18 sts)

ROUND 5: [K2, m1] 9 times. (27 sts)

ROUND 7: [K3, m1] 9 times. (36 sts)

ROUNDS 8-23: Knit.

Use end at base to neaten the joining round, then fasten it off on the inside.

ROUND 24: [K4, k2tog] 6 times. (30 sts)

ROUNDS 25-28: Knit.

ROUND 29: [K3, k2tog] 6 times. (24 sts)

ROUNDS 30-31: Knit.

ROUND 32: [K2tog] 12 times. (12 sts)

Slip sts onto contrast yarn and insert mold, rounder end first. Replace sts onto 3 dpn.

ROUND 33: [K2tog] 6 times. (6 sts)

Pull out marker yarn. Break off main yarn and take it through remaining 6 sts in the direction of work. Fasten off firmly.

GRAY NEST

Yarn: DK yarn in dark gray (A) and light gray (B)

Needles: 2 pairs, one pair a size smaller than the other

METHOD

Using A and larger needles, cast on 4 sts.

ROW 1 (RS): [Kfb] 4 times. (8 sts)

ROW 2 AND ALL WS ROWS: Purl.

ROW 3: [Kfb] 8 times. (16 sts)

ROW 5: [Kfb] 16 times. (32 sts)

ROW 7: [K1, make 10-st chain in next st, drop chain st, wyif slip next 5 sts purlwise, wyab put chain st onto left needle, then k this st, k next st] 4 times.

ROW 9: [K1, kfb, k2] 8 times. (40 sts)

ROW 11: As [ ] of row 7 five times.

ROW 13: [K2, kfb, k2] 8 times. (48 sts)

ROW 15: As [ ] of row 7 six times.

ROW 17: [K2, kfb, k3] 8 times. (56 sts)

ROW 19: As [ ] of row 7 seven times.

ROW 21: Knit.

ROW 23: As row 19.

Continue in B with smaller needles.

ROWS 25-27: Knit.

Beginning with a p row, work 5 rows st-st.

ROW 33: [K5, k2tog] 8 times. (48 sts)

Work 3 rows st-st.

ROW 37: [K4, k2tog] 8 times. (40 sts)

Work 3 rows st-st.

ROW 41: [K3, k2tog] 8 times. (32 sts)

ROW 42: Purl.

ROW 43: [K2tog] 16 times. (16 sts)

ROW 44: Purl.

ROW 45: [K2tog] 8 times. (8 sts)

ROW 46: [P2tog] 4 times.

Fasten off by running end of yarn through remaining 4 sts.

Finishing

With RS facing, join seam using mattress stitch. Tug chain loops and press lightly. With light gray lining turned in, use B to slightly gather top by running a thread around inside of edge sts.

SWANSDOWN

Yarn: DK yarn (preferably with a multi-strand construction)

Needles: Small-size knitting needles

METHOD

SPECIFIC INSTRUCTIONS

Single loop = *K1 st without slipping it off, bring yarn between needles to front, take yarn under and over left thumb, then back between needles,** k st remaining on left needle, drop loop, slip 2nd st on right needle over first st.

Double loop = Taking yarn under and over left thumb twice, work as single loop from * to **, then again taking yarn around thumb twice, repeat from * to **; k st remaining on left needle, slip 2nd and 3rd sts on right needle over first st.

Triple loop = Taking yarn around left thumb twice, work as single loop from * to **, then again taking yarn around thumb twice, repeat from * to ** twice; k st remaining on left needle, slip 2nd, 3rd, and 4th sts on right needle over first st.

Feather

Make a 6-st chain and, without turning, slip last st back onto left needle. Cast on 16 sts using the knitted method. (17 sts)

LOOP ROW: Make 3 single loops, 4 double loops, 3 triple loops, 4 double loops, 3 single loops. Slipping first st, bind off purlwise. Fasten off, leaving a long end.

Finishing

With cast-on edge facing, fold loop row so that chain remains free. Using long end and taking in one strand from each edge, join pairs of cast-on sts with overcasting. Turn over and join bound-off sts with backstitch. Fasten off first end by taking yarn through each st of chain to counteract any curve in the chain. Cut each loop at the halfway point. Trim lower loops and then use yarn needle to fray out all ends of yarn.

Yarn: Worsted-weight acrylic in orange (A) and white (B)

Needles: 4 double-pointed needles

Extras: Black yarn; batting

METHOD

NOTE: This fish is worked in the round. In the beginning when there are few stitches, work on 2 dpn as you would a cord (sliding the stitches to the other end of the needle when a round is completed). You can either splice the yarn to make the stripes when changing between the orange and white parts, or just leave the free end to pick up later.

Body

Using A, cast on 1 st.
ROUND 1: (K1, p1, k1) in same st. (3 sts)
ROUND 2: [Kfb] 3 times. (6 sts)
ROUND 3: [K1, m1] 5 times, k1. (11 sts)
Distribute sts onto 3 dpn.
ROUND 4: [K1, m1] 10 times, k1. (21 sts)
ROUNDS 5-6: Knit.
ROUND 7: [K6, m1] 3 times, k3. (24 sts)
ROUNDS 8-9: Using B, knit.
ROUND 10: [K6, m1] 4 times. (28 sts)
ROUNDS 11-14: Using A, knit.
ROUND 15: [K7, k2tog] 3 times, k1. (25 sts)
ROUND 16: Using B, knit. (25 sts)
ROUND 17: [K6, k2tog] 3 times, k1. (22 sts)
ROUND 18: Knit.
ROUND 19: [K9, k2tog] twice. (20 sts)
ROUND 20: Using A, knit.
ROUND 21: [K4, k2tog] 3 times, k2. (17 sts)
ROUND 22: Knit.

ROUND 23: [K4, k2tog] twice, k5. (15 sts)
ROUND 24: Knit.
ROUND 25: Using B, [k4, k2tog] twice, k3. (13 sts)
ROUND 26: Knit.
ROUND 27: [K3, k2tog] twice, k3. (11 sts)
ROUND 28: Using A, knit.
ROUND 29: K2tog, k9. (10 sts)
Stuff the fish.
To form the tail, distribute sts evenly onto 2 dpn and hold needles parallel together. On next row, use 3rd dpn to work sts alternately from front and back needles.
ROWS 30-31: [P1, k1] 5 times.
ROW 32: Kfb, [k1, p1] 5 times, kfb. (12 sts)
ROW 33: [K1, p1] 6 times. (12 sts)
Bind off.

Side fins (make 2)

Using A, cast on 6 sts.
ROW 1: Kfb, [p1, k1] twice, kfb. (8 sts)
ROWS 2-3: [P1, k1] 4 times.
Bind off.

Back fins (make 2)

Using A, cast on 4 sts.
Bind off.

Top fin

Using A, cast on 8 sts.
ROW 1: [K1, p1] 4 times.
Bind off.

Bottom fin

Using A, cast on 4 sts.
ROW 1: [K1, p1] twice.
Bind off.

Finishing

Using black yarn, sew large French knots for pupils, then sew yarn B around them to complete the eyes. Using A, add shaping to the mouth.

101 MYSTERY WRASSE V

Yarn: Superfine yarn in orange (A) and purple (B)

Needles: 3 double-pointed needles

Extras: Batting; 2 pony beads; sewing thread; embroidery thread

METHOD
Body
Using A, cast on 4 sts.

ROUND 1: [Kfb] 4 times. (8 sts)

ROUND 2: Knit.

ROUND 3: [Kfb, k3] twice. (10 sts)

ROUND 4: Knit.

ROUND 5: [K4, kfb] twice. (12 sts)

ROUND 6: Knit.

ROUND 7: [K5, kfb] twice. (14 sts)

ROUNDS 8-11: Knit.

ROUND 12: [K5, k2tog] twice. (12 sts)

ROUND 13: Knit.

ROUND 14: [K4, k2tog] twice. (10 sts)

ROUND 15: Knit.

Stuff the fish.

ROUND 16: [K2tog, k3] twice. (8 sts)

ROUND 17: Knit.

ROUND 18: [K2tog, k2] twice. (6 sts)

To form the tail, distribute sts evenly onto 2 dpn and hold needles parallel together. On next row, use 3rd dpn to work sts alternately from front and back needles.

ROWS 19-20: [K1, p1] 3 times.

Bind off knitwise.

Top fin
Using B, cast on 10 sts. Bind off knitwise.

Bottom fin
Using B, cast on 6 sts. Bind off knitwise.

Finishing
Sew on pony beads for eyes. using embroidery thread, work asymmetrical chain stitches or other surface embroidery onto the body in stripes.

102 FAIRY WRASSE I

Yarn: Lightweight yarn in pink (A) and yellow (B)

Needles: 3 double-pointed needles

Extras: Batting; 2 pony beads; black felt; sewing thread; embroidery thread

METHOD
Using A, cast on 3 sts.

ROUND 1: [Kfb] 3 times. (6 sts)

ROUND 2: [Kfb, k2] twice. (8 sts)

ROUND 3: Knit.

ROUND 4: [Kfb, k3] twice. (10 sts)

ROUND 5: Knit.

ROUND 6: [K4, kfb] twice. (12 sts)

ROUNDS 7-10: Knit.

Stuff the fish, then continue in B.

ROUNDS 11-12: Knit.

ROUND 13: [K4, k2tog] twice. (10 sts)

ROUND 14: Knit.

ROUND 15: [K2tog, k3] twice. (8 sts)

ROUND 16: Knit.

ROUND 17: [K2tog, k2] twice. (6 sts)

ROUND 18: [K2tog] 3 times. (3 sts)

ROUND 19: K2tog, k1. (2 sts)

ROUND 20: K2tog. (1 st)

Fasten off.

Finishing
Cut 1 dorsal, 1 ventral, 2 side fins, and 2 tail fins out of felt. Using sewing thread, stitch these to the body. Sew on pony beads for eyes. With embroidery thread, add designs to the fins.

Yarn: Worsted-weight acrylic in purple (A) and mustard (B)

Needles: 4 double-pointed needles

Extras: Contrasting and light-colored yarn; batting

METHOD

NOTE: This fish is worked in the round. In the beginning when there are few stitches, work on 2 dpn as you would a cord (sliding the stitches to the other end of the needle when a round is completed).

Body

Using A, cast on 1 st.

ROUND 1: (K1, p1, k1) in same st. (3 sts)

ROUND 2: [Kfb] 3 times. (6 sts)

ROUND 3: [Kfb] 6 times. (12 sts)

Distribute sts onto 3 dpn.

ROUNDS 4-14: Knit.

ROUND 15: K2tog, k10. (11 sts)

ROUND 16: K4, k2tog, k5. (10 sts)

ROUND 17: K2tog, k8. (9 sts)

Change to B.

ROUND 18: Knit.

ROUND 19: K5, k2tog, k2. (8 sts)

ROUNDS 20-21: Knit.

ROUND 22: K2tog, k6. (7 sts)

ROUNDS 23-24: Knit.

ROUND 25: K2tog, k5. (6 sts)

Stuff the fish.

To form the tail, distribute sts evenly onto 2 dpn and hold needles parallel together. On next row, use 3rd dpn to work sts alternately from front and back needles.

ROW 26: Knit.

ROW 27: [P1, k1] 3 times.

ROW 28: [P1, k1] 3 times.

ROW 29: Kfb, [k1, p1] twice, kfb. (8 sts)

ROW 30: [K1, p1] 4 times.

Bind off.

Top fin

Using A, cast on 6 sts.

Bind off.

Bottom fin

Using A, cast on 4 sts.

Bind off.

Side fins (make 2)

Using A, cast on 2 sts.

ROW 1: Knit.

ROW 2: [Kfb] twice. (4 sts)

Bind off.

Finishing

Sew fins to body. Using contrasting yarn, sew large French knots for pupils, then wrap light-colored yarn around them to complete the eyes.

Yarn: Worsted-weight acrylic in green (A) and yellow (B)

Needles: 4 double-pointed needles

Extras: Contrasting color yarn

METHOD

NOTE: This fish is worked in the round. In the beginning when there are few stitches, work on 2 dpn as you would a cord (sliding the stitches to the other end of the needle when a round is completed).

Body

Using A, cast on 3 sts.

ROUND 1: Knit.

ROUND 2: K2, m1, k1. (4 sts)

ROUND 3: Knit.

ROUND 4: K1, m1, k3. (5 sts)

ROUND 5: K2, m1, k2, m1, k1. (7 sts)

ROUNDS 6-7: Knit.

ROUND 8: M1, k7. (8 sts)

Distribute sts onto 3 dpn if you find this unwieldy.

ROUNDS 9-12: Knit.

ROUND 13: K4, m1, k4. (9 sts)

ROUNDS 14-16: Knit.

ROUND 17: K2tog, k7. (8 sts)

ROUND 18: Knit.

ROUND 19: K3, k2tog, k3. (7 sts)

ROUND 20: K2tog, k5. (6 sts)

ROUND 21: K2, k2tog, k2. (5 sts)

ROUNDS 22-23: Knit.

ROUND 24: K2tog, k3. (4 sts)

To form the tail, turn and continue in rows

ROWS 25-26: [K1, p1] twice.

ROW 27: Kfb, p1, k1, kfb. (6 sts)

Bind off.

Fins (make 2)

Cast on 2 sts.

ROW 1: [Kfb] twice. (4 sts)

Bind off.

Finishing

Sew fins to body. Stitch zebra stripes in B using duplicate stitch. Using contrasting yarn, sew large French knots for pupils, then wrap B around them to complete the eyes.

ANGELFISH \//

Yarn: Worsted-weight acrylic in turquoise (A) and indigo (B)

Needles: 4 double-pointed needles

Extras: Contrasting color yarn

METHOD

NOTE: This fish is worked in the round. In the beginning when there are few stitches, work on 2 dpn as you would a cord (sliding the stitches to the other end of the needle when a round is completed).

Body

Using A, cast on 3 sts.

ROUND 1: K1, m1, k2. (4 sts)

ROUND 2: K2, m1, k2. (5 sts)

ROUND 3: [K2, m1] twice, k1. (7 sts)

ROUND 4: [K2, m1] 3 times, k1. (10 sts)

ROUND 5: [K3, m1] 3 times, k1. (13 sts)

Distribute sts onto 3 dpn.

ROUND 6: [K4, m1] 3 times, k1. (16 sts)

ROUND 7: Using B, [k5, m1] 3 times, k1. (19 sts)

ROUND 8: [K6, m1] 3 times, k1. (22 sts)

ROUND 9: Using A, [k8, m1] 3 times, k1. (28 sts)

ROUNDS 10-13: Knit.

ROUND 14: Using B, [k6, m1] 4 times, k3. (31 sts)

ROUNDS 15-16: Knit.

ROUNDS 17-18: Using A, knit.

ROUND 19: [K4, k2tog] 5 times, k1. (26 sts)

ROUND 20: [K4, k2tog] 4 times, k2. (22 sts)

ROUND 21: [K3, k2tog] 4 times, k2. (18 sts)

ROUND 22: [K2, k2tog] 4 times, k2. (14 sts)

ROUND 23: [K1, k2tog] 4 times, k2. (10 sts)

ROUND 24: [K3, k2tog] twice. (8 sts)

To form the tail, distribute sts evenly onto 2 dpn and hold needles parallel together. On next row, use 3rd dpn to work sts alternately from front and back needles.

ROWS 25-26: [P1, k1] 4 times.

ROW 27: Kfb, [k1, p1] 3 times, kfb. (10 sts)

ROWS 28-29: [K1, p1] 5 times.

ROW 30: Kfb, [p1, k1] 4 times, kfb. (12 sts)

ROW 31: Kfb, [k1, p1] 5 times, kfb. (14 sts)

ROW 32: Using B, kfb, [p1, k1] 6 times, kfb. (16 sts)

Bind off.

Top and bottom fins (make 1 each)

Using B, cast on 12 sts.

ROW 1: [K1, p1] 6 times.

ROW 2: [K1, p1] 4 times, [k2tog] twice. (10 sts)

ROW 3: [K1, p1] 3 times, [k2tog] twice. (8 sts)

ROW 4: [K1, p1] twice, [k2tog] twice. (6 sts)

ROW 5: K1, p1, [k2tog] twice. (4 sts)

ROW 6: [K2tog] twice. (2 sts)

ROW 7: K2tog. (1 st)

Fasten off.

Thin front fins

Using B, cast on 24 sts.

Bind off.

Finishing

Pull the thin front fin halfway through the body and stitch in place. Sew top and bottom fins in place. Using B, sew French knots for pupils, then wrap a contrasting color around them to complete the eyes.

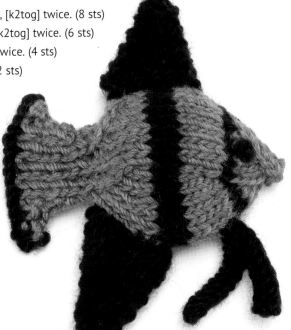

106 COURT JESTER GOBY

Yarn: Lightweight yarn

Needles: 3 double-pointed needles

Extras: Batting; lightweight orange yarn; 2 pony beads; black felt; sewing thread

METHOD

Cast on 3 sts.

ROUND 1: [Kfb] 3 times. (6 sts)

ROUND 2: [K1, kfb] 3 times. (9 sts)

ROUND 3: [K1, kfb] 3 times. (12 sts)

ROUND 4: Knit.

ROUND 5: [K5, kfb] twice. (14 sts)

ROUNDS 6-12: Knit.

ROUND 13: [K5, k2tog] twice. (12 sts)

ROUNDS 14-16: Knit.

ROUND 17: [K2tog, k4] twice. (10 sts)

ROUNDS 18-19: Knit.

ROUND 20: [K2tog, k3] twice. (8 sts)

ROUNDS 21-22: Knit.

Stuff the fish.

ROUND 23: [K2, k2tog] twice. (6 sts)

ROUNDS 24-25: Knit.

ROUND 26: [K2tog] 3 times. (3 sts)

Bind off knitwise.

Finishing

Cut fin shapes, 2 tail shapes, and 2 small circles out of felt for use behind eyes. Using sewing thread, couch stitch the orange yarn onto the body in stripes. Any loose ends can be left at the tail, since this will be covered with felt. For each eye, sew a pony bead on top of a felt circle. Sew fins to body, using 2 pieces on the tail to conceal any loose ends from the orange yarn.

107 SPRAT

Yarn: Sport-weight metallic yarn used double

Needles: 2 pairs, one pair a size smaller than the other

Extras: Batting; flat matte silver sequins; 2 larger faceted silver sequins; transparent sewing thread

METHOD

Using larger needles, cast on 3 sts.

ROW 1 & ALL WS ROWS: Purl.

ROW 2: K1, [m1, k1] twice. (5 sts)

ROW 4: K1, [m1, k1] 4 times. (9 sts)

ROW 6: [K1, m1] 3 times, k3, [m1, k1] 3 times. (15 sts)

Beginning with a p row, work 3 rows st-st.

ROW 10: [K3, m1] twice, k3, [m1, k3] twice. (19 sts)

Work 7 rows st-st.

ROW 18: K3, skpo, k2tog, k5, skpo, k2tog, k3. (15 sts)

Work 5 rows st-st.

ROW 24: K2, skpo, k2tog, k3, skpo, k2tog, k2. (11 sts)

Work 3 rows st-st.

ROW 28: K1, skpo, k2tog, k1, skpo, k2tog, k1. (7 sts)

Change to smaller needles.

Work 3 rows st-st.

ROW 32: Skpo, k1, [m1, k1] twice, k2tog. (7 sts)

ROWS 33 & 35: P1, [k1, p1] 3 times.

ROW 34: K1, [p1, k1] 3 times.

ROW 36: K1, [pfb, k1] 3 times. (10 sts)

Bind off knitwise.

Finishing

Taking in half a stitch from each edge, join back seam with mattress stitch, lightly filling with batting and finishing at decreases of row 32 to leave tail free. Starting 1in (2.5cm) from tail end, sew overlapping flat sequins onto the body. For each eye, sew a flat sequin over a faceted one.

Yarn: Lightweight yarn

Needles: 3 double-pointed needles

Extras: Yellow yarn; black sewing thread

METHOD

NOTE: This creature is worked as a cord, starting from the tail. When you reach the jaws, you will leave some of the stitches on one needle, and work the others in a row. After finishing, you can return to the other stitches and work them in a row as well.

Body

Cast on 4 sts.

ROUNDS 1-5: Knit.

ROUND 6: Kfb, k to end. (5 sts)

Repeat rounds 1–6 five times. (10 sts)

Knit 11 rounds.

NEXT ROUND: K4.

Turn and continue in rows on these 4 sts only, leaving the other 6 sts on needle (these will form upper jaw).

Lower jaw

ROW 1 (WS): Purl. (4 sts)

ROW 2: Knit.

ROW 3: Purl.

ROW 4: Ssk, k2tog. (2 sts)

ROW 5: Purl.

Bind off.

Upper jaw

Now return to 6 sts left on needle.

ROW 1: With RS facing, k2, m1, k2, m1, k2. (8 sts)

ROW 2: Purl. (8 sts)

ROW 3: Knit.

ROW 4: Purl.

ROW 5: [Ssk] twice, [k2tog] twice. (4 sts)

ROW 6: Purl.

ROW 7: Ssk, k2tog. (2 sts)

ROW 8: Purl.

Bind off.

Finishing

Using yellow yarn, make large French knots on top of the upper jaw for eyes. Using black sewing thread, make pupils for the eyes, and also cinch jaw together to close to desired level.

Yarn: Lightweight yarn

Needles: 3 double-pointed needles

Extras: Batting; 2 pony beads; gray and beige felt; sewing thread

METHOD

Cast on 3 sts.

ROUNDS 1-3: Knit.

ROUND 4: K1, m1, k2. (4 sts)

ROUND 5: Knit.

ROUND 6: K3, m1, k1. (5 sts)

ROUND 7: K1, m1, k4. (6 sts)

ROUND 8: K3, m1, k2, m1, k1. (8 sts)

ROUND 9: K1, m1, k4, m1, k3. (10 sts)

ROUND 10: K4, m1, k4, m1, k2. (12 sts)

ROUND 11: K1, m1, k10, m1, k1. (14 sts)

ROUND 12: K5, m1, k9. (15 sts)

ROUND 13: K1, m1, k14. (16 sts)

ROUNDS 14-16: Knit.

ROUND 17: K2tog, k14. (15 sts)

ROUND 18: K5, k2tog, k8. (14 sts)

ROUND 19: K10, k2tog, k2. (13 sts)

ROUND 20: K6, k2tog, k5. (12 sts)

ROUND 21: K3, k2tog, k7. (11 sts)

ROUND 22: K4, k2tog, k5. (10 sts)

ROUND 23: K1, k2tog, k7. (9 sts)

Stuff the fish.

ROUND 24: K6, k2tog, k1. (8 sts)

ROUND 25: [K2tog] 4 times. (4 sts)

To form the tail, distribute sts evenly onto 2 dpn and hold needles parallel together. On next row, use 3rd dpn to work sts alternately from front and back needles.

ROWS 26-27: [K1, p1] twice.

ROW 28: [Kfb, p1] twice. (6 sts)

Bind off knitwise.

Finishing

Cut 2 side fins and 1 dorsal fin out of beige felt, and 2 small circles out of gray felt for use behind eyes. Using same yarn used to knit fish, sew the fins to the body and embroider running stitches along the dorsal fin. Using sewing thread, sew the gray circles and pony beads onto the body for eyes.

Yarn: Worsted-weight yarn for large shark; superfine yarn for small shark

Needles: 3 double-pointed needles

Extras: Blue yarn; black permanent marker; batting

METHOD

Body

Cast on 1 st.

ROUND 1: Kfbf. (3 sts)

ROUND 2: [Kfb] 3 times. (6 sts)

ROUND 3: [Kfb, k2] twice. (8 sts)

ROUND 4: Knit.

ROUND 5: [K3, kfb] twice. (10 sts)

ROUND 6: Knit.

ROUND 7: [Kfb, k4] twice. (12 sts)

ROUND 8: Knit.

ROUND 9: [K5, kfb] twice. (14 sts)

ROUNDS 10-17: Knit.

ROUND 18: [K5, k2tog] twice. (12 st)

ROUND 19: Knit.

ROUND 20: [K2tog, k4] twice. (10 sts)

ROUND 21: Knit.

ROUND 22: [K3, k2tog] twice. (8 sts)

ROUND 23: Knit.

Stuff the shark.

ROUND 24: [K2, k2tog] twice. (6 sts)

ROUND 25: [K2tog] 3 times. (3 sts)

Bind off knitwise.

Dorsal fin

Cast on 4 sts.

ROW 1: K1, p1, k2tog. (3 sts)

ROW 2: Ssk, p1. (2 sts)

ROW 3: K2tog. (1 st)

Fasten off, leaving a long tail.

Side fins (make 2)

Cast on 3 sts.

ROW 1: K1, p1, k1.

ROW 2: P1, k1, p1.

ROW 3: K1, k2tog. (2 sts)

ROW 4: K2tog. (1 st)

Fasten off, leaving a long tail.

Back fins (make 2)

Cast on 3 sts.

ROW 1: K1, p1, k1.

ROW 2: P1, k2tog. (2 sts)

ROW 3: K2tog. (1 st)

Fasten off, leaving a long tail.

Finishing

Using tails of yarn, attach fins to body. Using same yarn used to knit fish, cinch a mouth in place (you may need to baste the yarn in place with additional stitches). Using blue yarn, sew French knots for eyes, and add pupils with the permanent marker.

BLUE WHALE \/

Yarn: Worsted-weight yarn

Needles: 3 double-pointed needles

Extras: Crochet hook (optional); black embroidery thread; seed beads; felt; sewing thread; batting

METHOD

Body

Cast on 1 st.

ROUND 1: Kfbf. (3 sts)

ROUND 2: K1, kfb, k1. (4 sts)

ROUND 3: K1, [kfb] twice, k1. (6 sts)

ROUND 4: K2, [kfb] twice, k2. (8 sts)

ROUND 5: K3, [kfb] twice, k3. (10 sts)

ROUND 6: Knit. (10 sts)

ROUND 7: K4, [kfb] twice, k4. (12 sts)

ROUND 8: Knit. (12 sts)

ROUND 9: K5, [kfb] twice, k5. (14 sts)

ROUNDS 10-18: Knit.

ROUND 19: K5, ssk, k2tog, k5. (12 sts)

ROUNDS 20-21: Knit.

ROUND 22: K4, ssk, k2tog, k4. (10 sts)

ROUNDS 23-24: Knit.

ROUND 25: K3, ssk, k2tog, k3. (8 sts)

Lightly stuff the body.

ROUNDS 26-27: Knit.

ROUND 28: K2, ssk, k2tog, k2. (6 sts)

ROUNDS 29-32: Knit.

ROUND 33: K1, ssk, k2tog, k1. (4 sts)

ROUND 34: Ssk, k2tog. (2 sts)

Bind off knitwise.

Side fin (make 2)

Cast on 2 sts.

ROW 1: Purl.

ROW 2: K1, m1, k1. (3 sts)

ROW 3: Purl.

ROW 4: K1, m1, k2. (4 sts)

ROW 5: Purl.

ROW 6: K2, k2tog. (3 sts)

ROW 7: Purl.

ROW 8: K1, k2tog. (2 sts)

Bind off purlwise, leaving a long tail.

Back fin (make 2)

Cast on 2 sts.

Beginning with a p row, work 5 rows st-st.

Bind off knitwise, leaving a long tail.

Finishing

Using tails of yarn and yarn needle or crochet hook, attach fins to body. Embroider a mouth in black thread. Cut small circles out of felt about the size of a lentil; these will stabilize seed bead eyes and prevent them from being pulled through the knitted fabric. Sew the beads and felt eyes in place, orienting the beads, if possible, so that the holes look like pupils.

Yarn: Jacquard sock yarn

Needles: 2 double-pointed needles

Extras: Batting; 2 two-hole buttons; contrasting color thread

METHOD

NOTE: The tentacles are worked as cords that are made to curve by slipping some of the stitches.

Body (make 2)

Cast on 4 sts.

ROW 1 (WS): Purl.

ROW 2: Kfb, k2, kfb. (6 sts)

ROW 3: Purl.

ROW 4: Kfb, k4, kfb. (8 sts)

ROW 5: Purl.

ROW 6: Kfb, k6, kfb. (10 sts)

ROW 7: Purl.

ROW 8: K3, m1, k4, m1, k3. (12 sts)

ROW 9: Purl.

ROW 10: Kfb, k10, kfb. (14 sts)

ROW 11: Purl.

ROW 12: K3, m1, k8, m1, k3. (16 sts)

ROW 13: Purl.

ROW 14: Kfb, k14, kfb. (18 sts)

ROW 15: Purl.

ROW 16: K3, m1, k12, m1, k3. (20 sts)

ROW 17: Purl.

Starting with a k row, work 6 rows st-st.

ROW 24: K3, ssk, k10, k2tog, k3. (18 sts)

ROW 25: Purl.

ROW 26: Ssk, k14, k2tog. (16 sts)

ROW 27: Purl.

ROW 28: Ssk, k1, ssk, k6, k2tog, k1, k2tog. (12 sts)

ROW 29: Purl.

ROW 30: Ssk, k1, ssk, k2, k2tog, k1, k2tog. (8 sts)

ROW 31: Purl.

Bind off.

Top tentacles (make 4)

Using dpn, make tentacles one at a time as cords, working into 2 sts along bound-off edge of front of body as follows:

ROUND 1: M1, k1, m1, k1. (4 sts)

ROUNDS 2-3: Knit.

ROUND 4: Slip 1, k2, slip 1.

ROUND 5: Knit.

ROUND 6: Slip 1, k2, slip 1.

ROUND 7: Knit.

ROUND 8: Slip 1, k2, slip 1.

ROUNDS 9-12: Knit.

ROUND 13: Ssk, k2tog. (2 sts)

Bind off.

Bottom tentacles (make 4)

Using dpn, make tentacles one at a time as cords, working into 2 sts along bound-off edge of back of body as follows:

ROUND 1: M1, k1, m1, k1. (4 sts)

ROUNDS 2-3: Knit.

ROUND 4: K1, slip 2, k1.

ROUND 5: Knit.

ROUND 6: K1, slip 2, k1.

ROUND 7: Knit.

ROUND 8: K1, slip 2, k1.

ROUNDS 9-12: Knit.

ROUND 13: Ssk, k2tog. (2 sts)

Bind off.

Yarn: Lightweight yarn in red

Needles: 2 double-pointed needles

Extras: Sewing thread; seed beads

METHOD

Working on dpn as you would a cord, cast on 1 st.

ROUND 1: Kfbf. (3 sts)

ROUND 2: [Kfb] 3 times. (6 sts)

ROUNDS 3-5: Knit.

ROUND 6: K2tog, k2, k2tog. (4 sts)

ROUND 7: [K2tog] twice. (2 sts)

To form the tail, turn and continue in rows.

ROW 8: [Kfb] twice. (4 sts)

Bind off.

Finishing

Sew on seed beads for eyes, with the bead hole pointing outward to look like a pupil.

Finishing

With WS of body facing and starting at the side of the mouth, sew the work together at the edge. After about ½in (1cm) of sewing, gradually start stitching closer to the center of the body. This "seam allowance" will form the fins. By the time you reach the tail, you should be stitching around ½in (1cm) in from the sides. Continue sewing along the other side, again sewing directly on the edge of the fabric as you approach the mouth. Stuff lightly, covering batting with fabric if desired. Sew buttons on for eyes, using contrasting thread to mimic the unique shape of a cuttlefish's pupil.

Yarn: Worsted-weight yarn

Needles: 3 double-pointed needles

Extras: White and black embroidery thread

METHOD

NOTE: The body and tentacles are both worked as cords. To form the mouth, bind off at the same time as you kfb in each stitch; this will create a slight pout.

Body

Cast on 2 sts.

ROUND 1: [Kfb] twice. (4 sts)
ROUND 2: [K1, kfb] twice. (6 sts)
ROUND 3: [Kfb, k2] twice. (8 sts)
ROUND 4: [K3, kfb] twice. (10 sts)
ROUND 5: [Kfb, k4] twice. (12 sts)
ROUND 6: Knit.
ROUND 7: [K5, kfb] twice. (14 sts)
ROUND 8: Knit.
ROUND 9: [K5, k2tog] twice. (12 sts)
ROUND 10: Knit.
ROUND 11: [K2tog, k4] twice. (10 sts)
ROUND 12: Knit.
ROUND 13: [K3, k2tog] twice. (8 sts)
ROUND 14: [K2tog, k2] twice. (6 sts)
ROUND 15: [K1, k2tog] twice. (4 sts)
ROUND 16: Knit.
ROUND 17: [Kfb] to end, binding off at the same time. (8 sts)

Tentacles (make 8)

Cut 4 pieces of yarn, 2ft (60cm) each. Using slipknots, attach them at the center of each length to the top of the head, giving 8 strands of yarn to make tentacles. To make a tentacle, use a strand of yarn to pick up a stitch nearby and knit a 1-st cord for 8 rounds, then bind off. Repeat until all 8 tentacles have been formed.

Finishing

Using yarn, sew 2 French knots on either side of the head for eyes. Using embroidery thread, add a black French knot on top for pupils, then wrap white thread around these to complete the eyes.

Yarn: Worsted-weight yarn

Needles: 3 double-pointed needles

Extras: White and black yarn

METHOD

Body

Cast on 3 sts.

ROUND 1: Knit.
ROUND 2: K1, m1, k2. (4 sts)
ROUND 3: M1, k4. (5 sts)
ROUND 4: K2, m1, k3. (6 sts)
ROUND 5: K6, m1. (7 sts)
ROUND 6: K4, m1, k3. (8 sts)
ROUND 7: M1, k8. (9 sts)
ROUND 8: K8, m1, k1. (10 sts)
ROUND 9: K5, m1, k5. (11 sts)
ROUND 10: K1, m1, k10. (12 sts)
ROUND 11: Knit.
ROUND 12: K5, k2tog, k5. (11 sts)
ROUND 13: K2tog, k9. (10 sts)
ROUND 14: K4, k2tog, k4. (9 sts)
ROUND 15: K2tog, k7. (8 sts)
ROUNDS 16-18: Knit.
Bind off knitwise.

Long tentacles (make 2)

Work each tentacle into 1 st on last round of body, opposite each other. Using dpn, knit each tentacle as a 1-st cord for 15 rounds or until cord is 2½in (6cm) long.

ROUND 16: Kfb. (2 sts)
ROUNDS 17-21: Knit.
Bind off knitwise.

Short tentacles (make 6)

Work 1 tentacle into each remaining st on last round of body. Using dpn, work each tentacle as a 1-st cord for 15 rounds or until cord is 2½in (6cm) long.

Finishing

Using black yarn, sew 2 French knots for pupils. Wrap white yarn around them, securing in place with a few stitches, to complete the eyes.

Yarn: Worsted-weight yarn in dark green (A) and brown (B)

Needles: 4 double-pointed needles

Extras: Light green yarn; black embroidery thread

METHOD

Shell (make 2)

Using A, cast on 3 sts.

ROUND 1: [Kfb] 3 times. (6 sts)

ROUND 2: [Kfb] 6 times. (12 sts)

ROUND 3: [Kfb, k2] 4 times. (16 sts)

ROUND 4: [K3, kfb] 4 times. (20 sts)

ROUND 5: [Kfb, k4] 4 times. (24 sts)

ROUND 6: [K3, kfb] 6 times. (30 sts)

ROUND 7: [Kfb, k4] 6 times. (36 sts)

ROUND 8: [K5, kfb] 6 times, binding off at the same time.

Limbs (make 2 pieces)

Using B, cast on 2 sts.

ROUND 1: Knit.

ROUND 2: Kfb, k1. (3 sts)

ROUND 3: Knit.

ROUND 4: Kfb, k2. (4 sts)

ROUNDS 5-15: Knit.

ROUND 16: K2tog, k2. (3 sts)

ROUND 17: Knit.

ROUND 18: K2tog, k1. (2 sts)

ROUND 19: Knit.

Bind off.

Head and tail

Using B, cast on 3 sts.

ROUND 1: [Kfb] 3 times. (6 sts)

ROUNDS 2-9: Knit.

ROUND 10: K2tog, k4. (5 sts)

ROUND 11: Knit.

ROUND 12: K2tog, k3. (4 sts)

ROUNDS 13-22: Knit.

ROUND 23: K2tog, k2. (3 sts)

ROUND 24: Knit.

ROUND 25: K2tog, k1. (2 sts)

ROUND 26: Knit.

Bind off.

Finishing

Using light green yarn, embroider a pattern on the knit side of one of the shells. Using the same yarn, sew the limbs to the head/tail piece, symmetrically in the middle as if skewering them on the "kebab" of your needle. Sew the edges of the shells to one another, sewing through and around the limbs. Use light green yarn to add French knot eyespots to the head, and finish these with French knot pupils made with black embroidery thread.

Yarn: Worsted-weight yarn

Needles: 2 or 3 double-pointed needles in usual size for the yarn; 2 more needles that are two sizes smaller

Extras: Dark and lighter colored yarn

METHOD

SPECIFIC INSTRUCTION

Loop 1 = k1 but do not slip st off needle, bring yarn between needles to front, take it clockwise around left thumb and between needles to back, k same st on left needle again, this time slipping it off needle, on right needle slip 2nd st over st just made.

Body (make 2)

Using smaller dpn, cast on 8 sts.

ROW 1 (WS): Purl.

ROW 2: Knit.

ROW 3: Purl.

ROW 4: Purl.

Repeat rows 1–4 once.

Rows 4 and 8 create the ridges on the body.

ROW 9: Purl.

ROW 10: Ssk, k4, k2tog. (6 sts)

ROW 11: Purl.

ROW 12: Ssk, k2, k2tog. (4 sts)

ROW 13: Purl.

ROW 14: Ssk, k2tog, binding off at the same time.

Large claws and front legs (make 2)

Using larger dpn, cast on 3 sts and knit a cord for 16 rounds. Continue using the cord technique with 2 dpn, or use a 3rd dpn to work in rounds as follows:

ROUND 17: [Loop 1, m1] twice, loop 1. (5 sts)

ROUND 18: [K1, m1] 3 times, k2. (8 sts)

ROUND 19: [Loop 1] 8 times.

ROUND 20: Knit.

Repeat rounds 19–20 three times, then round 19 once again.

Now continue in rows on first 4 sts only.

ROW 28: P4, turn.

ROW 29: K4, turn.

ROW 30: P4, turn.

ROW 31: Ssk, k2tog, binding off at the same time.

Repeat rows 28–31 on remaining 4 sts of leg.

Hind legs

Using larger dpn, cast on 3 sts and knit a cord for 24 rounds. Bind off.

Finishing

Sew the body together, sandwiching the legs in place as you go. You can decide how long you want each leg to be and conceal the rest in the body, which will also provide a little stuffing and shape. The hind leg piece stretches across the body from left to right, while the front legs do not. Each front leg piece forms a large claw and one leg behind it. Because the tips of the claws are worked in stockinette, they have a tendency to curl undesirably; you can cinch them in place with a few stitches if you like. Using dark yarn, sew French knots for pupils. Wrap lighter colored yarn around them to complete eyes.

Yarn: Lightweight yarn

Needles: 3 double-pointed needles

Extras: Crochet hook; black yarn; batting

METHOD

NOTE: The body and ends of the claws are worked in rows. The legs are worked in rounds as cords.

Right side

Cast on 12 sts.

ROWS 1, 3 & 5: Purl.

ROW 2: K6, [k2tog] 3 times. (9 sts)

ROW 4: K3, [k2tog] 3 times. (6 sts)

ROW 6: [K2tog] 3 times. (3 sts)

Bind off purlwise.

Left side

Cast on 12 sts.

ROWS 1, 3 & 5: Purl.

ROW 2: [Ssk] 3 times, k6. (9 sts)

ROW 4: [Ssk] 3 times, k3. (6 sts)

ROW 6: [Ssk] 3 times. (3 sts)

Bind off purlwise.

Bottom, front, and top

Cast on 14 sts.

Starting with a p row, work 12 rows st-st.

ROW 13 (WS): Knit.

Row 13 creates a ridge for the boundary between bottom and front of the crab.

Starting with a k row, work 7 rows st-st.

ROW 21 (WS): Knit.

Row 21 creates a ridge for the boundary between front and top of the crab.

Starting with a k row, work 15 rows st-st.

Bind off purlwise.

Back legs (make 2 pieces)

Cast on 2 sts.

ROUNDS 1-2: Knit.

ROUND 3: K1, m1, k1. (3 sts)

ROUNDS 4-5: Knit.

ROUND 6: K1, m1, k2. (4 sts)

ROUNDS 7-31: Knit.

ROUND 32: K2tog, k2. (3 sts)

ROUNDS 33-34: Knit.

ROUND 35: K2tog, k1. (2 sts)

ROUNDS 36-37: Knit.

Bind off knitwise.

Left claw and front leg

Work rounds 1–31 as for back legs.

ROUND 32: K1, m1, k3. (5 sts)

ROUND 33: Knit.

ROUND 34: K1, m1, k4. (6 sts)

ROUND 35: Knit.

ROUND 36: K1, m1, k5. (7 sts)

ROUNDS 37-41: Knit.

To form the claw, turn and continue in rows on first 4 sts only.

ROW A1: P4.

ROW A2: Knit.

ROW A3: Purl.

ROW A4: Ssk, k2tog. (2 sts)

Bind off purlwise.

With RS facing, rejoin yarn to remaining 3 sts.

ROW B1: K3.

ROW B2: Purl.

ROW B3: K1, k2tog. (2 sts)

Bind off purlwise.

Right claw and front leg

Work rounds 1–31 as for back legs.

ROUND 32: K1, m1, k3. (5 sts)

ROUND 33: Knit.

ROUND 34: K1, m1, k4. (6 sts)

ROUND 35: Knit.

ROUND 36: K1, m1, k5. (7 sts)

ROUND 37: Knit.

ROUND 38: K6, m1, k1. (8 sts)
ROUND 39: Knit.
ROUND 40: K1, m1, k7. (9 sts)
ROUND 41: Knit.
ROUND 42: K8, m1, k1. (10 sts)
ROUND 43: Knit.
ROUND 44: K1, m1, k9. (11 sts)
ROUNDS 45-49: Knit.
To form the claw, turn and continue in rows on first 4 sts only.
ROW A1: P4.
ROW A2: Knit.
ROW A3: Purl.
ROW A4: Ssk, k2tog. (2 sts)
Bind off purlwise.
With RS facing, rejoin yarn to remaining 7 sts.
ROW B1: K7.
ROW B2: Purl.
ROW B3: Knit.
ROW B4: Purl.

ROW B5: Ssk, k3, k2tog. (5 sts)
ROW B6: Purl.
ROW B7: Ssk, k1, k2tog. (3 sts)
Bind off purlwise.

Eyes
Cast on 4 sts.
ROUND 1: K1, m1, k1, m1, k2. (6 sts)
ROUND 2: Knit.
ROUND 3: K2tog, k2, k2tog. (4 sts)
ROUND 4: K2tog, k2. (3 sts)
ROUNDS 5-12: Knit.
ROUND 13: K1, m1, k2. (4 sts)

ROUND 14: K1, m1, k1, m1, k2. (6 sts)
ROUND 15: Knit.
ROUND 16: K2tog, k2, k2tog. (4 sts)
Bind off knitwise.

Finishing
Sew the side pieces to the bottom/front/top of the body and stuff it. Then sew up the back of the body in the same way. Each back leg piece forms two legs. Pull the back legs and front legs/claws through the sides of the body so that the center of each piece is concealed; the two halves of each piece should emerge about ¼–½in (0.5–1.5cm) apart. Sew in place if desired, and then sew bends in the legs to form the joints. Likewise, pull the eye piece through the front of the body and sew in place. Using black yarn, sew French knots for eyes.

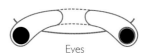

Eyes

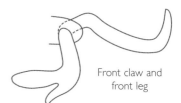

Front claw and front leg

Back legs

Pull the legs and claws through the sides of the body and the eyes through the front of the body.

119 BRINE SHRIMP |

Yarn: Lightweight yarn

Needles: 2 double-pointed needles

Extras: 2 pony beads

METHOD

Body

Using dpn, cast on 4 sts and knit a cord as follows, starting at the head:

ROUNDS 1-11: Knit.

ROUND 12: K2, k2tog. (3 sts)

ROUNDS 13-16: Knit.

ROUND 17: K1, k2tog. (2 sts)

ROUNDS 18-21: Knit.

Bind off.

Finishing

Cut 28 pieces of yarn, 5in (13cm) long. Knot them together in pairs with an overhand knot, 1½in (4cm) from one end. To attach one pair, slide the body between the long ends of yarn and knot them tightly together around the body with another overhand knot. Repeat this process down the back of the shrimp. Trim them to a pleasing shape. Sew 2 large French knots on either side of

the head to form the base for the eyes, then attach beads to these knots.

120 COMMON STARFISH |

Yarn: DK yarn

METHOD

Cast on 4 sts by knitted method.

ROW 1 (RS): [Kfb] 4 times. (8 sts)

ROW 2: Knit.

ROW 3: K1, [m1, k1] 7 times. (15 sts)

ROW 4: Knit.

ROW 5: K1, m1, [k3, m1] 4 times, k2. (20 sts)

ROW 6: Knit.

ROW 7: K1, m1, [k2, m1] 9 times, k1. (30 sts)

ROW 8: Knit.

*ROW 9: K3, m1, k3, turn. Continue on these 7 sts.

ROWS 10-12: Knit.

ROW 13: K2, sk2po, k2. (5 sts)

ROWS 14-16: Knit.

ROW 17: K1, sk2po, k1. (3 sts)

ROWS 18-20: Knit.

ROW 21: Sk2po. (1 st)

ROW 22: Knit.

Fasten off.

Rejoining yarn each time, repeat from * 4 times.

Finishing

Do not press. Gather cast-on edge, then seam first 8 rows. Lightly press the seam.

121 RED STAR |

Yarn: Lightweight yarn

Needles: 3 double-pointed needles

Extras: Accent color yarn

METHOD

Leg (make 5)

Cast on 8 sts and knit a cord as follows:

ROWS 1-3: Knit.

ROW 4: K2tog, k6. (7 sts)

ROW 5: Knit.

ROW 6: K4, k2tog, k1. (6 sts)

ROW 7: Knit.

ROW 8: K1, k2tog, k3. (5 sts)

ROW 9: Knit.

ROW 10: K3, k2tog. (4 sts)

ROW 11: Knit.

ROW 12: K2tog, k2. (3 sts)

ROW 13: Knit.

ROW 14: K1, k2tog. (2 sts)

Bind off knitwise.

Finishing

Using main yarn, sew the legs together at the base. Sew French knots in accent color on one side.

122 BRITTLE STAR |

Yarn: Worsted-weight acrylic in pale pink (A) and gray (B)

Needles: 2 double-pointed needles

METHOD

Leg (make 5)

Using A, cast on 4 sts and knit a cord as follows:

ROWS 1-3: Knit.

ROWS 4-6: Using B, knit, concealing working end of A within.

ROWS 7-9: Using A, knit, concealing B within.

ROWS 10-12: Using B, knit, concealing A within.

ROWS 13-14: Using A, knit.

ROW 15: [K2tog] twice. (2 sts)

Bind off.

Finishing

Using A, stitch legs together at the cast-on edges.

Yarn: Worsted-weight wool in ecru (A); worsted-weight bamboo yarn in pink (B)

Needles: 4 double-pointed needles

Extras: Crochet hook

METHOD

NOTE: After making the cap, you may wish to press the center flat before proceeding.

Cap

Using A, cast on 1 st.
ROUND 1: (K1, p1, k1) in same st. (3 sts)
ROUND 2: [Kfb] 3 times. (6 sts)
ROUND 3: [Kfb] 6 times. (12 sts)
ROUND 4: [Kfb, k2] 4 times. (16 sts)
ROUND 5: [Kfb, k3] 4 times. (20 sts)
ROUND 6: [K4, kfb] 4 times. (24 sts)
ROUND 7: [Kfb, k3] 6 times. (30 sts)
ROUND 8: [K4, kfb] 6 times. (36 sts)
ROUNDS 9-12: Knit.
Bind off knitwise.

Short tentacles (make 2)

Using B, cast on 15 sts.
ROW 1: [Kfb] 15 times, binding off at the same time.

Finishing

Using tails of yarn from tentacles, attach them to the inside center of cap. To make long tentacles, cut 6 pieces of yarn A, 22in (56cm) long. Knot these every ½in (1.5cm). To attach a pair of long tentacles, take one of these pieces and attach the middle along the inside edge of the cap. Repeat with the other tentacles, spacing them evenly around the cap.

124 SIMPLE SEA ANEMONE \/

Yarn: Worsted-weight yarn

Needles: 3 double-pointed needles

METHOD

Cast on 12 sts.

ROUNDS 1-8: Knit.

ROUND 9: [Cast on 10 sts in next st using knitted method, bind off 10 sts knitwise, making a tentacle. Cast on 8 sts in same st as first tentacle, bind off 9 sts knitwise] 12 times. When you finish a tentacle, pull the loop left on the working needle from the previous tentacle over it, so that, when beginning a new one, you always have only one loop on the working needle. Fasten off, and use some yarn to cinch the mouth of the anemone closed.

125 FANCY SEA ANEMONE \/

Yarn: Ultra-fine yarn in plum (A) and turquoise (B)

Needles: 3 double-pointed needles

METHOD

Using A, cast on 12 sts.

ROUNDS 1-8: Knit.

ROUND 9: [Cast on 12 sts in next st using knitted method, bind off 13 sts knitwise, making a tentacle. Cast on 9 sts in next st, bind off 10 sts knitwise (leaving loop from previous tentacle on working needle)] 6 times.

ROUND 10: Using B, [cast on 10 sts in next st, bind off 11 sts. Cast on 7 sts in next st, bind off 8 sts] 6 times. Unlike previous round, this time when you finish a tentacle, pull the loop left on the working needle from the previous tentacle over it, so that, when beginning a new tentacle, you always have only one loop on the working needle. Fasten off.

126 SNAIL SHELL |

Yarn: Worsted-weight 100% wool (preferably felting)

Needles: 2 or more double-pointed needles

METHOD

NOTE: It is important to use a wool that will felt. The texture of regular yarn (particularly one with a tight weave) will overwhelm the shape and make it difficult to distinguish the coiled form.

Using dpn, cast on 2 sts and work as a cord to begin, adding more needles if you need to.

ROUNDS 1-2: Knit.

ROUND 3: K1, m1, k1. (3 sts)

ROUNDS 4-5: Knit.

ROUND 6: K2, m1, k1. (4 sts)

ROUNDS 7-8: Knit.

ROUND 9: K1, m1, k3. (5 sts)

ROUNDS 10-11: Knit.

ROUND 12: K3, m1, k2. (6 sts)

ROUND 13: Knit.

ROUND 14: K2, m1, k4. (7 sts)

ROUND 15: Knit.

ROUND 16: K6, m1, k1. (8 sts)

ROUND 17: Knit.

ROUND 18: K1, m1, k7. (9 sts)

ROUNDS 19-20: Knit.

Bind off, leaving a long tail.

127 WENTLETRAP |

Yarn: Worsted-weight 100% wool (preferably felting)

Needles: 2 or 3 double-pointed needles

METHOD

NOTE: It is important to use 100% wool yarn so that the piece can be felted, concealing individual stitches and making the spiral more apparent.

Using dpn, cast on 3 sts and work as a cord to begin, adding more needles if you need to.

ROUNDS 1-3: Purl.

ROUND 4: P2, pfb. (4 sts)

ROUNDS 5-7: Purl.

ROUND 8: P3, pfb. (5 sts)

ROUND 9: Knit.

ROUND 10: Purl.

Repeat rounds 9-10 three times, then round 9 once again.

ROUND 18: P3, pfb, p1. (6 sts)

ROUNDS 19-20: Knit.

ROUND 21: Purl.

Repeat rounds 19–21 twice, then rounds 19–20 once again.

ROUND 30: Pfb, p5. (7 sts)

ROUNDS 31-33: Knit.

ROUND 34: Purl.

Repeat rounds 31–34 once.

Bind off knitwise.

Finishing

Rub the work vigorously between your fingers to create a light felted appearance; this will help make the finished shape of the shell appear more defined. Using the long ends of yarn, sew the shell in place after coiling it into a pleasing form.

Finishing

Rub the work vigorously between your fingers to create a light felted appearance. Form the shell by curling the knitted piece up, then pin and sew in place.

Yarn: Superfine yarn in darker color (A) and lighter color (B)

Extras: Accent color yarn

METHOD

NOTE: For striped shell, use A to cast on and work row 1, then use B to work the next 2 rows. Continue alternating A and B every 2 rows. For the Fair Isle shell, use A to cast on and then use colors shown on chart.

Each shell

Cast on 15 sts.
ROW 1 (RS): K to last 2 sts, k2tog. (14 sts)
ROW 2: Purl.
Repeat rows 1–2 three times. (11 sts)
ROW 9: Knit.
ROW 10: Purl.
ROW 11: K to last 2 sts, k2tog. (10 sts)

Striped shell

ROW 12: Purl.
ROW 13: Knit.
ROW 14: Purl.
Repeat rows 11–14 five times. (5 sts)
Bind off.

Finishing

Using accent color, backstitch along both straight edges of the piece. Roll up with the cast-on stitches forming the "mouth" of the shell and sew in place.

Fair Isle shell

Color key
■ A
□ B

Stitch key
□ k on RS, p on WS
⊿ k2tog

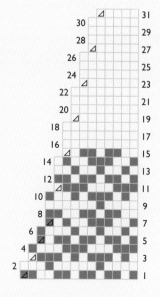

129 BARNACLE I

Yarn: Bulky-weight wool

Needles: 4 double-pointed needles

METHOD
Body

Cast on 16 sts.

ROUND 1: [K1, p1] 8 times.

ROUND 2: As round 1.

ROUND 3: [K2tog, (k1, p1)
3 times] twice. (14 sts)

ROUND 4: [K2, p1, k2tog, k1, p1]
twice. (12 sts)

ROUND 5: [K2, p1, k1, k2tog]
twice. (10 sts)

Bind off.

Mouth

Cast on 5 sts.

Starting with a k row, work
4 rows st-st.

Bind off.

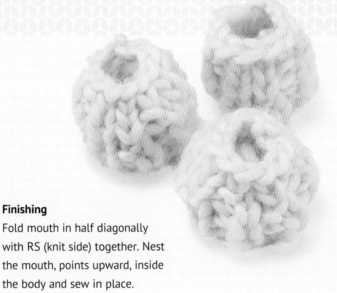

Finishing

Fold mouth in half diagonally
with RS (knit side) together. Nest
the mouth, points upward, inside
the body and sew in place.

130 PLAIN SCALLOP V

Yarn: Worsted-weight acrylic

METHOD

Cast on 11 sts.

ROW 1 (RS): Purl.

ROW 2: [Ssk] 3 times, k1,
[k2tog] twice. (6 sts)

ROW 3: Purl.

ROW 4: Knit.

ROW 5: [P1, m1] 5 times, p1.
(11 sts)

ROW 6: [K1, p1] 5 times, k1.

ROW 7: [P1, m1, k1] 5 times, p1.
(16 sts)

ROW 8: [K1, p2] 5 times, k1.

ROW 9: [P1, k1, m1, k1] 5 times,
p1. (21 sts)

ROW 10: [K1, p3] 5 times, k1.

ROW 11: [P1, k3] 5 times, p1.

ROW 12: [K1, p3] 5 times, k1.

ROW 13: [P1, ssk, k1] twice,
[p1, k1, k2tog] 3 times, p1.
(16 sts)

ROW 14: [K1, p2] 5 times, k1.

ROW 15: [P1, ssk] twice,
[p1, k2tog] 3 times, p1. (11 sts)

ROW 16: [K1, p1] 5 times, k1.

ROW 17: P1, [ssk] twice, [k2tog]
3 times. (6 sts)

ROW 18: [Ssk] twice, k2tog.
(3 sts)

Bind off.

Yarn: DK yarn in pink (A) and pale pink (B)

Needles: 2 pairs, one pair a size smaller than the other

METHOD

Using A and larger needles, cast on 5 sts by knitted method.

ROW 1 (RS): Knit.

ROW 2: Purl.

ROW 3: Cast on 3 sts, p3, k5. (8 sts)

ROW 4: Cast on 3 sts, k3, p5, k3. (11 sts)

ROW 5: Cast on 5 sts, [k5, p3] twice. (16 sts)

ROW 6: Cast on 5 sts, p5, [k3, p5] twice. (21 sts)

ROW 7: Cast on 3 sts, [p3, k5] 3 times. (24 sts)

ROW 8: Cast on 3 sts, k3, [p5, k3] 3 times. (27 sts)

ROW 9: Cast on 3 sts, k3, [p3, k5] 3 times, p3. (30 sts)

ROW 10: Cast on 3 sts, p3, [k3, p5] 3 times, k3, p3. (33 sts)

ROW 11: K3, p3, ssk, k1, k2tog, p3, k5, p3, ssk, k1, k2tog, p3, k3. (29 sts)

ROW 12: [P3, k3] twice, p5, [k3, p3] twice.

ROW 13: [K3, p3] twice, ssk, k1, k2tog, [p3, k3] twice. (27 sts)

ROW 14: P3, [k3, p3] 4 times.

Change to B.

ROW 15: K3, [p3, k3] 4 times.

ROW 16: As row 14.

ROW 17: K3, p3tog, [k3, p3tog] 3 times, k3. (19 sts)

Change to A.

ROW 18: P3, [k1, p3] 4 times.

ROW 19: K3, [p1, k3] 4 times.

Change to B.

ROW 20: As row 18.

ROW 21: S2kpo, [p1, s2kpo] 4 times. (9 sts)

ROW 22: P1, [k1, p1] 4 times.

ROW 23: K1, [p1, k1] 4 times.

ROW 24: As row 22.

ROW 25: S2kpo, p1, k1, p1, k2tog, slip st just made onto left needle, pass next st over it, slip it back onto right needle. (5 sts)

ROW 26: P1, [k1, p1] twice.

ROW 27: K1, s2kpo, k1. (3 sts)

ROW 28: Purl.

ROW 29: S2kpo. (1 st)

Fasten off.

Wings

Using A and smaller needles, with RS facing and starting at row 28, pick up and k7 sts along B row-ends of right-hand edge.

ROWS 1, 3 & 5 (WS): Knit.

ROW 2: Ssk, k3, k2tog. (5 sts)

ROW 4: Ssk, k1, k2tog. (3 sts)

ROW 6: Sk2po. (1 st)

Fasten off.

Work left-hand edge to match.

Top edge

Using A and smaller needles, with RS facing and working into each cast-on st, pick up and k36 sts around top edge, taking 1 st from each st plus 1 extra st from cast-on of each 5-st rib.

NEXT ROW: Using larger needles, k4, kfb, [k8, kfb] 3 times, k4. (40 sts)

Bind off knitwise. Press to shape.

Yarn: DK cotton

Needles: 3 double-pointed needles

Extras: Pipe cleaner

METHOD

Main stem

Using 2 dpn, cast on 6 sts.
*ROW 1 (RS): [K1, p1] 3 times.
Without turning, slide sts to opposite end of needle, take yarn firmly across back of work.
ROW 2 (RS): [P1, k1] 3 times.
Without turning, slide sts to opposite end of needle, take yarn firmly across back of work.**

These 2 rows form seed st pattern. Repeat from * to ** 6 times.

First branch

Do not turn, cast on 6 sts by knitted method. Do not turn, continue on these 6 sts only:
ROW 1 (RS): [K1, p1] 3 times.
Without turning, slide sts to opposite end of needle, take yarn firmly across back of work.
ROW 2: Using 3rd dpn and leaving 6 sts of main stem on left needle: [p1, k1] 3 times.
Without turning, slide sts to opposite end of needle, take yarn firmly across back of work.
Repeat these 2 rows 3 times.
Turn (WS facing), bind off these 6 sts in pattern. Fasten off.
Turn to RS and rejoin yarn to 6 sts of main stem.
Pattern 8 rows as before.

2nd branch

Cast on 4 sts by knitted method. Do not turn, continue on these 4 sts only. Using 3rd dpn and leaving 6 sts of main stem on left needle as before, pattern 4 rows. Turn (WS facing),

Yarn: Worsted-weight yarn in turquoise (A) and lime (B) for large coral, or magenta (A) and pale pink (B) for small coral

Needles: 4 double-pointed needles

METHOD

Large coral—body

Using A, cast on 3 sts.
ROUND 1: [Kfb] 3 times. (6 sts)
ROUND 2: [Kfb] 6 times. (12 sts)
ROUND 3: [Kfb, k1] 6 times. (18 sts)
ROUND 4: [Kfb, k2] 6 times. (24 sts)
ROUND 5: [Kfb, k3] 6 times. (30 sts)
ROUND 6: [Kfb, k4] 6 times. (36 sts)
ROUNDS 7 - 11: Knit.
Bind off.

Trim

Using B, cast on 2 sts, leaving a very long tail, and knit a 4ft (120cm) long cord. Do not bind off.

Finishing

Turn the body inside out so that the purl side shows. Using the long tail of yarn, sew the trim to the body in a labyrinthine

Large coral

bind off these 4 sts in pattern. Fasten off. Turn to RS and rejoin yarn to 6 sts of main stem. Pattern 8 rows. Turn and bind off as before.

Finishing

From the top, insert pipe cleaner into 2nd branch and a little way into main stem. Trim pipe cleaner at the top. Do the same with first branch. Insert pipe

cleaner in main stem and trim. Use ends of yarn to firm joins at base of branches and to close main stem and branches. If the strand at the back forms a ladder, backstitch over this to look like seed st.

Small coral

pattern. When you have covered the whole surface of the body with trim, unravel the excess trim and bind off the end. Conceal all ends of yarn in the underside of the body.

Small coral

Work as for large coral but omit rounds 6–7 of the body. The remaining rounds of the body will have only 30 sts. The trim only needs to be 3ft (90cm) long.

Yarn: Worsted-weight acrylic in khaki (A) and mustard (B)

Needles: 4 double-pointed needles

METHOD

NOTE: This is worked in the round. In the beginning when there are few stitches, work on 2 dpn as you would a cord (sliding the stitches to the other end of the needle when a round is completed).

Large buttonweed

Using A, cast on 1 st.
ROUND 1: (K1, p1, k1) in same st. (3 sts)
ROUND 2: Knit.
ROUND 3: Kfb. (6 sts)
ROUND 4: Knit.
ROUND 5: Kfb. (12 sts)
Distribute sts onto 3 dpn.
ROUND 6: Knit.

ROUND 7: [Kfb, k1] 6 times. (18 sts)
ROUND 8: Knit.
ROUND 9: [Kfb, k2] 6 times. (24 sts)
Bind off.

Medium buttonweed

Make as large, omitting rounds 2 and 9.

Small buttonweed

Make as large, omitting rounds 2, 4, 8, and 9.

Finishing

Using B, sew two enlarged French knots in the center of the buttonweeds (wrapping yarn around the needle 4–6 times instead of the usual 2).

AGARUM SEAWEED V

Yarn: Worsted-weight acrylic

Needles: 2 double-pointed needles

METHOD

Small seaweed

Cast on 3 sts and knit a cord for 10 rounds. Now start working in rows as follows:

ROW 1 (RS): K1, m1, k1, m1, k1. (5 sts)

ROW 2 & ALL WS ROWS: Purl.

ROW 3: K1, [m1, k1] 4 times. (9 sts)

ROW 5: K1, yo, ssk, k1, [k2tog, yo] twice, k1. (9 sts)

ROW 7: K1, [yo, ssk] twice, k2tog, yo, k2. (9 sts)

ROW 9: K2, yo, ssk, [k2tog, yo] twice, k1. (9 sts)

ROW 11: K1, [yo, ssk] twice, k2tog, yo, k2. (9 sts)

ROW 13: Ssk, yo, ssk, k1, k2tog, yo, k2tog. (7 sts)

ROW 15: K1, yo, ssk, k1, k2tog, yo, k1. (7 sts)

ROW 17: Ssk, yo, ssk, k1, k2tog. (5 sts)

ROW 19: [K2tog, yo] twice, k1. (5 sts)

ROW 21: Ssk, k1, k2tog. (3 sts)

ROW 23: Knit.

ROW 24: Purl.

Bind off.

Large seaweed

Cast on 3 sts and knit a cord for 12 rounds.

ROWS 1-4: As small seaweed.

ROW 5: [K1, m1] twice, yo, ssk, k1, k2tog, yo, [m1, k1] twice. (13 sts)

ROW 7: K1, [yo, ssk] twice, k3, [k2tog, yo] twice, k1. (13 sts)

ROW 9: K2, [yo, ssk] twice, k1, [k2tog, yo] twice, k2. (13 sts)

ROW 11: K1, [yo, ssk] twice, k3, [k2tog, yo] twice, k1. (13 sts)

ROW 13: K2, [yo, ssk] twice, k1, [k2tog, yo] twice, k2. (13 sts)

ROW 15: K1, [yo, ssk] twice, k3, [k2tog, yo] twice, k1. (13 sts)

ROW 17: Ssk, [yo, ssk] twice, k1, [k2tog, yo] twice, k2tog. (11 sts)

ROW 19: K1, [yo, ssk] twice, [k2tog, yo] twice, k2. (11 sts)

ROW 21: Ssk, k1, yo, ssk, k1, k2tog, yo, k1, k2tog. (9 sts)

ROW 23: K1, yo, ssk, k3, k2tog, yo, k1. (9 sts)

ROW 25: Ssk, yo, ssk, k1, k2tog, yo, k2tog. (7 sts)

ROW 27: K3, k2tog, yo, k2. (7 sts)

ROW 29: Ssk, k3, k2tog. (5 sts)

ROW 31: K1, yo, ssk, k2. (5 sts)

ROW 33: Ssk, k1, k2tog. (3 sts)

ROW 35: Knit.

ROW 36: Purl.

Bind off.

Large seaweed

Small seaweed

136 NEREOCYSTIS SEAWEED \/

Yarn: Worsted-weight acrylic

Needles: At least 3 double-pointed needles

Extras: Batting (optional)

METHOD

Cast on 3 sts and knit a cord for 11 rounds.

ROUND 12: [K1, m1] twice. k1. (5 sts)

ROUND 13: [K1, m1] 4 times, k1. (9 sts)

Distribute sts onto 2 dpn.

ROUND 14: [K3, m1] 3 times. (12 sts)

ROUND 15: [K2, m1] 6 times. (18 sts)

ROUNDS 16-17: Knit.

ROUND 18: [K4, k2tog] 3 times. (15 sts)

ROUND 19: K3, [k2tog] 6 times. (9 sts)

ROUND 20: Knit.

To close the bulb, distribute sts evenly onto 2 dpn and hold needles parallel together. As you do this, you can put a bit of batting inside the bulb to help hold its shape. On next row, use 3rd dpn to work sts alternately from front and back needles. In first 2 sts, work 24 rows st-st. Bind off. In next 3 sts, work 31 rows st-st. Bind off. In next 2 sts, work 30 rows st-st. Bind off. In last 2 sts, work 18 rows st-st. Bind off.

137 FAN SEAWEED |

Yarn: Sport-weight yarn

METHOD

Cast on 55 sts by thumb method.

ROW 1 (RS): K7, [p5, k7] 4 times.

ROW 2: P7, [k5, p7] 4 times.

ROW 3: K7, [p2tog, p1, p2tog, k7] 4 times. (47 sts)

ROW 4: P7, [k3, p7] 4 times.

ROW 5: Ssk, k3, k2tog, [p3, ssk, k3, k2tog] 4 times. (37 sts)

ROW 6: P5, [k3, p5] 4 times.

ROW 7: K5, [p3tog, k5] 4 times. (29 sts)

ROW 8: P5, [k1, p5] 4 times.

ROW 9: Ssk, k1, k2tog, [p1, ssk, k1, k2tog] 4 times. (19 sts)

ROWS 10 & 12: P3, [k1, p3] 4 times.

ROW 11: K3, [p1, k3] 4 times.

ROW 13: S2kpo, [p1, s2kpo] 4 times. (9 sts)

ROWS 14 & 16: P1, [k1, p1] 4 times.

ROW 15: K1, [p1, k1] 4 times.

ROW 17: Sk2po, p1, k1, p1, k2tog, slip st just made onto left needle, pass next st over it, slip it back onto right needle. (5 sts)

ROW 18: P1, [k1, p1] twice.

ROW 19: K1, s2kpo, k1. (3 sts)

ROW 20: P3.

ROW 21: S2kpo. (1 st)

Slip remaining st onto left needle and make a 6-st chain. Press lightly.

Yarn: DK cotton

METHOD

Cast on 27 sts by thumb method.

ROW 1 (RS): Purl.

ROW 2: Knit.

Repeat rows 1–2 three times.

ROW 9: P13, k1, p13.

ROW 10: K13, p1, k13.

ROW 11: P12, k3, p12.

ROW 12: K12, p3, k12.

ROW 13: P11, k2tog, yo, k1, yo, skpo, p11.

ROW 14: K11, p5, k11.

ROW 15: P10, k2tog, k1, [yo] twice, k1, [yo] twice, k1, skpo, p10. (29 sts)

ROW 16: K10, p2, (k1, p1) in double yo, p1, (p1, k1) in double yo, p2, k10.

ROW 17: P9, k2tog, k2, yo, k1, [yo] twice, k1, [yo] twice, k1, yo, k2, skpo, p9. (33 sts)

ROW 18: K9, p5, (k1, p1) in double yo, p1, (p1, k1) in double yo, p5, k9.

ROW 19: P8, k2tog, k5, yo, [k1, yo] 3 times, k5, skpo, p8. (35 sts)

ROWS 20 & 22: K8, p19, k8.

ROW 21: P8, k19, p8.

ROW 23: P8, k5, yo, skpo, k5, k2tog, yo, k5, p8.

ROW 24: K8, p5, k1tbl, p7, k1tbl, p5, k8.

ROW 25: P8, k2, k2sso, yo, p1, yo, skpo, k3, k2tog, yo, p1, yo, sk2po, k2, p8. (33 sts)

ROW 26: K8, p3, k1tbl, k1, k1tbl, p5, k1tbl, k1, k1tbl, p3, k8.

ROW 27: P8, k2sso, p3, yo, skpo, k1, k2tog, yo, p3, sk2po, p8. (29 sts)

ROW 28: K12, k1tbl, p3, k1tbl, k12.

ROW 29: P13, s2kpo, p13. (27 sts)

ROW 30: K13, p1, k13.

Beginning with a p row, work 6 rows reverse st-st to complete 36 rows.

Bind off purlwise.

Finishing

To neaten the sides, RS facing, pick up and k27 sts along one edge and then bind off knitwise. Do the same along 2nd edge.

FORMAL FLOWER \/

Yarn: DK cotton

Extras: Cable needle

METHOD
SPECIFIC ABBREVIATIONS

c3bp = slip next 2 sts onto cable needle and hold at back, k1, then p2 from cable needle.

c3fp = slip next st onto cable needle and hold at front, p2, then k1 from cable needle.

MB = make bobble: (k1, p1, k1, p1, k1) in next st, turn, p5, turn, pass 2nd, 3rd, 4th, and 5th sts over first st, k this st tbl.

Cast on 27 sts.
ROW 1 (RS): Purl.
ROW 2: Knit.
Repeat rows 1–2 three times.
ROW 9: P12, k3, p12.
ROW 10: K12, p3, k12.
ROW 11: P10, c3bp, k1, c3fp, p10.
ROW 12: K10, p1, [k2, p1] twice, k10.
ROW 13: P8, c3bp, p2, k1, p2, c3fp, p8.
ROW 14: K8, p1, [k4, p1] twice, k8.
ROW 15: P8, yo, k1, yo, p4, k1, p4, yo, k1, yo, p8. (31 sts)
ROW 16: K8, p3, k4, p1, k4, p3, k8.

ROW 17: P8, k1, [yo, k1] twice, [p4, k1] twice, [yo, k1] twice, p8. (35 sts)
ROW 18: K8, p5, k4, p1, k4, p5, k8.
ROW 19: P8, k2, yo, k1, yo, k2, p4, k1, p4, k2, yo, k1, yo, k2, p8. (39 sts)
ROW 20: K8, p7, k4, p1, k4, p7, k8.
ROW 21: P8, k5, k2tog, p4, k1, p4, skpo, k5, p8. (37 sts)
ROW 22: K8, p6, k4, p1, k4, p6, k8.
ROW 23: P8, k4, k2tog, p3, MB, k1, MB, p3, skpo, k4, p8. (35 sts)
ROW 24: K8, p5, k3, p3, k3, p5, k8.
ROW 25: P8, k2, k2sso, p2, MB, k3, MB, p2, sk2po, k2, p8. (31 sts)

ROW 26: K8, p3, k2, p5, k2, p3, k8.
ROW 27: P8, k2sso, p2, MB, k3, MB, p2, sk2po, p8. (27 sts)
ROW 28: K8, p1, k2, p5, k2, p1, k8.
ROW 29: P12, MB, k1, MB, p12.
Beginning with a k row, work 7 rows reverse st-st to complete 36 rows.
Bind off purlwise.

Finishing

To neaten the sides, RS facing, pick up and k27 sts along one edge and then bind off knitwise. Do the same along 2nd edge.

Mix and match
138 + 139 + 140

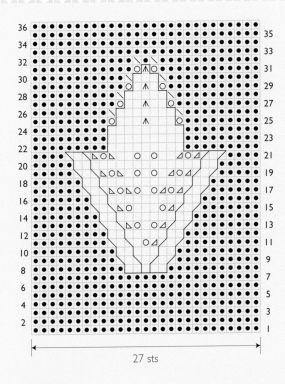

27 sts

Yarn: DK cotton

Extras: Cable needle

METHOD

Cast on 27 sts by thumb method. Beginning with a p row, work 7 rows reverse st-st. Now continue from row 8 of the chart, noting that this is a WS row. Read WS rows from left to right and RS rows from right to left, as indicated by the row numbering. When row 36 has been completed, bind off purlwise. To neaten the sides, RS facing, pick up and k27 sts along one edge and then bind off knitwise. Do the same along 2nd edge.

Stitch key

☐ k on RS, p on WS

● p on RS, k on WS

○ yarn over

◢ k2tog

◳ skpo

⋀ s2kpo

◺ k1tbl (WS)

◢◢ c3b: slip next st onto cable needle and hold at back, k2, then k1 from cable needle

◳◳ c3f: slip next 2 sts onto cable needle and hold at front, k1, then k2 from cable needle

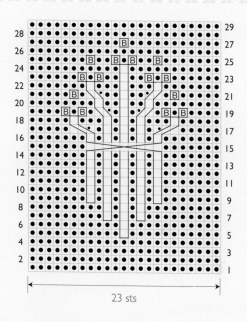

23 sts

Yarn: DK wool

Extras: Cable needle

METHOD

Cast on 23 sts by thumb method. Beginning with a p row, work in reverse st-st from the chart, reading RS rows from right to left and WS rows from left to right, as indicated by the row numbering. When row 29 has been completed, bind off knitwise.

Stitch key

☐ k on RS, p on WS

● p on RS, k on WS

c3bp: slip next 2 sts onto cable needle and hold at back, k1, then p2 from cable needle

c3fp: slip next st onto cable needle and hold at front, p2, then k1 from cable needle

c2bp: slip next st onto cable needle and hold at back, k1, then p1 from cable needle

c2fp: slip next st onto cable needle and hold at front, p1, then k1 from cable needle

slip next 6 sts onto cable needle and hold at back, k1, p1, k1, then work 6 sts from cable needle: [p1, k1] 3 times

B make bobble: (k1, yo, k1) in next st, turn, k3, turn, pass 2nd and 3rd sts over first st, k this st tbl

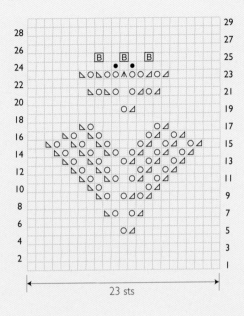

23 sts

Stitch key

☐ k on RS, p on WS

● k on WS

O yarn over

⊿ k2tog on RS, p2tog on WS

◣ skpo on RS, p2tog tbl on WS

⋀ s2kpo

Ⓑ make bobble: (k1, yo, k1) in next st, turn, p3, turn,
pass 2nd and 3rd sts over first st, k this st tbl

Yarn: Sport-weight cotton

METHOD

Cast on 23 sts by thumb method.
Beginning with a k row, work
in st-st from the chart, reading
RS rows from right to left and
WS rows from left to right, as
indicated by row numbering.

When row 29 has been
completed, bind off knitwise.
To neaten the sides, RS facing,
pick up and k23 sts along one
edge and then bind off knitwise.
Do the same along 2nd edge.

Mix and match
142 + 143

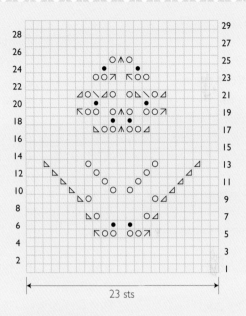

23 sts

Yarn: Sport-weight cotton

METHOD

Cast on 23 sts by thumb method.
Beginning with a k row, work
in st-st from the chart, reading
RS rows from right to left and
WS rows from left to right, as
indicated by row numbering.

When row 29 has been
completed, bind off knitwise.
To neaten the sides, RS facing,
pick up and k23 sts along one
edge and then bind off knitwise.
Do the same along 2nd edge.

Stitch key

☐ k on RS, p on WS
● k on WS
O yarn over
⟋ k2sso
⟍ sk2po
⟋ k2tog on RS, p2tog on WS
⟍ skpo on RS, p2tog tbl on WS
⟍ k1 tbl
⋀ s2kpo

Yarn: Sport-weight cotton

METHOD
SPECIFIC ABBREVIATION

MB = make bobble: (k1, yo, k1, yo, k1) in next st, turn, [p5, turn, k5, turn] twice, p1, [p2tog] twice, turn, sk2po.

NOTE: Slip stitches knitwise.

Bobble segments (make 4)

Cast on 2 sts.

ROW 1 (RS): Kfb, k1. (3 sts)
ROW 2: Slip 1, kfb, k1. (4 sts)
ROW 3: Slip 1, k3.
ROW 4: Slip 1, k1, yo, k2. (5 sts)
ROW 5: Slip 1, k4.
ROW 6: Slip 1, [k1, yo] twice, k2. (7 sts)

ROW 7: Slip 1, k6.
ROW 8: Slip 1, k1, yo, k3, yo, k2. (9 sts)
ROW 9: Slip 1, k8.
ROW 10: Slip 1, k1, yo, k5, yo, k2. (11 sts)
ROW 11: Slip 1, k10.
ROW 12: Slip 1, k1, yo, k7, yo, k2. (13 sts)
ROW 13: Slip 1, k5, MB, k6.
ROW 14: Slip 1, k1, yo, k9, yo, k2. (15 sts)
ROW 15: Slip 1, k14.
ROW 16: Slip 1, k1, yo, k11, yo, k2. (17 sts)
ROW 17: Slip 1, k5, MB, k3, MB, k6.
ROW 18: Slip 1, k1, yo, k13, yo, k2. (19 sts)
ROW 19: Slip 1, k18.

ROW 20: Slip 1, k1, yo, k15, yo, k2. (21 sts)
ROW 21: Slip 1, k9, MB, k10.
ROW 22: Slip 1, k1, yo, k17, yo, k2. (23 sts)
ROW 23: Slip 1, k22.
ROW 24: Slip 1, k1, yo, k19, yo, k2. (25 sts)
ROW 25: Slip 1, k24.
ROW 26: Slip 1, k1, yo, p2, [yo, p2tog] 9 times, p1, yo, k2. (27 sts)
ROW 27: Slip 1, k26.
ROW 28: Slip 1, k1, yo, k23, yo, k2. (29 sts)

ROW 29: Slip 1, k1, p25, k2.
ROW 30: Slip 1, k1, yo, p25, yo, k2. (31 sts)
ROW 31: Slip 1, k30.
ROW 32: Slip 1, k1, yo, k27, yo, k2. (33 sts)
ROW 33: Slip 1, k1, p29, k2.
Bind off knitwise.

Finishing

With cast-on to center and taking in 1 st from each section, join sections to form a square.

145 LEAF QUARTET \||

Yarn: DK wool in green (A) and turquoise (B)

METHOD

NOTE: Taking yarn to opposite side of work as necessary, use stranding technique for rows 4–6, then use intarsia technique.

Leaf segments (make 4)

Using A, cast on 3 sts.
ROW 1 (RS): Knit.
ROW 2: K1, p1, k1.
ROW 3: [Kfb] twice, k1. (5 sts)
ROW 4: KfbA, k1A, p1B, kfbA, k1A. (7 sts)
ROW 5: KfbA, p1A, k3B, pfbA, k1A. (9 sts)
ROW 6: K3A, p3B, k3A.
ROW 7: K2A, p1A, using B: [k1, yo] twice, k1; p1A, k2A. (11 sts)
ROW 8: K3A, p5B, k3A.
ROW 9: K2A, p1A, using B: k2, yo, k1, yo, k2; p1A, k2A. (13 sts)
ROW 10: K2A, kfbA, p7B, kfbA, k2A. (15 sts)
ROW 11: K2A, p2A, using B: k3, yo, k1, yo, k3; p2A, k2A. (17 sts)
ROW 12: K4A, p9B, k4A.
ROW 13: K2A, p2A, using B: k4, yo, k1, yo, k4; p2A, k2A. (19 sts)
ROW 14: K3A, kfbA, p11B, kfbA, k3A. (21 sts)
ROW 15: K2A, p3A, using B: k5, yo, k1, yo, k5; p3A, k2A. (23 sts)

ROW 16: K5A, p13B, k5A.
ROW 17: K2A, p3A, using B: k6, yo, k1, yo, k6; p3A, k2A. (25 sts)
ROW 18: K4A, kfbA, p15B, kfbA, k4A. (27 sts)
ROW 19: K1A, kfbA, p4A, using B: k7, yo, k1, yo, k7; p4A, pfbA, k1A. (29 sts)
ROW 20: K7A, p17B, k7A.
ROW 21: K1A, k2togA, p4A, using B: k7, s2kpo, k7; p4A, k2togA, k1A. (27 sts)
ROW 22: K4A, k2togA, p15B, k2togA, k4A. (25 sts)
ROW 23: K2A, p3A, using B: k6, s2kpo, k6; p3A, k2A. (23 sts)
ROW 24: As row 16.
ROW 25: K2A, p3A, using B: k5, s2kpo, k5; p3A, k2A. (21 sts)
ROW 26: K3A, k2togA, p11B, k2togA, k3A. (19 sts)
ROW 27: K2A, p2A, using B: k4, s2kpo, k4; p2A, k2A. (17 sts)
ROW 28: As row 12.
ROW 29: K2A, p2A, using B: k3, s2kpo, k3; p2A, k2A. (15 sts)
ROW 30: K2A, k2togA, p7B, k2togA, k2A. (13 sts)
ROW 31: K2A, p1A, using B: k2, s2kpo, k2; p1A, k2A. (11 sts)
ROW 32: As row 8.
ROW 33: K2A, p1A, using B: k1, s2kpo, k1; p1A, k2A. (9 sts)
ROW 34: As row 6.
Continue in A.

ROW 35: K2, p1, s2kpo, p1, k2. (7 sts)
ROW 36: K1, k2tog, p1, k2tog, k1. (5 sts)
ROW 37: K2tog, p1, k2tog. (3 sts)
ROW 38: Sk2po.
Fasten off.

Finishing

Square up segments and press edges only. With cast-on to center, taking in half a stitch from each edge, join segments to form a square.

Yarn: DK wool in sky blue (A), soft orange (B), yellow (C), brown (D), black (E), and white (F)

Needles: 2 pairs, one pair a size smaller than the other

METHOD

Flower block

Using larger needles and A, cast on 35 sts by thumb method. Beginning with a k row, work mainly in st-st from the chart, reading RS rows from right to left and WS rows from left to right, as indicated by row numbering. When row 41 has been completed, bind off knitwise.

Finishing

To neaten the sides, RS facing, pick up and k35 sts along one edge and then bind off knitwise. Do the same along 2nd edge.

Butterfly body and first wing

Using smaller needles and E, cast on 6 sts by knitted method.
ROW 1 (RS): Bind off 3 sts, k to end. (3 sts)
Change to F.
ROW 2: Purl.
ROW 3: K1, [yo, k1] twice. (5 sts)
ROW 4: K1, [k1tbl, k1] twice.
ROW 5: K1, yo, k3, yo, k1. (7 sts)

ROW 6: K1, k1tbl, k3, k1tbl, k1.
ROW 7: K1, yo, k5, yo, k1. (9 sts)
ROW 8: K1, k1tbl, k5, k1tbl, k1.
ROW 9: Knit.
ROW 10: K6, turn, wyab slip 1 purlwise, k5.
ROW 11: K3, turn, wyab slip 1 purlwise, k2.
Bind off knitwise.

Butterfly 2nd wing

RS facing and using F, pick up and k1 st in each of first 3 sts of body.
ROW 1 (WS): Purl.
ROW 2: K1, [yo, k1] twice. (5 sts)
ROW 3: K1, [k1tbl, k1] twice.
ROW 4: K1, yo, k3, yo, k1. (7 sts)
ROW 5: K1, k1tbl, k3, k1tbl, k1.
ROW 6: K1, yo, k5, yo, k1. (9 sts)
ROW 7: K1, k1tbl, k5, k1tbl, k1.
ROW 8: K6, turn, wyab slip 1 purlwise, k5.
ROW 9: K3, turn, wyab slip 1 purlwise, k2.
ROW 10: Knit.
Bind off knitwise.

Finishing

Using E, sew a French knot on each wing. Use E to stitch the butterfly in place, leaving the wings free and making a straight stitch for each antenna.

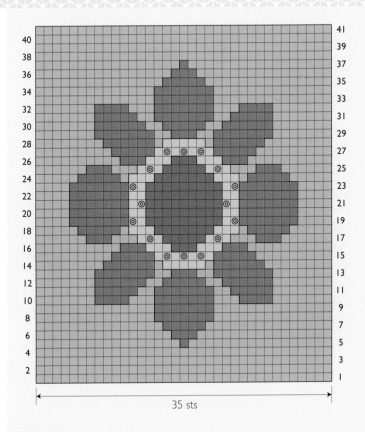

35 sts

Color key
- A
- B
- C
- D

Stitch key
- ☐ k on RS, p on WS
- ◎ make loop: k1 but do not slip st off needle, bring yarn between needles to front, take it clockwise around left thumb and between needles to back, k same st on left needle again, this time slipping it from needle, drop loop and slip 2 sts just made onto left needle, k2tog tbl

Yarn: Worsted-weight wool in soft white (A), blue-green (B), and mauve (C)

METHOD

NOTE: Use stranding technique for color not in use.

Using A, cast on 15 sts by thumb method.
ROWS 1 & 3: Knit.
ROWS 2 & 4: Purl.
ROW 5: K7A, k1B, k7A.
ROW 6: P7A, p1B, p7A.
Repeat rows 5–6 once.
ROW 9: K3A, insert right needle in space to right of first center st B (on row 5), pull through a loop of B, using A: k next st then pass loop over this st without twisting it, k3A, k1B, k3A, insert right needle in space to left of first center st B, pull through a loop of B, using A: k next st then pass loop over this st without twisting it, k3A.
ROW 10: P7A, p1B, p7A.
ROW 11: K7A, using B: (k1, yo, k1, yo, k1, yo, k1) in next st, k7A. (21 sts)
ROW 12: P7A, p7C, p7A.
ROW 13: K7A, using C: ssk, s2kpo, k2tog, k7A. (17 sts)
ROW 14: P7A, p3togC, p7A. (15 sts)
Continue in A.
ROWS 15 & 17: Knit.
ROWS 16 & 18: Purl.
ROW 19: Knit.
Bind off knitwise.

Finishing

To neaten the sides, RS facing, pick up and k15 sts along one edge and then bind off knitwise. Do the same along 2nd edge.

Yarn: DK wool in olive-brown (A), yellow (B), and olive (C)

Needles: 5 double-pointed needles

METHOD

Center

Using pair of needles and A, cast on 8 sts.

ROW 1 (RS): Kfb, k to last 2 sts, kfb, k1. (10 sts)

ROW 2: Knit.

Repeat rows 1–2 three times. (16 sts)

Work 8 rows g-st.

ROW 17: K1, k2tog, k to last 3 sts, k2tog, k1. (14 sts)

ROW 18: Knit.

Repeat rows 17–18 three times. (8 sts)

Bind off.

Petals

RS facing, using dpn and B, distributing 16 sts onto each of 4 dpn, pick up and k8 sts from cast-on edge, 8 sts from shaped edge, 8 sts from row-ends, 8 sts from shaped edge, 8 sts from bound-off edge, 8 sts from shaped edge, 8 sts from row-ends, and 8 sts from shaped edge. (64 sts)

ROUND 1 (RS): Knit.

Turn in order to work round 2 on WS.

*ROUND 2: Cast on 3 sts, bind off 5 sts, slip st from right needle to left needle; repeat from * to end.

Fasten off.

Border

*RS facing and folding petals forward, using pair of needles and C, pick up and k1 st in back loop of each of 8 sts of one group in round 1 of petal, turn.

ROWS 1-3: Knit.

ROW 4 (RS): Kfb, k5, kfb, k1. (10 sts)

ROWS 5-8: Knit.

Bind off knitwise.

Repeat from * 7 times.

Finishing

RS together, backstitch pairs of row-ends to complete the border. Lightly press the center to a circle. On WS, press the seams of the border.

Yarn: DK wool in pea green (A), yellow-green (B), cream (C), and deep turquoise (D)

METHOD

NOTE: Do not break yarn between colors.
On the petals, slip stitches knitwise.

Center

Using A, cast on 9 sts by thumb method.
ROW 1 (RS): Using B, k7, turn, wyab slip 1 purlwise, k6.
ROW 2 (RS): K5, turn, wyab slip 1 purlwise, k4.
ROW 3 (RS): Using A, k all 9 sts.
ROW 4 (WS): Slip 1 knitwise, k to end.
Repeat rows 1–4, 14 times, then rows 1–2 again. Using A, bind off knitwise.

Petals

Using C, cast on 4 sts.
ROW 1 (RS): Slip 1, kfb, k2. (5 sts)
ROW 2: Slip 1, k2, kfb, k1. (6 sts)
ROW 3: Slip 1, kfb, k4. (7 sts)
ROW 4: Slip 1, k4, kfb, k1. (8 sts)
ROWS 5-8: Slip 1, k7.
ROW 9: Slip 1, k2tog, k5. (7 sts)
ROW 10: Slip 1, k3, k2tog, k1. (6 sts)
ROW 11: Slip 1, k2tog, k3. (5 sts)
ROW 12: Slip 1, k1, k2tog, k1. (4 sts)
ROW 13: Slipping first st, bind off 2 sts, k remaining 1 st. (2 sts)
ROW 14: Slip 1, k1, turn, cast on 2 sts by knitted method. (4 sts)
Do not turn.
Repeat rows 1–14 seven times, then rows 1–13 again.
Bind off remaining 2 sts.

Block

Using D, cast on 31 sts.
ROW 1 (RS): K1, [p1, k1] 15 times.
ROW 2: As row 1.
Repeat these 2 rows until 51 rows have been completed or until block is square. Bind off knitwise.
To neaten the sides, RS facing and using D, pick up and k31 sts along one edge and then bind off knitwise. Do the same along 2nd edge.

Finishing

Seam the center, using A and taking in the chain edge of the bind-off and the single back strand of the cast-on. Gently stretch the outer edge and gather the inner edge tightly. Seam the petals by joining the 2 bound-off stitches and the inner 2 cast-on stitches. Attach the center to the block by overcasting the outer edge. Set the petals on top and, using C, backstitch on RS around slip stitch edge. Press the nose of the iron into each petal to make it concave.

Yarn: DK wool in yellow (A), purple (B), and gray-blue (C)

METHOD

Flower center

Using A, cast on 5 sts by knitted method.

ROW 1 (WS): Purl.

ROW 2: K1, [m1, k1] 4 times. (9 sts)

ROWS 3 & 5: Purl.

ROW 4: K1, [m1, k2] 4 times. (13 sts)

ROW 6: K1, [yo, k1] 12 times. (25 sts)

Bind off knitwise.

Flower petals

ROW 1: RS facing and using B, insert needle in first eyelet of row 6, pick up and k1 st, [yo, pick up and k1 st in next eyelet] 11 times. (23 sts)

ROW 2: Purl.

ROW 3: K1, [yo, k1] 12 times. (45 sts)

BIND-OFF ROW: *Cast on 2 sts, bind off 4 sts, slip remaining st back onto left needle; repeat from *, ending bind off 5 sts.

Block

Using C, cast on 32 sts by thumb method.

Beginning with a k row, work 39 rows st-st, or until work is square.

Bind off knitwise.

To neaten the sides, RS facing and using C, pick up and k23 sts along one edge and then bind off knitwise. Do the same along 2nd edge.

Finishing

Gather the cast-on stitches in the flower center and then seam the row-ends. Center the flower on the block and, using B, backstitch in place between the B eyelets.

Mix and match 150 (different colorways)

Yarn: Sport-weight wool in purple (A), mauve (B), acid yellow (C), and dull lime green (D)

Extras: Crochet hook

METHOD
SPECIFIC ABBREVIATION

MB = make bobble: [insert crochet hook in last ch, yo, pull loop through, make 1ch] twice, yo, pull yarn through all loops on hook, fasten off.

Petals (make 5)

Using A, cast on 25 sts by thumb method.

ROW 1 (RS): K11, s2kpo, k11. (23 sts)

ROW 2: K11, wyif slip 1 purlwise, wyab k11.

ROW 3: K10, s2kpo, k10. (21 sts)

ROW 4 & ALL WS ROWS: K to center st, wyif slip 1 purlwise, wyab k to end.

ROW 5: K9, s2kpo, k9. (19 sts)

ROW 7: K8, s2kpo, k8. (17 sts)

ROW 9: K7, s2kpo, k7. (15 sts)

ROW 11: K6, s2kpo, k6. (13 sts)

ROW 13: K5, s2kpo, k5. (11 sts)

ROW 14: As row 4.

Change to B.

ROW 15: K4, s2kpo, k4. (9 sts)

ROW 17: K3, s2kpo, k3. (7 sts)

ROW 19: K2, s2kpo, k2. (5 sts)

ROW 21: K1, s2kpo, k1. (3 sts)

ROW 23: S2kpo. (1 st)

Fasten off.

Block

Using D, cast on 43 sts. Work 85 rows g-st, or until work is square.

Bind off knitwise.

Finishing

With RS together and using yarn ends, backstitch the petals, with yarn B to the center. Starting at the center, RS facing, use crochet hook and C to surface crochet a chain halfway along one seam. End by breaking off the yarn, leaving a long end, and pull this through to RS. MB and then take yarn to WS. Alternatively, use yarn needle to make chain st and end with a large French knot. Do the same along remaining seams. Use A to attach the flower to the block, leaving cast-on edges of petals free.

Yarn: Sport-weight wool in scarlet (A) and black (B)

METHOD

SPECIFIC INSTRUCTION

Loop 1 = k1 but do not slip st off needle, bring yarn between needles to front, take it clockwise around left thumb and between needles to back, k same st on left needle again, this time slipping it from needle, drop loop and slip 2 sts just made onto left needle, k2tog tbl.

Petals

Using A, cast on 10 sts by cable method.
ROW 1 (RS): Kfb, k8, w&t, p to end. (11 sts)
ROW 2 (RS): As row 1. (12 sts)
ROWS 3 & 5: Knit.
ROWS 4 & 6: Purl.
ROW 7: Ssk, k9, w&t, p to end.
ROW 8: Ssk, k7, w&t, p to end. (10 sts)
ROW 9: Slipping first st knitwise, bind off 4 sts, k to end. (6 sts)
ROW 10: P6, turn, cast on 4 sts by cable method. (10 sts)
Repeat rows 1–10 four times, then work rows 1–9 again.
Bind off purlwise.

Center

RS facing and using A, pick up and k6 sts from inside edge of each petal. (36 sts)
Change to B.
ROW 1: Purl.
ROW 2: K1, [loop 1] 34 times, k1.
ROW 3: [K4, k2tog] 6 times. (30 sts)
ROW 4: [K3, k2tog] 6 times. (24 sts)
ROW 5: [K2, k2tog] 6 times. (18 sts)

ROW 6: [K1, k2tog] 6 times. (12 sts)
ROW 7: [K2tog] 6 times. (6 sts)
Break off yarn, leaving a long end, and thread this through sts.

Finishing

Pull yarn end B to gather the center, then use it to seam the row-ends of the center. Join the 6 sts of bind-off of the last petal to inner 6 sts of cast-on of the first petal. Press petals to shape.

Yarn: DK wool in magenta (A) and blue-pink (B)

Extras: Crochet hook

METHOD

Center

Using crochet hook and A, make a slip ring. Working in the round with RS facing, make 2ch, work 7sc into ring, pull yarn end to close ring, join with ss in top ch of 2ch. (8 sts)

ROUND 2: 1ch, [5ch, skip 1sc, 1sc in next sc] 4 times, ending ss in first ch. (4 ch loops) Fasten off.

Inner petals

RS facing and using A, in one loop: *insert hook under ch, yo, pull yarn through, yo, pull loop through to enclose ch, slip loop from hook onto knitting needle; in same ch loop repeat from * 8 times. (9 sts on needle) Turn.**

Beginning with a WS row, work 7 rows g-st.

ROW 8: [K2tog] twice, k1, [k2tog] twice. (5 sts)

Bind off knitwise.

Make 3 more petals in the same way.

Outer petals

RS facing, fold a petal forward and, using crochet hook and A, insert the hook in one of the free sc of round 1, 1ch, [7ch, fold next petal forward, 1sc in next free sc of round 1] 4 times, ending ss in first ch. (4 ch loops) Fasten off.

RS facing, fold a petal forward in order to work into the ch loop behind and, using crochet hook and B, making 13 sts instead of 9 sts, work as inner petal from * to **.

Beginning with a WS row, work 3 rows g-st.

ROW 4 (RS): Kfb, k10, kfb, k1. (15 sts)

ROWS 5-9: Knit.

ROW 10: K2tog, k11, k2tog. (13 sts)

ROW 11: Knit.

ROW 12: K2tog, k9, k2tog. (11 sts)

Bind off knitwise.

Make 3 more petals in the same way.

Yarn: DK wool in purple (A); sport-weight wool in shocking pink (B)

Needles: 2 double-pointed needles

METHOD

Block

Using pair of needles and A, cast on 2 sts.

ROW 1 (RS): Kfb, k1. (3 sts)

ROW 2 & ALL WS ROWS: Knit.

ROW 3: [Kfb] twice, k1. (5 sts)

ROW 5: Kfb, k2, kfb, k1. (7 sts)

ROW 7: Kfb, k4, kfb, k1. (9 sts)

ROW 9: Kfb, k6, kfb, k1. (11 sts)

Continue to increase in this way on RS rows until there are 43 sts.

NEXT RS ROW: K1, k2tog, k to last 3 sts, k2tog, k1. (41 sts)

Continue to decrease in this way on RS rows until 7 sts remain.

NEXT RS ROW: K1, [k2tog, k1] twice. (5 sts)

NEXT RS ROW: K1, sk2po, k1. (3 sts)

NEXT RS ROW: Sk2po. (1 st)

Fasten off.

Cord

Using dpn and B, cast on 5 sts and knit a cord approximately 33in (84cm) long or length required. Break off yarn, leaving an end long enough to sew with. Join the cord into a ring by grafting the loop of each stitch at the end of the cord to a stitch of the cast-on.

Finishing

Square up the block and press lightly. Hiding the join in a curve, pin the cord in position on the block and then baste it, using sport-weight yarn (this will grip better than smooth sewing thread). Making small stitches on the underside of the cord, use B to sew the cord in place.

Yarn: DK wool in blue-green (A); sport-weight wool in apple green (B)

Needles: 2 double-pointed needles

METHOD

Block

Using pair of needles and A, cast on 2 sts.

ROW 1 (RS): Kfb, k1. (3 sts)

ROW 2 & ALL WS ROWS: Knit.

ROW 3: [Kfb] twice, k1. (5 sts)

ROW 5: Kfb, k2, kfb, k1. (7 sts)

ROW 7: Kfb, k4, kfb, k1. (9 sts)

ROW 9: Kfb, k6, kfb, k1. (11 sts)

Continue to increase in this way on RS rows until there are 43 sts.

NEXT RS ROW: K1, k2tog, k to last 3 sts, k2tog, k1. (41 sts)

Continue to decrease in this way on RS rows until 7 sts remain.

NEXT RS ROW: K1, [k2tog, k1] twice. (5 sts)

NEXT RS ROW: K1, sk2po, k1. (3 sts)

NEXT RS ROW: Sk2po. (1 st)

Fasten off.

Cord

Using dpn and B, cast on 5 sts and knit a cord approximately 30in (76cm) long or length required. Bind off.

Finishing

Square up the block and press lightly. Pin the cord in position on the block and then baste it, using sport-weight yarn (this will grip better than smooth sewing thread). Making small stitches on the underside of the cord, use B to sew the cord in place.

Mix and match
154 + 155

Yarn: Sport-weight cotton in pale green (A) and dull green (B)

METHOD

Stem

Using A, cast on 3 sts.

ROW 1 (RS): K1, slip 1 purlwise, k1.

ROW 2: Purl.

Repeat rows 1–2 four times.

Do not break off yarn.

Leaf

ROW 1 (RS): Cast on 3 sts by knitted method, k4, slip 1 purlwise, k1. (6 sts)

ROW 2: Cast on 3 sts as before, p9. (9 sts)

ROW 3: K2, k2tog, [yo] 4 times, k1, [yo] 4 times, ssk, k2.

ROW 4: P3, (k1, yo, k1, yo, k1, yo, k1) in multiple yo, p1, (k1, yo, k1, yo, k1, yo, k1) in multiple yo, p3. (21 sts)

ROW 5: K8, k2tog, [yo] 3 times, k1, [yo] 3 times, ssk, k8.

ROW 6: P9, (k1, yo, k1, yo, k1) in multiple yo, p1, (k1, yo, k1, yo, k1) in multiple yo, p9. (29 sts)

ROW 7: K12, k2tog, [yo] twice, k1, [yo] twice, ssk, k12.

ROW 8: P13, (k1, yo, k1) in double yo, p1, (k1, yo, k1) in double yo, p13. (33 sts)

ROW 9: K14, k2tog, yo, k1, yo, ssk, k14.

ROWS 10, 12, 14, 16 & 18: Purl.

ROWS 11, 13, 15 & 17: Knit.

*ROW 19: Ssk, k7, k2tog, turn. (9 sts)

Continue on these sts only.

ROWS 20, 22, 24 & 26: Purl.

ROW 21: Ssk, k5, k2tog. (7 sts)

ROW 23: Ssk, k3, k2tog. (5 sts)

ROW 25: Ssk, k1, k2tog. (3 sts)

ROW 27: Sk2po. (1 st)

Fasten off.

RS facing, rejoin yarn to remaining sts and repeat from * twice.

Block

Using B, cast on 42 sts. Beginning with a k row, work 51 rows st-st, or until block is square. Bind off knitwise.

To neaten the sides, RS facing and using B, pick up and k42 sts along one edge and then bind off knitwise. Do the same along 2nd edge.

Finishing

Press to shape. Pin and then baste the leaf to the block. Using A, backstitch around edges of leaf 1 st in from the edge. Catch down center stitches of stem.

Yarn: Sport-weight cotton in pale mauve (A) and deep lilac (B)

Needles: 4 double-pointed needles

METHOD

Flower

Using A, cast 2 sts onto each of 3 dpn. (6 sts)

ROUND 1: Knit.

ROUND 2: [Yo, k1] 6 times. (12 sts)

ROUNDS 3 & 5: Knit.

ROUND 4: [Yo, k1] 12 times. (24 sts)

ROUND 6: [Yo, k3, yo, k1] 6 times. (36 sts)

ROUNDS 7-8: Knit.

ROUND 9: *K1, k2tog, [yo] 4 times, skpo, k1; repeat from * 5 times. (48 sts)

ROUND 10: [K2, (k1, yo, k1, yo, k1, yo, k1) in multiple yo, k2] 6 times. (66 sts)

ROUNDS 11-12: Knit.

**ROUND 13: Ssk, k7, k2tog, turn. (9 sts)

Continue in rows on these 9 sts only.

ROWS 14, 16, 18 & 20: Purl.

ROW 15: Ssk, k5, k2tog. (7 sts)

ROW 17: Ssk, k3, k2tog. (5 sts)

ROW 19: Ssk, k1, k2tog. (3 sts)

ROW 21: Sk2po. (1 st)

Fasten off.

RS facing, rejoin yarn to remaining sts and repeat from ** 5 times.

Block

Using B and pair of needles, cast on 42 sts. Beginning with a k row, work 51 rows st-st, or until block is square. Bind off knitwise. To neaten the sides, RS facing and using B, pick up and k42 sts along one edge and then bind off knitwise. Do the same along 2nd edge.

Finishing

Press to shape. Pin and baste the flower in position on the block. Using A, backstitch around edge of the flower, 1 st in from the edge.

Mix and match
156 + 157

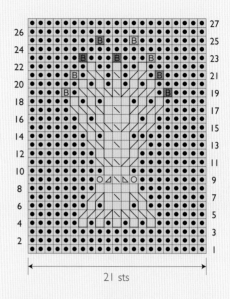

21 sts

Color key

- A
- B
- C
- D
- E
- F

Stitch key

- ☐ k on RS, p on WS
- • p on RS, k on WS
- ◩ k1tbl
- ○ yarn over
- B make bobble: take A to back, then using contrast color indicated, (k1, yo, k1) in next st, turn, k1, [yo, k1] twice to make 5 sts, turn, p5, turn, k5, turn, pass 2nd, 3rd, 4th, and 5th sts over first st, then using A, k this st tbl, break off contrast yarn, bring A to front
- ◺ ssk
- ◿ k2tog
- ⟍⟍ t2L
- ⟋⟋ t2R

Yarn: DK wool in pale green (A), shocking pink (B), pale pink (C), lilac (D), mauve (E), and plum (F)

Extras: Ribbon, approximately 12in (30cm) long

METHOD

Using A, cast on 21 sts by thumb method.

Beginning with a p row, work 3 rows reverse st-st.

Now continue from the row 4 of the chart, noting that this is a WS row. Read WS rows from left to right and RS rows from right to left, as indicated by the row numbering. When row 27 has been completed, bind off knitwise.

To neaten the sides, RS facing and using A, pick up and k21 sts along one edge and then bind off knitwise. Do the same along 2nd edge.

Finishing

Press reverse st-st only. Thread the ribbon through the eyelet holes on row 9, tie a bow, and trim the ends.

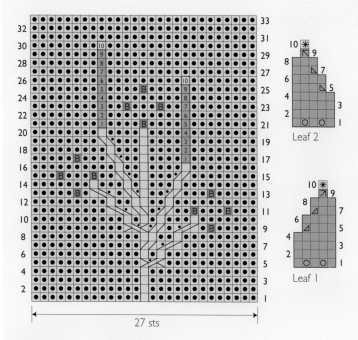

Leaf 2

Leaf 1

27 sts

Yarn: Sport-weight wool in lime green (A), fuchsia (B), and bright green (C)

Extras: Cable needle

METHOD

Using A, cast on 27 sts by thumb method. Now pattern from the chart, reading RS rows from right to left and WS rows from left to right, as indicated by the row numbering.
On row 17 begin leaf 1. On row 21 begin leaf 2. The first row of each leaf is worked (k1, yo, k1, yo, k1) in 1 st. The st count is then as shown on the charts.

The last st of each leaf is p1A on WS. When row 33 has been completed, bind off knitwise. To neaten the sides, RS facing and using A, pick up and k27 sts along one edge and then bind off knitwise. Do the same along 2nd edge.

Color key

■ A

■ B

■ C

Stitch key

□ k on RS, p on WS
● p on RS, k on WS
◿ k2tog
◺ skpo
◹ k2sso
◸ sk2po

✳ p1A (WS)
○ yarn over needle
⁄⁄ c2b
⟍⟍ c2f
⁄⁄ c2bp
⟍⟍ c2fp

⟩⟩⟨ slip next 2 sts onto cable needle and hold at back, k1, then p1, k1 from cable needle

⟩⟨ slip next st onto cable needle and hold at front, k1, p1, then k1 from cable needle

⁄⟨ slip next 2 sts onto cable needle and hold at back, k1, then p2 from cable needle

⟍⟨ slip next st onto cable needle and hold at front, p2, then k1 from cable needle

B make bobble: using B, (k1, yo, k1, yo, k1) in next st, turn, p5, turn, pass 2nd, 3rd, 4th, and 5th sts over first st, then using A, k this st tbl

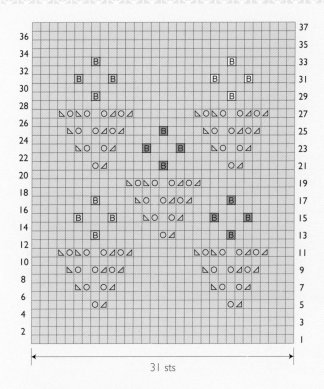

31 sts

Yarn: DK wool in lime green (A), bright blue (B), sky blue (C), royal blue (D), pale blue (E), and periwinkle (F)

METHOD

Using A, cast on 31 sts by thumb method.

Beginning with a k row, work 4 rows st-st. Now continue from row 5 of the chart, reading RS rows from right to left and WS rows from left to right, as indicated by the row numbering. When row 37 has been completed, bind off knitwise.

Finishing

To neaten the sides, RS facing and using A, pick up and k31 sts along one edge and then bind off knitwise. Do the same along 2nd edge.

Color key

A
B
C
D
E
F

Stitch key

☐ k on RS, p on WS
Ⓞ yarn over
◿ k2tog
◺ skpo
Ⓑ make bobble: using contrast color, (k1, p1, k1) in next st, turn, p3, turn, using A, sk2po

161 FLOWER BED V

Yarn: DK wool in pale gray (A), four shades of green (B), and four shades of mauve and pink (C)

METHOD

NOTE: Slip stitches purlwise.

SPECIFIC ABBREVIATION

MB = make bobble: p3, turn, k3, turn, p3tog, take yarn to back.

Using A, cast on 33 sts.

ROWS 1 & 3 (RS): Knit.

ROWS 2 & 4: Purl.

Change to first shade B.

ROW 5: Knit.

ROW 6: K5, [wrapping yarn 3 times for each st: k3, k7] twice, wrapping yarn 3 times for each st: k3, k5. Change to A.

ROW 7: K1, [slip 1, k3, slip 3 dropping extra wraps, k3] 3 times, slip 1, k1.

ROW 8: P1, [wyif slip 1, p3, wyif slip 3, p3] 3 times, wyif slip 1, p1.

ROW 9: K5, [slip 3, k7] twice, slip 3, k5.

ROW 10: P5, [wyif slip 3, p7] twice, wyif slip 3, p5.

ROW 11: K3, [slip 2, drop next st off needle to front, slip same 2 slip sts back onto left needle, pick up and k dropped st without twisting it, k3, drop next st off needle to front, k2, pick up and k dropped st without twisting it, k3] 3 times. Change to first shade C.

ROW 12: P1, wyif slip 2, *[(p1, k1, p1) in next st, wyif slip 2] twice, (p1, k1, p1) in next st, wyif slip 3; repeat from * once, [(p1, k1, p1) in next st, wyif slip 2] 3 times, p1.

ROW 13: K1, slip 2, *MB, [slip 2, MB] twice, slip 3; repeat from * once, [MB, slip 2] 3 times, k1. Change to A.

ROW 14: Purl, working each bobble st tbl.

Repeat rows 3–14 three times, substituting shades B and C each time.

Beginning with a k row, work 3 rows st-st.

Bind off knitwise.

Yarn: DK wool in sap green (A), soft white (B), candy pink (C), and teal (D)

METHOD

Stem

Using A, cast on 3 sts. Beginning with a k row, work 18 rows st-st. Do not break off yarn.

Flower

ROW 1 (RS): [Kfb] twice, k1. (5 sts)

ROW 2: [Pfkb] 4 times, p1. (9 sts)

ROW 3: [K1, p1] 4 times, k1.

ROW 4: [P1, k1] 4 times, p1.

ROW 5: [K1, m1, p1] 4 times, k1. (13 sts)

ROW 6: [P1, k2] 4 times, p1.

ROW 7: [K1, p2] 4 times, k1.

ROW 8: As row 6.

Change to B.

ROW 9: Knit.

ROW 10: Purl.

ROW 11: K2, [m1, k3] 3 times, m1, k2. (17 sts)

ROW 12: P2, [k1, p3] 3 times, k1, p2.

ROW 13: K2, [p1, k3] 3 times, p1, k2.

ROW 14: As row 12.

Change to C.

ROW 15: Knit.

ROW 16: Purl.

ROW 17: [K2tog, yo] 8 times, k1.

ROW 18: Purl.

Bind off loosely knitwise.

Fold along row 17 to make picots and catch down along color-change row on WS.

Block

Using D, cast on 2 sts.

ROW 1 (RS): Kfb, k1. (3 sts)

ROW 2 & ALL WS ROWS: Knit.

ROW 3: [Kfb] twice, k1. (5 sts)

ROW 5: Kfb, k2, kfb, k1. (7 sts)

ROW 7: Kfb, k4, kfb, k1. (9 sts)

ROW 9: Kfb, k6, kfb, k1. (11 sts)

Continue to increase in this way on RS rows until there are 31 sts.

NEXT RS ROW: K1, k2tog, k to last 3 sts, k2tog, k1.

Continue to decrease in this way on RS rows until 7 sts remain.

NEXT RS ROW: K1, [k2tog, k1] twice. (5 sts)

NEXT RS ROW: K1, sk2po, k1. (3 sts)

NEXT RS ROW: Sk2po. (1 st)

Fasten off.

Finishing

Square up the block and press lightly. Attach daisy by using matching yarn to overcast along edges, taking in only the outermost strand of each edge stitch.

Mix and match
162 + 163

Yarn: DK wool in pale green (A) and leaf green (B)

METHOD

NOTE: Slip stitches purlwise.

Stem

Using A, cast on 3 sts. Beginning with a k row, work 12 rows st-st. Do not break off yarn.

Leaf

ROW 1 (RS): K1, slip 1, k1.

ROW 2: K1, p1, k1.

ROW 3: K1, m1R, slip 1, m1L, k1. (5 sts)

ROW 4: K1, p3, k1.

ROW 5: K1, m1R, k1, slip 1, k1, m1L, k1. (7 sts)

ROW 6 & ALL WS ROWS: K1, p to last st, k1.

ROW 7: K1, m1R, t2R, slip 1, t2L, m1L, k1. (9 sts)

ROW 9: K1, m1R, t2R, k1, slip 1, k1, t2L, m1L, k1. (11 sts)

ROW 11: K1, m1R, [t2R] twice, slip 1, [t2L] twice, m1L, k1. (13 sts)

ROW 13: K1, m1R, [t2R] twice, k1, slip 1, k1, [t2L] twice, m1L, k1. (15 sts)

ROW 15: K1, m1R, [t2R] 3 times, slip 1, [t2L] 3 times, m1L, k1. (17 sts)

ROW 17: K1, [t2R] 3 times, k1, slip 1, k1, [t2L] 3 times, k1.

ROW 19: K2, [t2R] 3 times, slip 1, [t2L] 3 times, k2.

ROW 21: As row 17.

ROW 23: As row 19.

ROW 25: K1, k2tog, [t2R] twice, k1, slip 1, k1, [t2L] twice, ssk, k1. (15 sts)

ROW 27: K1, k2tog, [t2R] twice, slip 1, [t2L] twice, ssk, k1. (13 sts)

ROW 29: K3tog, t2R, k1, slip 1, k1, t2L, sk2po. (9 sts)

ROW 31: K3tog, s2kpo, sk2po. (3 sts)

ROW 32: K1, p1, k1.

ROW 33: S2kpo. (1 st)

Fasten off.

Block

Using B, cast on 2 sts.

ROW 1 (RS): Kfb, k1. (3 sts)

ROW 2 & ALL WS ROWS: Knit.

ROW 3: [Kfb] twice, k1. (5 sts)

ROW 5: Kfb, k2, kfb, k1. (7 sts)

ROW 7: Kfb, k4, kfb, k1. 9 sts

ROW 9: Kfb, k6, kfb, k1. (11 sts)

Continue to increase in this way on RS rows until there are 31 sts.

NEXT RS ROW: K1, k2tog, k to last 3 sts, k2tog, k1. Continue to decrease in this way on RS rows until 7 sts remain.

NEXT RS ROW: K1, [k2tog, k1] twice. (5 sts)

NEXT RS ROW: K1, sk2po, k1. (3 sts)

NEXT RS ROW: Sk2po. (1 st)

Fasten off.

Finishing

Square up the block and press lightly. Using A, backstitch the leaf in place on RS, 1 st in from the edge stitch. Catch down the edge stitches of the stem.

Yarn: Worsted-weight wool

METHOD
SPECIFIC ABBREVIATION
t2Rp = k 2nd st on left needle, p first st, slip both sts off together.

Block
Cast on 17 sts by thumb method.
ROWS 1, 3 & 5: Purl.
ROWS 2 & 4: Knit.
ROW 6 (WS): K4, p7, k6.
ROW 7: P6, t2R, k3, t2R, p4.
ROW 8: K4, p8, k5.
ROW 9: P5, t2R, k3, t2R, k1, p4.
ROW 10: K4, p9, k4.
ROW 11: P4, t2R, k3, t2R, k2, p4.
ROW 12: As row 10.
ROW 13: P4, k4, t2R, k1, t2Rp, p4.
ROW 14: K5, p8, k4.
ROW 15: P4, k6, t2Rp, p5.
ROW 16: K6, p7, k4.
ROW 17: P4, k5, t2Rp, p6.
ROWS 18 & 20: Knit.
ROWS 19 & 21: Purl.
ROW 22: Knit.
Bind off purlwise.

Picot edging
Cast on 37 sts, leaving a long end for sewing.
ROW 1 (WS): P18, m1, p1, m1, p18. (39 sts)
ROW 2: [K2tog, yo] 19 times, k1.
ROW 3: P18, p3tog, p18. (37 sts)
ROW 4: Form picots by folding widthwise along row 2, then join by binding off knitwise each stitch on the needle together with a single strand of each corresponding stitch of the cast-on edge.

Finishing
Take the 2nd yarn end under the first chain of the bound-off edge and back again (as for invisible fastening off), and then use this end to join the picots into a ring. Position this join at the base of the leaf, pinch the point at the top, and use the first yarn end to sew the picots around the outline of the leaf, making a backstitch underneath alternate chains of the bound-off edge. To neaten the sides, RS facing, pick up and k17 sts along one edge and then bind off knitwise. Do the same along 2nd edge.

Yarn: Worsted-weight wool

Extras: Cable needle

METHOD

SPECIFIC ABBREVIATIONS

c3bp = slip next st onto cable needle and hold at back, k2, then p1 from cable needle.

c3fp = slip next 2 sts onto cable needle and hold at front, p1, then k2 from cable needle.

c4bp = slip next 2 sts onto cable needle and hold at back, k2, then p2 from cable needle.

c4fp = slip next 2 sts onto cable needle and hold at front, p2, then k2 from cable needle.

dec4 = decrease 4: wyab slip 3 sts purlwise, *on right needle pass 2nd st over first st, slip this st back onto left needle, pass next st over it,** slip this st back onto right needle; repeat from * to ** once to leave 1 st on left needle, k this st tbl.

inc2 = increase 2: (k1tbl, k1) in next st, insert left needle behind vertical strand between the 2 sts just made and k this tbl.

Block

Cast on 17 sts by thumb method.

ROW 1 (RS): Purl.

ROW 2: Knit.

Repeat rows 1–2 twice more.

ROW 7: P8, m1, inc2, m1, p8. (21 sts)

ROW 8: K8, p2, k1, p2, k8.

ROW 9: P6, c4bp, p1, c4fp, p6.

ROW 10: K6, p2, k5, p2, k6.

ROW 11: P5, c3bp, p5, c3fp, p5.

ROW 12: K5, p2, k7, p2, k5.

ROW 13: P5, k2, p7, k2, p5.

ROW 14: As row 12.

ROW 15: P5, c3fp, p5, c3bp, p5.

ROW 16: As row 10.

ROW 17: P6, c4fp, p1, c4bp, p6.

ROW 18: K8, dec4, k8. (17 sts)

ROWS 19 & 21: Purl.

ROWS 20 & 22: Knit.

Bind off purlwise.

Picot petals

Cast on 31 sts, leaving a long end for sewing.

ROW 1 (WS): Purl.

ROW 2: [K2tog, yo] 15 times, k1.

ROW 3: Purl.

ROW 4: Form picots by folding widthwise along row 2, then join by binding off knitwise each stitch on the needle together with a single strand of each corresponding stitch of the cast-on edge. Fasten off, leaving a long end.

Finishing

Take the 2nd yarn end under the first chain of the bound-off edge and back again (as for invisible fastening off), and then use this end to join the picots into a ring. Use the first yarn end to sew the petal ring around the cabled ring, making a backstitch underneath alternate chains of the bound-off edge.

To neaten the sides, RS facing, pick up and k17 sts along side edge and then bind off knitwise. Do the same along 2nd edge.

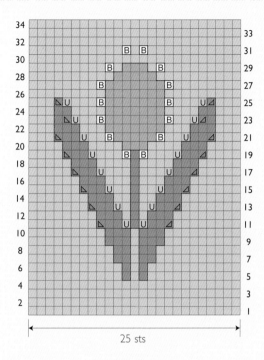

Yarn: DK wool in gray-blue (A), bright green (B), soft white (C), yellow (D), and pale green (E)

METHOD

Block

Using A, cast on 25 sts. Beginning with a k row, work in st-st from the chart, reading RS rows from right to left and WS rows from left to right as indicated by row numbering on chart. Use a separate length of yarn for each leaf from row 20 onward. When row 34 has been completed, bind off.

Border

RS facing and using E, pick up and k25 sts along cast-on edge.
ROW 1: Knit.
ROW 2: Kfb, k to last 2 sts, kfb, k1. (27 sts)
Repeat rows 1–2 once. (29 sts)
Bind off knitwise.
Edge remaining 3 sides to match. Join the mitered corners.

Color key

■ A
■ B
□ C
■ D

Stitch key

□ k on RS, p on WS
◢ k2tog
◣ skpo
U make a st by inserting left needle under strand A between sts from front to back and k this tbl
B make bobble: (k1, p1, k1) in next st, turn, p3, turn, k3, pass 2nd and 3rd sts over first st

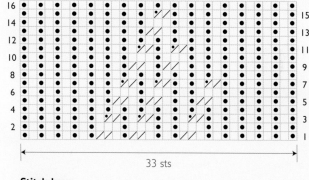

33 sts

Stitch key

☐ k1tbl on RS, p1tbl on WS

● p1 on RS, k1 on WS

⧄ t2R

⧄ t2Rp: k in front of 2nd st, then p in front of first st, slip both sts off needle together

Yarn: Sport-weight wool in grass green (A), yellow (B), and soft white (C)

METHOD

Block

Using A, cast on 33 sts.

ROW 1 (RS): P1, [k1tbl, p1] 16 times.

ROW 2: K1, [p1tbl, k1] 16 times.

Rows 1–2 set twisted rib pattern. Repeat rows 1–2 three times.

Now work from chart, reading RS rows from right to left and WS rows from left to right as indicated by row numbering on chart. When row 16 of chart has been completed, work 10 rows twisted rib. Bind off in rib.

Daisies (make 3)

Using B, cast on 4 sts by thumb method.

ROW 1 (RS): K1, [yo, k1] 3 times. (7 sts)

ROW 2: K1, [k1tbl, k1] 3 times. Change to C.

ROW 3: Knit.

ROW 4: *Cast on 3 sts by cable method, bind off 4 sts knitwise, slip remaining st from right needle to left needle; repeat from * 5 times.

Fasten off.

Half daisies (make 2)

Using C, cast on 5 sts.

ROW 1 (RS): Knit.

ROW 2: *Cast on 3 sts, bind off 4 sts, slip remaining st from right needle to left needle; repeat from * 3 times.

Fasten off.

Finishing

For each daisy, use first yarn end B to gather the cast-on edge tightly, then join the row-ends. For each half daisy, use first yarn end C to slightly gather the cast-on edge. Stitch all the flowers in place on the block, leaving the petals free.

Yarn: Sport-weight wool in shocking pink (A), pale pink (B), and green (C)

METHOD

Rose

Using A and leaving a long yarn end, cast on 94 sts.

ROW 1: K2, [p2, k2] to end.

ROW 2: P2, [k2, p2] to end.

Change to B.

Repeat rows 1–2 twice, then row 1 again.

Leaving a long yarn end, bind off loosely in rib.

Block

Using C, cast on 2 sts.

ROW 1 (RS): Kfb, k1. (3 sts)

ROW 2 & ALL WS ROWS: Knit.

ROW 3: [Kfb] twice, k1. (5 sts)

ROW 5: Kfb, k2, kfb, k1. (7 sts)

ROW 7: Kfb, k4, kfb, k1. (9 sts)

ROW 9: Kfb, k6, kfb, k1. (11 sts)

Continue to increase in this way on RS rows until there are 27 sts.

NEXT RS ROW: K1, k2tog, k to last 3 sts, k2tog, k1.

Continue to decrease in this way on RS rows until 7 sts remain.

NEXT RS ROW: K1, [k2tog, k1] twice. (5 sts)

NEXT RS ROW: K1, sk2po, k1. (3 sts)

NEXT RS ROW: Sk2po. (1 st)

Fasten off.

Finishing

Square up the block and press lightly. Use long yarn end A to gather the cast-on sts of rib. Coil the rib and sew cast-on edge to the block. Take last yarn end B through the center of the flower and through the block to tuck this end of the rib into the center of the flower.

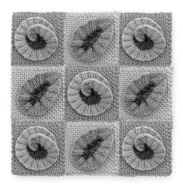

Mix and match
168 + 169

Yarn: Sport-weight wool in olive (A), leaf green (B), and sky blue (C)

METHOD

Leaf

Using A and leaving a long end, cast on 32 sts.

ROW 1 (RS): K2, [yo, p1, k2] 10 times. (42 sts)

ROW 2: P2, [k1, k1tbl, p2] 10 times.

Change to B.

ROW 3: K2, [p2, k2] 10 times.

ROW 4: P2, yo, k2, yo, [p2, k2] twice, [p2, yo, k2, yo]
4 times, p2, [k2, p2] twice, yo, k2, yo, p2. (54 sts)

ROW 5: K2, p1tbl, p2, p1tbl, [k2, p2] twice, k2, [p1tbl, p2,
p1tbl, k2] 4 times, [p2, k2] twice, p1tbl, p2, p1tbl, k2.

ROW 6: P2, k4, [p2, k2] twice, [p2, k4] 4 times, p2, [k2, p2]
twice, k4, p2.

ROW 7: K2, p4, [k2, p2] twice, [k2, p4] 4 times, k2, [p2, k2]
twice, p4, k2.

ROW 8: As row 6.

Bind off in pattern.

Block

Using C, cast on 2 sts.

ROW 1 (RS): Kfb, k1. (3 sts)

ROW 2 & ALL WS ROWS: Knit.

ROW 3: [Kfb] twice, k1. (5 sts)

ROW 5: Kfb, k2, kfb, k1. (7 sts)

ROW 7: Kfb, k4, kfb, k1. (9 sts)

ROW 9: Kfb, k6, kfb, k1. (11 sts)

Continue to increase in this way on RS rows until there
are 27 sts.

NEXT RS ROW: K1, k2tog, k to last 3 sts, k2tog, k1.

Continue to decrease in this way on RS rows until
7 sts remain.

NEXT RS ROW: K1, [k2tog, k1] twice. (5 sts)

NEXT RS ROW: K1, sk2po, k1. (3 sts)

NEXT RS ROW: Sk2po. (1 st)

Fasten off.

Finishing

Square up the block and press lightly. Using
matching yarn, join the row-ends of the ribbed
leaf and, gathering slightly, join the two
halves of the cast-on edge. Sew the leaf
to the block, leaving the edges free.

Yarn: DK wool in pink (A), turquoise (B), and pale yellow (C)

METHOD

Petals

Using A, cast on 4 sts by knitted method.

SET-UP ROW: Purl.

Now pattern as follows:

ROW 1 (RS): K1, yo, k3. (5 sts)

ROW 2: P3, p1tbl, p1.

ROW 3: [K1, yo] twice, k3. (7 sts)

ROW 4: P3, [p1tbl, p1] twice.

ROW 5: Cast on 2 sts, bind off 2 sts, k to end.

ROWS 6 & 8: Purl.

ROW 7: Ssk, k2tog, k3. (5 sts)

ROW 9: Ssk, k3. (4 sts)

ROW 10: Purl.

Repeat rows 1–10 seven times. Bind off.

Pin out petals and press.

RS facing and using A, pick up and k1 st in each alternate row-end along straight edge. (41 sts)

ROW 1: Knit.

ROW 2: K1, [k2tog] 20 times. (21 sts)

Break off yarn and take thread through sts to lightly gather them. Join cast-on and bound-off edges.

Block

Using B, cast on 29 sts.

ROW 1 (RS): K1, [p1, k1] 14 times.

ROW 2: As row 1.

Repeat these 2 rows until 45 rows have been completed. Bind off knitwise.

To neaten the sides, RS facing and using B, pick up and k29 sts along one edge and then bind off knitwise. Do the same along 2nd edge.

Finishing

Arrange the fluted petals so that the seam is hidden in a fold, then catch down in the center of the block and by stitching underneath the tip of each petal. Using C, make a fairly full pompom, trim it, use the point of a needle to separate the strands of yarn to fluff it up, and then sew it in the center of the flower.

Mix and match 170 (different colorways)

Yarn: DK wool in sky blue (A) and lime green (B)

Extras: Crochet hook

METHOD

Flower center

Using crochet hook and A, make 5ch, join with ss into a ring.

ROUND 1 (RS): 6ch, [1sc in ring, 5ch] 7 times, ss in first ch of 6ch. (8 ch loops)

Do not fasten off, do not turn. Slip loop from hook onto a knitting needle, with the needle pointing left to right.

First petal

Cast on 5 sts by cable method. (6 sts)

*ROW 1 (RS): K6, pick up and k1 st from ch loop below, turn. (7 sts)

ROW 2: K5, k2tog. (6 sts)

ROW 3: K6, pick up and k1 st from same ch loop. (7 sts)

ROW 4: As row 2.

ROW 5: As row 3.

ROW 6: As row 2.

ROW 7: Bind off 5 sts knitwise.

Do not turn, do not break off yarn.**

2nd petal

Pick up and k1 st from next ch loop, slip 2nd st on needle over first st. Slip remaining st onto left needle and then cast on 5 sts as before. (6 sts)

Work as first petal from * to **.

Make 3rd, 4th, 5th, 6th, and 7th petals as 2nd petal.

8th petal

Work as 2nd petal to row 6.

Bind off 6 sts knitwise.

Fasten off.

Join yarn end to base of first petal. Pin out petals and press. Turn flower to WS.

Block

To make the first quarter of the block, working into the front of the sc around the center ch ring and using B, [pick up and k1 st in each of the 2 strands that form 1sc] twice, turn. (4 sts)

ROW 1 (RS): [Kfb] 3 times, k1. (7 sts)

ROW 2: Purl.

ROW 3: Kfb, k to last 2 sts, kfb, k1. (9 sts)

Repeat rows 2–3 six times. (21 sts)

NEXT ROW: Purl.

Bind off knitwise.

Work 3 more quarters in this way, noting that in the ch that stands for the first sc, it will be necessary to pick up 1 st in the ch and 1 st in the ch ring.

Finishing

Join the quarters with mattress stitch, taking in half a stitch from each edge. Press.

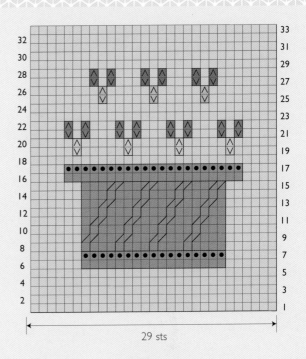

29 sts

Yarn: DK wool in lime (A), olive (B), pink-mauve (C), eggplant (D), mauve (E), and plum (F)

METHOD

NOTE: Use the intarsia color change technique for the window box and the stranding technique for the bobbles.

Using A, cast on 29 sts by thumb method. Beginning with a k row, work 5 rows st-st. Now continue from row 6 of the chart, noting that this is a WS row, reading WS rows from left to right and RS rows from right to left as indicated by row numbering on chart. When row 33 has been completed, bind off knitwise. To neaten the sides, RS facing and using A, pick up and k29 sts along one edge and then bind off knitwise. Do the same along 2nd edge.

Color key

- A
- B
- C
- E
- F
- G

Stitch key

- ☐ k on RS, p on WS
- • p on RS
- ⧄ t2R
- ⋁ (k1, yo, k1, yo, k1) in next st to make 5 sts from one
- ⋀ k5, then pass 2nd, 3rd, 4th, and 5th sts over first st

Yarn: DK wool in white (A), leaf green (B), sky blue (C), and yellow (D)

METHOD

Flower

Using A, cast on 14 sts.

SET-UP ROW: Purl.

Now pattern as follows:

ROW 1 (RS): P1, pfb, p9, w&t, k9, kfb, k2. (16 sts)

ROW 2 (RS): P1, pfb, p8, w&t, k8, kfb, k2. (18 sts)

ROW 3 (RS): Cast on 2 sts by cable method, bind off 2 sts knitwise, p2tog, p6, w&t, k5, k2tog, k1. (16 sts)

ROW 4 (RS): P1, p2tog, p1, w&t, k2tog, k1. (14 sts)

ROW 5 (RS): Knit.

ROW 6 (WS): Slip 1 purlwise, p13.

Repeat rows 1–6 twice, then rows 1–5 once again.

Bind off knitwise.

Stem

RS facing and using A, pick up and k6 sts along st-st row-ends, one and a half sts from edge.

Change to B.

ROWS 1 & 3: Purl.

ROW 2: Knit.

ROW 4: [K2tog] 3 times. (3 sts)

Beginning with a p row, work 17 rows st-st.

Bind off.

Block

Using C, cast on 2 sts.

ROW 1 (RS): Kfb, k1. (3 sts)

ROW 2 & ALL WS ROWS: Knit.

ROW 3: [Kfb] twice, k1. (5 sts)

ROW 5: Kfb, k2, kfb, k1. (7 sts)

ROW 7: Kfb, k4, kfb, k1. (9 sts)

ROW 9: Kfb, k6, kfb, k1. (11 sts)

Continue to increase in this way on RS rows until there are 31 sts.

NEXT RS ROW: K1, k2tog, k to last 3 sts, k2tog, k1.

Continue to decrease in this way on RS rows until 7 sts remain.

NEXT RS ROW: K1, [k2tog, k1] twice. (5 sts)

NEXT RS ROW: K1, sk2po, k1. (3 sts)

NEXT RS ROW: Sk2po. (1 st)

Fasten off.

Finishing

Using matching yarn and working underneath the stitches as far as possible, sew the stem and sides of the flower to the block. Catch down the tips of the petals and the inner points between. Using D double, sew three French knots on the block between the center petals.

174 BUTTON FLOWER

Yarn: Sport-weight wool in ocher (A), bright yellow (B), and teal (C)

Extras: Button

METHOD

Flower

Using A, cast on 42 sts.

ROW 1 (RS): K2, [p2, k2] 10 times.

ROW 2: P2, [k2, p2] 10 times.

Change to B.

ROW 3: As row 1.

ROW 4: P2, [yo, k2, yo, p2] 10 times. (62 sts)

ROW 5: K2, [p1tbl, p2, p1tbl, k2] 10 times.

ROW 6: P2, [k4, p2] 10 times.

ROW 7: K2, [p4, k2] 10 times.

ROW 8: As row 6.

Bind off in k2, p4 rib.

Block

Using C, cast on 2 sts.

ROW 1 (RS): Kfb, k1. (3 sts)

ROW 2 & ALL WS ROWS: Knit.

ROW 3: [Kfb] twice, k1. (5 sts)

ROW 5: Kfb, k2, kfb, k1. (7 sts)

ROW 7: Kfb, k4, kfb, k1. (9 sts)

ROW 9: Kfb, k6, kfb, k1. (11 sts)

Continue to increase in this way on RS rows until there are 27 sts.

NEXT RS ROW: K1, k2tog, k to last 3 sts, k2tog, k1. Continue to decrease in this way on RS rows until 7 sts remain.

NEXT RS ROW: K1, [k2tog, k1] twice. (5 sts)

NEXT RS ROW: K1, sk2po, k1. (3 sts)

NEXT RS ROW: Sk2po. (1 st)

Fasten off.

Finishing

Square up the block and press lightly. Using yarn ends or matching yarn, lightly gather the cast-on edge of the flower and join the side edges, taking in 1 st from each edge. Place the flower on the block and sew button through the center of both.

175 ZINNIA |

Yarn: DK wool in lime (A), mauve (B), and orange (C)

METHOD

SPECIFIC ABBREVIATION

MB = make bobble: (k1, yo, k1, yo, k1) in next st, pass 2nd, 3rd, 4th, and 5th sts over first st.

Using A, cast on 74 sts by thumb method.

ROW 1 (RS): Purl.

Change to B.

ROWS 2 & 4: K2, [p7, k2] 8 times.

ROW 3: P2, [k7, p2] 8 times.

ROW 5: P2, [k2, s2kpo, k2, p2] 8 times. (58 sts)

ROW 6: K2, [p5, k2] 8 times.

ROW 7: P2, [k1, s2kpo, k1, p2] 8 times. (42 sts)

ROW 8: K2, [p3, k2] 8 times.

ROW 9: P2, [s2kpo, p2] 8 times. (26 sts)

ROW 10: K2tog, [p1, k2tog] 8 times. (17 sts)

Change to C.

ROW 11: Knit.

ROW 12: [K2tog, MB] 5 times, k2tog. (11 sts)

ROW 13: Purl.

ROW 14: K1, [k2tog] 5 times. (6 sts)

Break off yarn and take it through remaining sts to gather them up.

Finishing

Using yarn ends or matching yarn, join row-ends. Press lightly.

Yarn: Sport-weight wool in dull yellow (A), burnt orange (B), soft white (C), and mauve (D)

Needles: Pair of needles; circular needle or 5 double-pointed needles

METHOD

Center

Using pair of needles and A, cast on 20 sts by thumb method.

ROW 1 (RS): K16, w&t, k16.

ROW 2 (RS): K12, w&t, k12.

ROW 3 (RS): K8, w&t, k8.

ROW 4 (RS): K4, w&t, k4.

ROW 5 (RS): K all 20 sts.

ROW 6 (WS): Slip 1 knitwise, k19.

Repeat rows 1–6, 20 times, then rows 1–4 again.

Bind off knitwise.

Join cast-on and bound-off edges, taking in the back strand of the cast-on and the chain of the bind-off to create a g-st ridge.

Gather the center tightly by taking A through all the slip stitches.

Band

RS facing, using circular needle or dpn and B, pick up and k1 st between each g-st ridge around edge. (111 sts)

Marking beginning of rounds, work in rounds with RS facing.

ROUND 1: Purl.

ROUND 2: Kfb, k5, [kfb, k7, kfb, k6] 7 times. (126 sts)

ROUND 3: Purl.

Petals

Change to pair of needles and C.

*ROW 1 (RS): K9, w&t.

Continue on these 9 sts only.

ROWS 2, 4, 6 & 8: Knit.

ROW 3: K2tog, k5, k2tog. (7 sts)

ROW 5: K2tog, k3, k2tog. (5 sts)

ROW 7: K2tog, k1, k2tog. (3 sts)

ROW 9: S2kpo. (1 st)

Fasten off, leaving an end for sewing.**

Repeat from * to ** 13 times. (14 petals)

Fasten off.

Border

RS facing, using circular needle or dpn and D, fold petals forward to pick up and k1 st in back loop of each st of last round B, in this way picking up and knitting 9 sts from behind each petal. (126 sts)

Marking beginning of rounds, work in rounds with RS facing.

ROUNDS 1 & 3: Purl.

ROUND 2: Knit.

ROUND 4: [Kfb, k8] 14 times. (140 sts)

ROUNDS 5 & 7: Purl.

ROUND 6: Knit.

ROUND 8: [Kfb, k6] 20 times. (160 sts)

ROUNDS 9 & 11: Purl.

ROUND 10: Knit.

ROUND 12: [Kfb, k7] 20 times. (180 sts)

ROUND 13: Purl.

ROUND 14: Knit.

Turn to WS and bind off knitwise.

Finishing

Using yarn ends, sew tip of each petal to the border.

Yarn: DK wool

Needles: 2 pairs, one pair a size smaller than the other

METHOD

NOTE: Slip single stitches on WS rows purlwise with yarn in front.

Block

Using larger needles, cast on 65 sts.
ROW 1 (RS): K30, ssk, k1, k2tog, k30. (63 sts)
ROW 2: K31, slip 1, k31.
ROW 3: K to center 5 sts, ssk, k1, k2tog, k to end. (61 sts)
ROW 4: K to center st, slip 1, k to end.
Repeat rows 3–4 until 5 sts remain.
NEXT RS ROW: Ssk, k1, k2tog. (3 sts)
NEXT ROW: K1, slip 1, k1.
NEXT ROW: S2kpo. (1 st)
Fasten off.

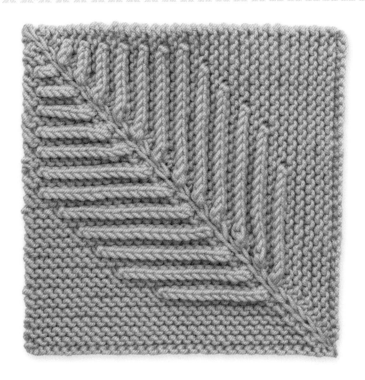

First pair of veins

RS facing and bound-off corner to top, using smaller needles, in 3rd g-st ridge from bind-off: *insert needle in top loop of st immediately to left of center slip st, fold work along g-st ridge, pick up and k1 in this st. Pick up and k1 in top loop of each of next 2 sts, turn. Slipping the first st knitwise, bind off all 3 sts knitwise.**
Fasten off, leaving an end at least 6 times the length of the vein or long enough to repeat the pick-up/bind-off process. Break off yarn, thread it onto a yarn needle, and take it underneath the center slip st. Swivel the block to start in the top loop of st immediately to opposite side of center and repeat from * to **.
Fasten off, leaving a short end. Take this to WS and weave it in.

2nd pair of veins

Skip 1 g-st ridge, in next ridge work as first pair of veins from * to ** but picking up 5 sts each side of center.

Remaining veins

Continue to make pairs of veins every 2nd ridge, making each pair 2 sts longer than previous pair until 7 pairs have been completed (15 sts in veins of 7th pair). Repeat last pair 4 times, then work one pair 2 sts shorter than the previous pair.

Yarn: Sport-weight wool in ocher (A) and rust (B)

Extras: Crochet hook

METHOD

Using A, cast on 25 sts by thumb method.

*Change to B.

ROW 1 (RS): Knit.

ROW 2: Purl.

ROW 3: K1, m1, k10, s2kpo, k10, m1, k1.

ROW 4: Purl.

Change to A.

ROW 5: K1, m1, k10, s2kpo, k10, m1, k1.

ROW 6: Knit.**

Repeat from * to ** 3 times.

Change to B and work rows 1–2 again.

Now decrease as follows:

ROW 1 (RS): K1, k2tog, k8, s2kpo, k8, skpo, k1. (21 sts)

ROW 2: Purl.

Change to A.

ROW 3: K9, s2kpo, k9. (19 sts)

ROW 4: Knit.

Change to B.

ROW 5: Knit.

ROW 6: Purl.

ROW 7: K1, k2tog, k5, s2kpo, k5, skpo, k1. (15 sts)

ROW 8: Purl.

Change to A.

ROW 9: K6, s2kpo, k6. (13 sts)

ROW 10: Knit.

Change to B.

ROW 11: Knit.

ROW 12: Purl.

ROW 13: K1, k2tog, k2, s2kpo, k2, skpo, k1. (9 sts)

ROW 14: Purl.

Change to A.

ROW 15: K3, s2kpo, k3. (7 sts)

ROW 16: Knit.

Change to B.

ROW 17: Knit.

ROW 18: Purl.

ROW 19: K2tog, s2kpo, skpo. (3 sts)

ROW 20: Purl.

ROW 21: S2kpo. (1 st)

Fasten off.

Stem and center vein

Using crochet hook and A, make 10ch, skip 1ch, ss in back strand of each of 9ch. Do not fasten off. RS of leaf facing, surface crochet 1ch in each of center B sts.

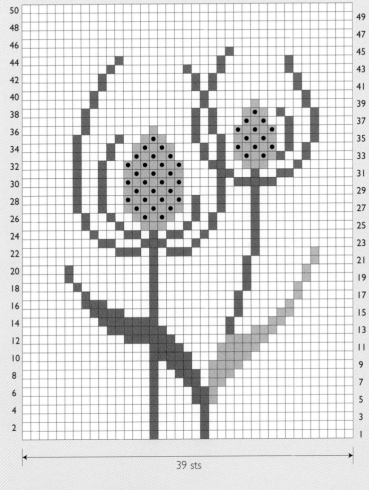

Yarn: DK wool in soft white (A), charcoal gray (B), silver gray (C), and dull red (D)

METHOD

Using A, cast on 39 sts. Beginning with a k row, work in st-st from the chart, reading RS rows from right to left and WS rows from left to right as indicated by row numbering on chart. When row 50 has been completed, bind off.

Border

RS facing and using A, pick up and k39 sts along cast-on edge. Change to D.

ROW 1: Purl.

ROW 2: Pfb, p to last 2 sts, pfb, p1. (41 sts)

ROW 3: Purl.

Bind off purlwise. Work remaining edges to match. Join the mitered corners. Press carefully, avoiding seed stitch.

39 sts

Color key

☐ A

■ B

■ C

Stitch key

☐ k on RS, p on WS

● p on RS, k on WS

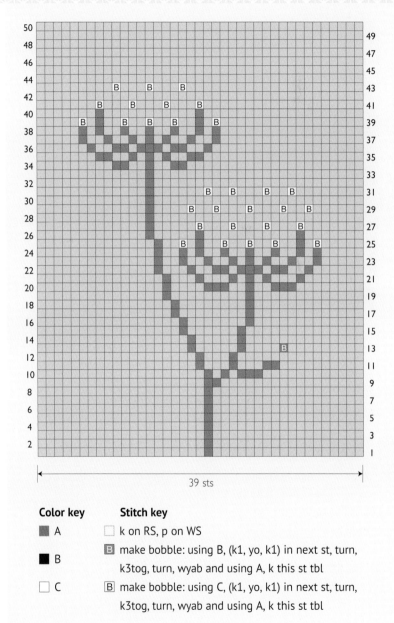

Yarn: DK wool in pale gray (A), charcoal gray (B), soft white (C), and dull red (D)

METHOD

Using A, cast on 39 sts. Beginning with a k row, work in st-st from the chart, reading RS rows from right to left and WS rows from left to right as indicated by row numbering on chart. When row 50 has been completed, bind off.

Border

RS facing and using A, pick up and k39 sts along cast-on edge.

Change to D.

ROW 1: Purl.

ROW 2: Pfb, p to last 2 sts, pfb, p1. (41 sts)

ROW 3: Purl.

Bind off purlwise.

Work remaining edges to match. Join the mitered corners. Press carefully, avoiding bobbles.

Color key

- ■ A
- ■ B
- □ C

Stitch key

- □ k on RS, p on WS
- ⊞ make bobble: using B, (k1, yo, k1) in next st, turn, k3tog, turn, wyab and using A, k this st tbl
- ⊞ make bobble: using C, (k1, yo, k1) in next st, turn, k3tog, turn, wyab and using A, k this st tbl

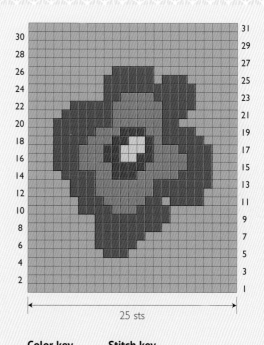

25 sts

Color key

- A
- B
- C
- D
- E

Stitch key

- ☐ k on RS, p on WS

Yarn: DK wool in turquoise (A), eggplant (B), orange (C), claret (D), and lemon yellow (E)

METHOD

Using A, cast on 25 sts by thumb method. Beginning with a k row, work in st-st from the chart, reading RS rows from right to left and WS rows from left to right as indicated by row numbering on chart. When row 31 has been completed, bind off knitwise.

To neaten the sides, RS facing and using A, pick up and k25 sts along one edge and then bind off knitwise. Do the same along 2nd edge.

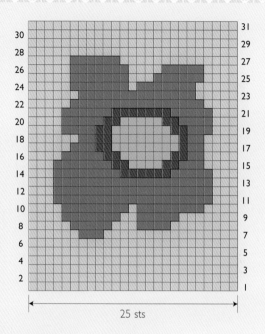

25 sts

Yarn: DK Wool in yellow (A), teal (B), crimson (C), and duck egg (D)

METHOD

Using A, cast on 25 sts by thumb method. Beginning with a k row, work in st-st from the chart, reading RS rows from right to left and WS rows from left to right as indicated by row numbering on chart. When row 31 has been completed, bind off knitwise.

To neaten the sides, RS facing and using A, pick up and k25 sts along one edge and then bind off knitwise. Do the same along 2nd edge.

Color key

▨ A

■ B

■ C

▨ D

Stitch key

☐ k on RS, p on WS

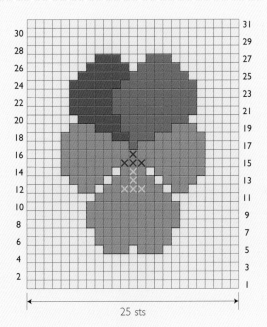

25 sts

Yarn: DK wool in yellow-green (A), purple (B), deep purple (C), eggplant (D), acid yellow (E), and burnt orange (F)

METHOD

Using A, cast on 25 sts by thumb method. Beginning with a k row, work in st-st from the chart, reading RS rows from right to left and WS rows from left to right as indicated by row numbering on chart. When row 31 has been completed, bind off knitwise.

To neaten the sides, RS facing and using A, pick up and k25 sts along one edge and then bind off knitwise. Do the same along 2nd edge.

Following the chart, use E and F to work the duplicate stitch detail.

Color key

A
B
C
D
E
F

Stitch key

☐ k on RS, p on WS
☒ duplicate stitch

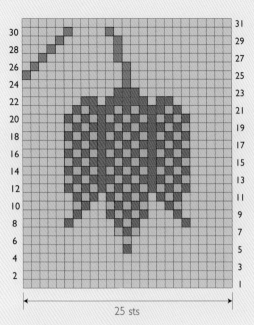

25 sts

Yarn: DK wool in leaf green (A), damson (B), dull pink (C), and dark green (D)

METHOD

Using A, cast on 25 sts by thumb method. Beginning with a k row, work in st-st from the chart, reading RS rows from right to left and WS rows from left to right as indicated by row numbering on chart. When row 31 has been completed, bind off knitwise.

Note that the last row is entirely in A so that no contrast color is shown in the bind-off.

To neaten the sides, RS facing and using A, pick up and k25 sts along one edge and then bind off knitwise. Do the same along 2nd edge.

Color key

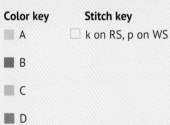

A

B

C

D

Stitch key

☐ k on RS, p on WS

25 sts

Color key

- A
- B
- C
- D

Stitch key

- ☐ k on RS, p on WS
- ☒ duplicate stitch

Yarn: DK wool in gray-blue (A), lime green (B), bright blue (C), and bright green (D)

METHOD

Using A, cast on 25 sts by thumb method. Beginning with a k row, work in st-st from the chart, reading odd-numbered RS rows from right to left and even-numbered WS rows from left to right as indicated by row numbering on chart. When row 31 has been completed, bind off knitwise.

To neaten the sides, with RS facing and using A, pick up and k25 sts along one edge and then bind off knitwise. Do the same along 2nd edge.

Following the chart, use D to work the duplicate stitch detail.

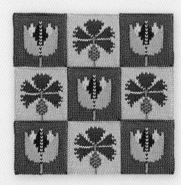

Mix and match
185 + 186

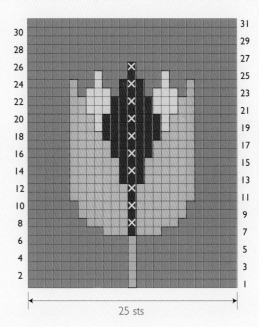

Yarn: DK wool in violet (A), leaf green (B), gold (C), burnt orange (D), and yellow-green (E)

METHOD

Using A, cast on 25 sts by thumb method. Beginning with a k row, work in st-st from the chart, reading RS rows from right to left and WS rows from left to right as indicated by row numbering on chart. When row 31 has been completed, bind off knitwise.

To neaten the sides, RS facing and using A, pick up and k25 sts along one edge and then bind off knitwise. Do the same along 2nd edge.
Following the chart, use E to work the duplicate stitch detail.

Color key

- A
- B
- C
- D
- E

Stitch key

- ☐ k on RS, p on WS
- ☒ duplicate stitch

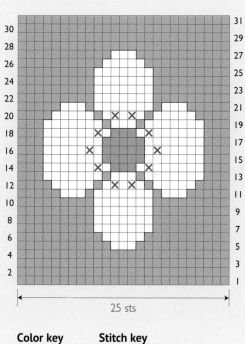

25 sts

Yarn: DK wool in sky blue (A), white (B), gold (C), and dark green (D)

METHOD

Using A, cast on 25 sts by thumb method. Beginning with a k row, work in st-st from the chart, reading RS rows from right to left and WS rows from left to right as indicated by row numbering on chart. When row 31 has been completed, bind off knitwise.

To neaten the sides, RS facing and using A, pick up and k25 sts along one edge and then bind off knitwise. Do the same along 2nd edge.

Following the chart, use D to work the duplicate stitch detail.

Color key

A
B
C
D

Stitch key

☐ k on RS, p on WS
☒ duplicate stitch

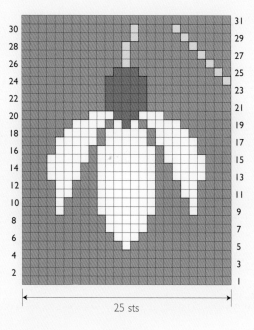

25 sts

Color key

- ▨ A
- ☐ B
- ▨ C
- ▨ D

Stitch key

- ☐ k on RS, p on WS

Yarn: DK wool in pea green (A), white (B), dark green (C), and pale green (D)

METHOD

Using A, cast on 25 sts by thumb method. Beginning with a k row, work in st-st from the chart, reading RS rows from right to left and WS rows from left to right as indicated by row numbering on chart. When row 31 has been completed, bind off knitwise.

Note that the last row is entirely in A so that no contrast color is shown in the bind-off.

To neaten the sides, RS facing and using A, pick up and k25 sts along one edge and then bind off knitwise. Do the same along 2nd edge.

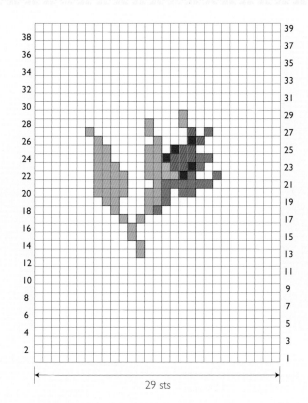

38
39
36
37
34
35
32
33
30
31
28
29
26
27
24
25
22
23
20
21
18
19
16
17
14
15
12
13
10
9
8
7
6
5
4
3
2
1

29 sts

Yarn: Sport-weight wool in white (A), mid-green (B), dark green (C), pale pink (D), raspberry (E), and hot pink (F)

METHOD

Using A, cast on 29 sts by thumb method. Beginning with a k row, work in st-st from the chart, reading RS rows from right to left and WS rows from left to right as indicated by row numbering on chart. When row 39 has been completed, bind off knitwise.

To neaten the sides, RS facing and using A, pick up and k29 sts along one edge and then bind off knitwise. Do the same along 2nd edge.

Color key

☐ A   ▨ D

▨ B   ■ E

▨ C   ▨ F

Stitch key

☐ k on RS, p on WS

Mix and match
189 + 190

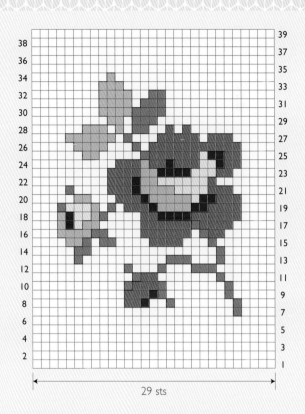

29 sts

Yarn: Sport-weight wool in white (A), dark green (B), hot pink (C), raspberry (D), pale pink (E), faded pink (F), and mid-green (G)

METHOD

Using A, cast on 29 sts by thumb method. Beginning with a k row, work in st-st from the chart, reading RS rows from right to left and WS rows from left to right as indicated by row numbering on chart. When row 39 has been completed, bind off knitwise.

To neaten the sides, RS facing and using A, pick up and k29 sts along one edge and then bind off knitwise. Do the same along 2nd edge.

Color key

☐ A   ▨ E

◼ B   ▨ F

◼ C   ▨ G

◼ D

Stitch key

☐ k on RS, p on WS

Yarn: DK wool in pale green (A), bright green (B), dark green (C), and ocher (D)

METHOD

Using A, cast on 45 sts.

ROW 1 (RS): P1, [k1, p1] to end.

ROW 2: As row 1.

Continue from row 3 of the chart, reading RS rows from right to left and WS rows from left to right as indicated by row numbering on chart. When row 56 has been completed, bind off in pattern.

Following the chart, use C and D to work the duplicate stitch detail.

Color key

- A
- B
- C
- D

Stitch key

- ☐ k on RS, p on WS
- ● p on RS, k on WS
- ☒ duplicate stitch

192 OAK LEAF \/

Yarn: DK wool in pale green (A), soft orange (B), rust (C), and pea green (D)

METHOD

Using A, cast on 45 sts.

ROW 1 (RS): P1, [k1, p1] to end.

ROW 2: As row 1.

Continue from row 3 of the chart, reading RS rows from right to left and WS rows from left to right as indicated by row numbering on chart. When row 56 has been completed, bind off in pattern.

Following the chart, use C and D to work the duplicate stitch detail.

45 sts

Color key

- A
- B
- C
- D

Stitch key

- ☐ k on RS, p on WS
- ● p on RS, k on WS
- ☒ duplicate stitch

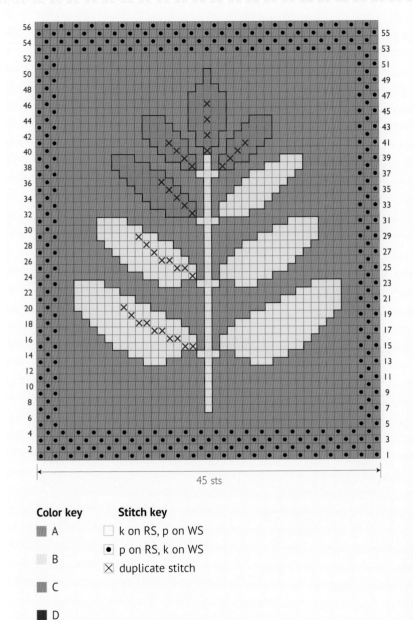

Yarn: DK wool in olive (A), lime (B), soft orange (C), and rust (D)

METHOD

Using A, cast on 45 sts.

ROW 1 (RS): P1, [k1, p1] to end.

ROW 2: As row 1.

Continue from row 3 of the chart, reading RS rows from right to left and WS rows from left to right as indicated by row numbering on chart. When row 56 has been completed, bind off in pattern.

Following the chart, use D to work the duplicate stitch detail.

Color key

- A
- B
- C
- D

Stitch key

- ☐ k on RS, p on WS
- ⦿ p on RS, k on WS
- ☒ duplicate stitch

Yarn: DK wool in pale green (A), leaf green (B), dark green (C), and soft green (D)

METHOD

Using A, cast on 45 sts.

ROW 1 (RS): P1, [k1, p1] to end.

ROW 2: As row 1.

Continue from row 3 of the chart, reading RS rows from right to left and WS rows from left to right as indicated by row numbering on chart. When row 56 has been completed, bind off in pattern.

Following the chart, use C and D to work the duplicate stitch detail.

Color key

A

B

C

D

Stitch key

☐ k on RS, p on WS

● p on RS, k on WS

☒ duplicate stitch

Yarn: DK wool in olive (A), lime (B), bright green (C), and pale green (D)

METHOD

Using A, cast on 45 sts.

ROW 1 (RS): P1, [k1, p1] to end.

ROW 2: As row 1.

Continue from row 3 of the chart, reading RS rows from right to left and WS rows from left to right as indicated by row numbering on chart. When row 56 has been completed, bind off in pattern.

Following the chart, use C and D to work the duplicate stitch detail.

Color key

▨ A

▨ B

▨ C

☐ D

Stitch key

☐ k on RS, p on WS

• p on RS, k on WS

☒ duplicate stitch

45 sts

Yarn: DK wool in leaf green (A), bright green (B), dark green (C), and blue-green (D)

METHOD

Using A, cast on 45 sts.

ROW 1 (RS): P1, [k1, p1] to end.

ROW 2: As row 1.

Continue from row 3 of the chart, reading RS rows from right to left and WS rows from left to right as indicated by row numbering on chart. When row 56 has been completed. bind off in pattern.

Following the chart, use D to work the duplicate stitch detail.

Color key

■ A
■ B
■ C
■ D

Stitch key

☐ k on RS, p on WS
● p on RS, k on WS
☒ duplicate stitch

45 sts

Yarn: DK wool in scarlet (A), black (B), charcoal gray (C), gray-blue (D), apple green (E), maroon (F), and steel gray (G)

METHOD

Using A, cast on 39 sts. Beginning with a k row, work in st-st from the chart, reading RS rows from right to left and WS rows from left to right as indicated by row numbering on chart. When row 50 has been completed, bind off.
Following the chart, use G to work the duplicate stitch detail.

Border

RS facing and using B, pick up and k39 sts along cast-on edge.
ROW 1: Knit.
ROW 2: Kfb, k to last 2 sts, kfb, k1. (41 sts)
Bind off knitwise.
Work remaining edges to match. Join the mitered corners.

Color key

■ A   ■ E
■ B   ■ F
■ C   ■ G
■ D

Stitch key

☐ k on RS, p on WS
☒ duplicate stitch

Yarn: DK wool in pale lime (A), purple (B), dark green (C), pale mauve (D), deep purple (E), gray-mauve (F), violet (G), gold (H), heliotrope (I), blue-mauve (J), and black (K)

METHOD

Using A, cast on 39 sts. Beginning with a k row, work in st-st from the chart, reading RS rows from right to left and WS rows from left to right as indicated by row numbering on chart. When row 50 has been completed, bind off.

Following the chart, use J to work the duplicate stitch detail.

Border

RS facing and using K, pick up and k39 sts along cast-on edge.

ROW 1: Knit.

ROW 2: Kfb, k to last 2 sts, kfb, k1. (41 sts)

Bind off knitwise.

Work remaining edges to match. Join the mitered corners.

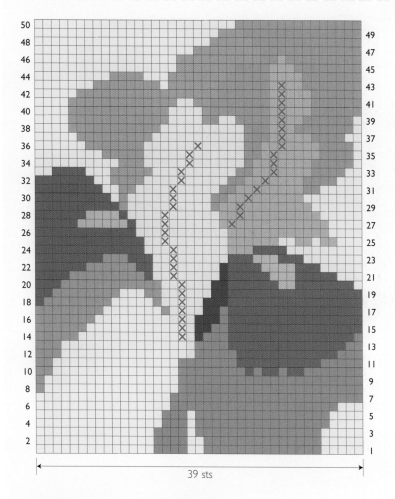

39 sts

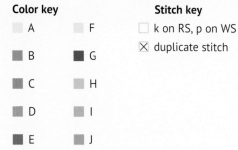

Color key

A   F

B   G

C   H

D   I

E   J

Stitch key

☐ k on RS, p on WS

☒ duplicate stitch

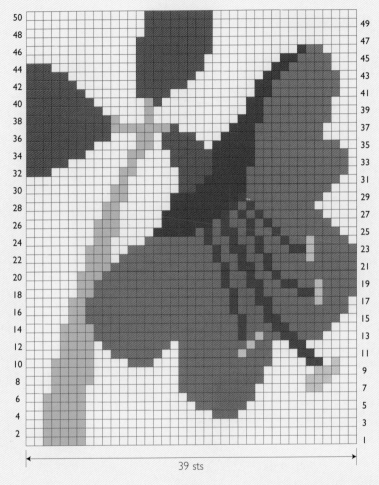

Yarn: DK wool in lime green (A),
leaf green (B), shocking pink (C),
gold (D), maroon (E), crimson (F),
fuchsia pink (G), and black (H)

METHOD

Using A, cast on 39 sts.
Beginning with a k row,
work in st-st from the chart,
reading RS rows from right
to left and WS rows from left
to right as indicated by row
numbering on chart. When
row 50 has been completed,
bind off.

Border

RS facing and using H,
pick up and k39 sts along
cast-on edge.
ROW 1: Knit.
ROW 2: Kfb, k to last 2 sts,
kfb, k1. (41 sts)
Bind off knitwise.
Work remaining edges
to match. Join the
mitered corners.

39 sts

Color key

A   ■ E

■ B   ■ F

■ C   ■ G

■ D

Stitch key

☐ k on RS, p on WS

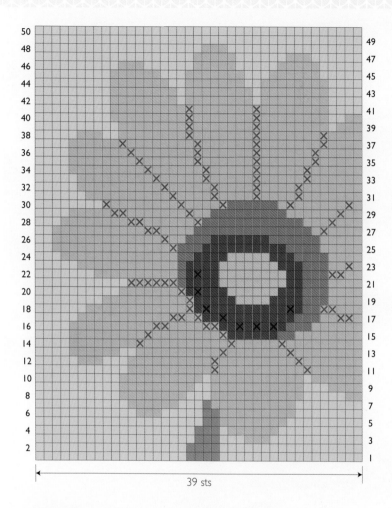

Yarn: DK wool in leaf green (A), dark green (B), mauve-pink (C), shocking pink (D), orange-rust (E), gold (F), gray-mauve (G), crimson (H), and black (I)

METHOD

Using A, cast on 39 sts. Beginning with a k row, work in st-st from the chart, reading RS rows from right to left and WS rows from left to right as indicated by row numbering on chart. When row 50 has been completed, bind off.

Following the chart, use G and H to work the duplicate stitch detail.

Border

RS facing and using I, pick up and k39 sts along cast-on edge.

ROW 1: Knit.

ROW 2: Kfb, k to last 2 sts, kfb, k1. (41 sts)

Bind off knitwise.

Work remaining edges to match. Join the mitered corners.

39 sts

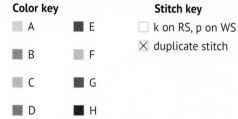

Color key

A E

B F

C G

D H

Stitch key

□ k on RS, p on WS

☒ duplicate stitch

TECHNIQUES

This chapter provides useful information about yarns, needles, abbreviations, and chart symbols. There are also some notes to help you brush up on your knitting skills, as well as advice on assembling and finishing off your work for the best results.

EQUIPMENT

The basic tools for knitting are simple, portable, and relatively inexpensive.

KNITTING NEEDLES

For most of the designs in this book, a conventional pair of knitting needles is used. If a pattern does not specify otherwise, this is what you should use. Pairs of needles are made in a variety of lengths, and the length you prefer will depend on the way you hold the needles. A few of the designs require double-pointed needles, and the pattern indicates when this is the case. You will need two double-pointed needles to make a cord, and three, four, or sometimes five double-pointed needles when knitting in the round.

Needle sizes

Needle sizes are not specified in this book, and the size of needle you choose will vary depending on the type of yarn you are using. Check the ball band of the yarn for the recommended size. For a tighter knit on small items, use the smallest size recommended or a size smaller than usual for all of the designs in this book except for the blocks. If particularly small needles are required, this is indicated in the instructions. If in doubt, use a smaller needle size than usual.

Metal needles may be either steel or aluminum. These strong, smooth materials are particularly suited to speedy knitting for anyone who likes their needles to be completely rigid.

Double-pointed needles are sold in sets of four or five in most of the same sizes as pairs of needles.

Wood or bamboo needles are lightweight and some knitters find them less tiring to the hands than metal. They are also useful for knitting with smooth yarns because there is less tendency for them to slip out of the stitches.

Cable needles (short double-pointed needles used to transfer groups of stitches) may slip out of the stitches if you knit loosely, so look for those with a curve in the middle.

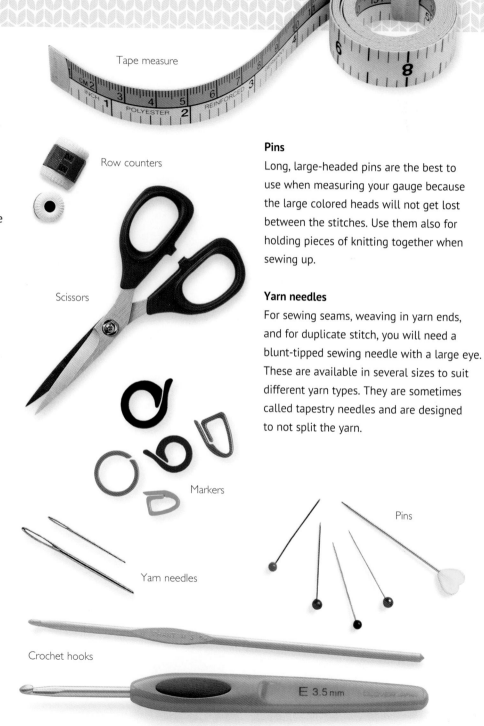

ADDITIONAL EQUIPMENT

Tape measure

Preferably choose a tape measure that features both inches and centimeters on the same side, to familiarize yourself with both systems of measurement.

Tape measure

Markers

Ready-made markers can be used to indicate a repeat, to help count stitches, or to mark the beginning of rounds. Alternatively, use a short length of yarn in a contrasting color as a soft, flexible marker.

Row counters

Row counter

A row counter may help you to keep track of the rows or rounds you have worked, but counting rows is easy if you remember to include the stitches on the needle as a row. Also remember that in garter stitch (knit every row), each ridge on the right side represents two rows.

Scissors

Crochet hooks

A few designs in this book require a crochet hook. Crochet hooks usually have a flange where they are to be held. Some newer hooks are made with a soft-grip handle.

Markers

Scissors

Choose a small, sharp-pointed pair of scissors to cut yarn and trim ends neatly.

Pins

Long, large-headed pins are the best to use when measuring your gauge because the large colored heads will not get lost between the stitches. Use them also for holding pieces of knitting together when sewing up.

Yarn needles

For sewing seams, weaving in yarn ends, and for duplicate stitch, you will need a blunt-tipped sewing needle with a large eye. These are available in several sizes to suit different yarn types. They are sometimes called tapestry needles and are designed to not split the yarn.

Yarn needles

Pins

Crochet hooks

YARN

There are abundant yarn types and colors to choose from. Changing the type of yarn will produce a different result and scale, so it can be very rewarding to experiment.

Yarns come in a wide range of different fibers and fiber combinations.

YARN CHOICE

Yarns are available in a range of weights, from lace weight to super bulky. Because yarns may vary from one manufacturer to another and certainly change from one fiber to another, generic yarn types are used in this book. You should be aware of the characteristics of different fibers, however, from the fullness of cotton to the elasticity of wool. Because the construction of a yarn will affect its behavior, this will also influence the end result. Try using as many different yarns as possible until you are confident.

FABRIC

When knitting blocks, the fabric is usually more critical than the size, so use a yarn and needle size that are compatible for your project. For example, a firm fabric would be suitable if you plan to use the blocks to make a bag, whereas a scarf would need to be soft and supple. Obviously, using a finer yarn will produce a daintier result and a thicker yarn will produce something chunkier.

BALL BANDS

Most yarns have a paper band or tag that gives you the information you need to make the right choice for any project. The ball band usually contains details about fiber content, recommended needle size, length of yarn on each ball, and washing instructions.

Care instructions are usually provided as symbols that tell you if the yarn can be hand- or machine-washed, dry-cleaned, pressed, and so on. Keep a ball band from each project for future reference, and if the item is a gift, make sure you pass on the details.

Yarn colors

If you really want to create a florist's shop or greengrocer's counter, separate your yarns into color groups and keep these in transparent plastic containers so that you have a palette of colors to work with. Don't limit yourself to knitting yarns and look out for interesting colors among embroidery wools.

CALCULATING SIZE

For most of the designs in this book, size really does not matter. However, if it is important to know the finished size of your knitting, some preparatory calculations will need to be made.

Gauge is the key to size in knitting and the starting point is usually the information given on the ball band, which states a recommended stitch and row count to 4in (10cm) over stockinette stitch. So, for example, if the stitch gauge is 22 sts to 4in (10cm), divide the number of stitches in your knitting by 22 and multiply by 4 (10) to calculate the width. Similarly, if the row gauge is 28 rows to 4in (10cm), divide the number of rows in your knitting by 28 and multiply by 4 (10) to calculate the depth.

Note that stranded knitting, garter stitch, and seed stitch will all differ in gauge from stockinette stitch.

Estimating size when knitting in the round is trickier. If knitting a round block, for example, you could take the number of stitches at the outside edge and use a stitch calculation like the one above to give the approximate circumference. Similarly, the outside edges of a hexagon or octagon could be estimated by taking the gauge along one edge and multiplying it by 6 or 8, as appropriate. The row gauge would give, very roughly, the depth of the rounds from center to outside edge.

The 60s Flower block made with sport-weight yarn measures approx. 8in (20cm) in diameter, whereas the same design in worsted-weight yarn measures approx. 14in (34cm) across.

Measuring gauge

To see if you are matching the gauge given on a ball band, or to measure the gauge of a swatch made in your chosen needle size and yarn, follow these instructions.

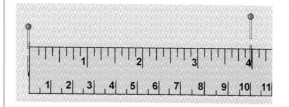

1 Lay the swatch on a flat surface. Using a ruler or tape measure, place two pins exactly 4in (10cm) apart at the center of the swatch as shown. Count the number of stitches (including any half stitches) along a straight row between the pins.

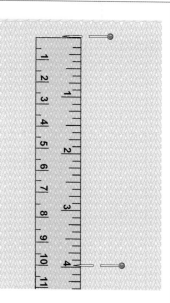

2 Now place the pins 4in (10cm) apart vertically and count the number of rows between them along a straight line of stitches.

KNITTING TECHNIQUES

This section is not a lesson in knitting. It is simply a reminder of a few basics, together with some suggestions and techniques that might be new to an inexperienced knitter.

The knitted cast-on method is used to make the swallowtails on the Swallowtail Butterfly.

SLIPKNOT

A slipknot forms the first stitch on the needle before casting on.

1 Loop the yarn around two fingers of your left hand, with the ball end on top. Dip the needle into the loop, catch the ball end of the yarn, and pull it through the loop.

2 Pull the ends of the yarn to tighten the knot. Tighten the ball end to bring the knot up to the needle.

CASTING ON

There are several cast-on methods, each with its own merits. Generally, you can use whichever method you prefer, but the following techniques are specified in this book whenever they would be the most appropriate method to use.

Thumb cast-on

Also called the long-tail cast-on or loop cast-on technique, this simple method uses a single needle and produces an elastic edge.

1 Leaving an end about three times the length of the required cast-on, put a slipknot on the needle. Holding the yarn end in the left hand, take the left thumb under the yarn and upward. Insert the needle in the loop made on the thumb.

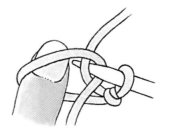

2 Use the ball end of the yarn to make a knit stitch, slipping the loop off the thumb. Pull the yarn end to close the stitch up to the needle. Continue making stitches in this way. The result looks like a row of garter stitch because the yarn has been knitted off the thumb.

Cable cast-on

This two-needle method gives a firm edge with the appearance of a rope.

1 Put a slipknot on one needle. Use the other needle and the ball end of the yarn to knit into the loop on the left needle without slipping it off. Transfer the new stitch to the left needle.

2 Insert the right needle between the new stitch and the next stitch, and then make another stitch as before. Continue making stitches in this way.

Knitted cast-on

This is similar to the cable method, but gives a softer edge. It is useful for making a smooth hem, as well as for starting in the round. It is also used when you need to add stitches to those already on the left needle.

1 Put a slipknot on one needle. Using the other needle and the ball end of the yarn, knit into the first stitch on the left needle, but do not slip the stitch off the left needle afterward.

2 Transfer the new stitch to the left needle. Insert the right needle into the new stitch, and then make another stitch as before. Continue making stitches in this way.

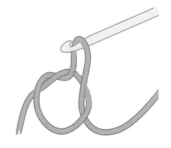

Crochet cast-on

Casting on with a crochet hook is an alternative method. Choose a hook that will make stitches compatible with the size of your knitting needles. Make a ring as for a slipknot. Insert the hook in the ring and pull a loop through (shown above), then catch the yarn and pull it through the loop just made on the hook. Continue in this way until the required number of stitches is on the hook. Pull the short yarn end to close the ring, then slip the stitches onto the knitting needle.

Ends of yarn

The end of yarn left after making the slipknot should be a reasonable length so that it can be used for sewing up. It can also be useful for covering up imperfections, such as awkward color changes. The same applies to the end left after binding off. Ends left when a new color is joined in should be woven in along a seam or row end on the wrong side.

KNITTING IN THE ROUND

If you are accustomed to knitting in rows with a pair of needles, don't be daunted by the prospect of knitting in continuous rounds using multiple double-pointed needles. Remember that you will be knitting stitches from the left needle onto the free needle in the usual way, and the right side will always be toward you.

Getting started is the trickiest part, as you need to learn to hold the needles in a comfortable way, not to let the needles slip out of the stitches, and not to twist the stitches of the cast-on and early rounds. To practice using a set of double-pointed needles, it may be useful to knit a tube (simply knit in rounds without shaping) before attempting a more complex design.

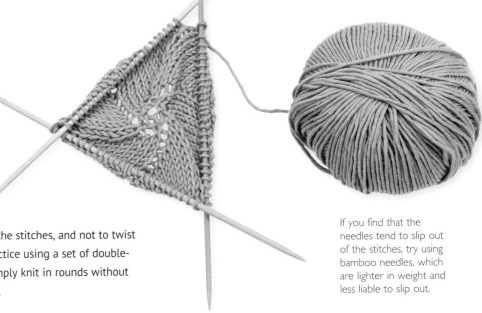

If you find that the needles tend to slip out of the stitches, try using bamboo needles, which are lighter in weight and less liable to slip out.

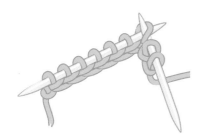

1 Preferably using the knitted cast-on method, cast the stitches onto one needle, and from this distribute the stitches onto the required number of double-pointed needles. Take care not to twist the cast-on stitches because this cannot be corrected later.

2 Overlapping the tips of the needles (the sequence can be changed later if necessary), arrange the needles so that the opening is toward you and the yarn is above and not below the needles.

3 Join the round by working the first set of stitches with the free needle. Position the needles as closely as possible and take the yarn across to make the first stitch. This should be done very firmly between needles, especially in knit rounds, otherwise a gap or ladder will appear. If the first stitch on the needle is a yarn over, this can be worked more loosely.

SWITCHING FROM ROUNDS TO ROWS

Several projects in this book require you to start by working in rounds and then switch to rows to complete the project.

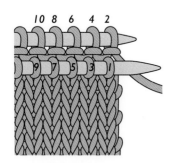

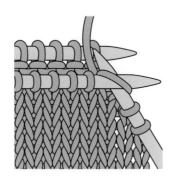

1 Distribute the stitches as evenly as possible between two needles and hold the needles parallel together. Think of the stitches on the front needle as being odd-numbered and those on the back needle as being even-numbered.

2 Knit into stitches from alternating needles, first working an odd-numbered stitch from the front needle.

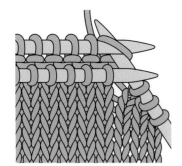

3 Then work an even-numbered stitch from the back needle. Continue until all the stitches are transferred onto a single needle.

Joining new yarn

Joining in a new yarn inconspicuously is sometimes tricky. Try leaving both ends hanging for a little way, tension the ends to neaten the stitches either side, and then tie a neat reef knot on the wrong side, weaving in the ends later.

WRAP AND TURN (W&T)

Short-row shaping is when you turn the needles partway through a row, leaving some of the stitches unworked. This wrap and turn technique can be used to prevent a hole from forming when making a mid-row turn.

1 Work the number of stitches required before the turn. Take the yarn to the opposite side of the work, slip the next stitch purlwise from left to right needle, and return the yarn to the original side of the work.

2 Slip the wrapped stitch back onto the left needle, turn, and tension the yarn ready to work the next row.

BOBBLES

Different sizes of bobbles are used in this book and are explained with each pattern, but they all use the same basic technique. This example is a simple five-stitch bobble.

1 Work (k1, yo, k1, yo, k1) into the next stitch, making five stitches from one.

2 Turn, p5, turn, k5, turn, p5. With the five bobble stitches on the right needle, lift the 2nd, 3rd, 4th, and 5th stitches over the first stitch and off the right needle. With yarn in front, slip the remaining bobble stitch onto the left needle. Pushing the bobble to the RS of the work if necessary, turn and continue the row.

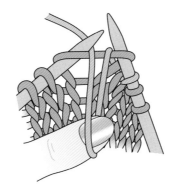

LOOP STITCH

1 Insert the right needle into a stitch on the left needle. Bring the yarn to the front between the needles, loop it around a thumb, then take it to the back again between the needles.

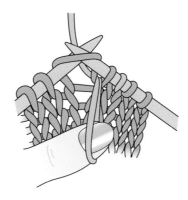

2 Apply tension to the loop with your thumb as you knit the part of the stitch that remains on the left needle as normal.

Loop stitches are used to make the center of the Clematis flower.

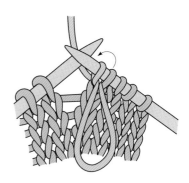

3 You have now made two stitches on the right needle, with a loop between them, so you have an extra stitch. Either lift the first stitch over the second, or slip both stitches onto the left needle and knit them together through the back loops.

PICK UP AND KNIT

This technique involves knitting up new stitches along the edge of a knitted piece, ready to work in another direction. With right side facing, insert the right needle under an edge stitch, then work a knit stitch in the usual way. Repeat for the number of stitches required, spacing the picked up stitches evenly along the edge.

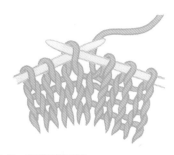

SLIP STITCHES

To slip a stitch knitwise, insert the right needle into the stitch as if to knit it, but simply transfer the stitch across. To slip a stitch purlwise (shown above), insert the needle as if to purl the stitch. As a rule of thumb, slip stitches purlwise unless instructed otherwise. The exception is when it is part of a decrease (such as ssk), in which case slip stitches knitwise.

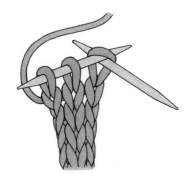

CORD

Sometimes called an i-cord, this round cord is made using two double-pointed needles. Cast on the specified number of stitches and knit one row in the usual way. The stitches are now on the right needle. Do not turn, but instead slide the stitches to the other end of the right needle. Transfer this needle with the stitches to your left hand, carry the yarn tightly across the wrong side of the work, and use the empty needle to knit the next row. Continue in this way for the length required, then bind off.

Some designs, such as the Zebra Dartfish, are worked in the round on double-pointed needles. In the beginning when there are few stitches, you work on two needles as you would a cord. As the number of stitches increase, you should add more needles and start working in the round in the usual way.

CHAIN

Put a slipknot on the needle. Knit one stitch. Transfer the stitch just made from the right to the left needle. Continue in this way for the length required. A similar fine chain can be made using a yarn needle and starting in the last stitch of a cast-off. Bring the yarn end through the stitch from back to front. Loop the yarn. Insert the needle into the stitch loop from front to back and then into the new loop from back to front. Continue in this way, making loops from left to right and right to left alternately.

COLOR KNITTING

There are two methods of changing color within a row for working the colorwork floral block designs, although both can be used in one design where this is appropriate. The blocks are worked in stockinette and the color changes are indicated on a chart.

Intarsia

For color changes between larger groups of stitches, it is better to use a separate length of yarn for each area of color and cross the yarns firmly at each change in order to lock the stitches together. If only two lengths of one color are needed, pull the end out of the center of the ball and use both the inside and outside ends of yarn. Don't worry too much about tangling when using a lot of colors—gently pull each end out of the snarl as you need it, then, leaving not too short an end, cut and remove it when it is finished with.

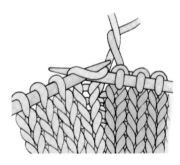

1 To change color on a knit row, drop the first color. Pick up the second color from beneath the first color and knit along the row to the next color change.

2 To change color on a purl row, drop the first color. Pick up the second color from beneath the first color and purl along the row to the next color change.

Stranding

If the color not in use is to be used again after a few stitches (say, up to six stitches), it can be carried across the wrong side. Avoid taking the yarn across too tightly by spreading the stitches on the right needle.

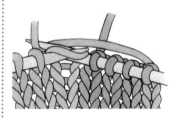

1 On knit rows, knit the first group of stitches in the first color, then let the yarn drop. Bring the new color over the top of the dropped yarn and knit the next group of stitches.

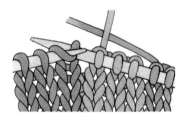

2 Let the second yarn drop, bring the first color under the dropped yarn, and knit the next group in the second color.

3 On purl rows, purl the first group of stitches in the first color, then let the yarn drop. Bring the new color over the top of the dropped yarn and purl the next group of stitches.

4 Let the second yarn drop, bring the first color under the dropped yarn, and purl the next group of stitches in the second color.

BINDING OFF

Once you have finished your knitting, you need to secure the stitches by binding them off. Binding off is also used to finish a group of stitches to shape the work. Use the chain method unless specified otherwise.

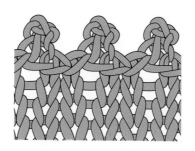

Picot bind-off

In a decorative picot bind-off, additional stitches are cast on and then bound off, followed by one or more stitches of the last row. Slip the stitch remaining from the bind-off onto the left needle, ready to make the next cast-on. Obviously, the number of stitches bound off must exceed the number of stitches cast on, but both can be varied. The closer the picots are spaced, the more the edge will flute. In the illustration, two stitches have been cast on and four stitches bound off.

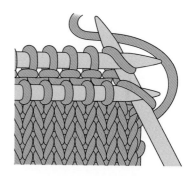

Binding off two sets of stitches together

Hold the two sets of stitches on parallel needles, right sides or wrong sides together according to the instructions. Using a third needle, knit together the first stitch from each needle, and then the next pair. Take the first stitch made on the third needle over the second stitch in the same way as for a chain bind-off. Continue to knit together pairs of stitches and bind them off along the row. This joins edges in a very neat, flexible way.

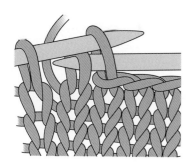

Chain bind-off

Knit two stitches. With the left needle, lift the first stitch over the second and off the needle. Knit the next stitch. Continue in this way until one stitch remains. To fasten off, break off the yarn, take the end through this stitch, and tighten.

Partial binding off

Sometimes a pattern requires part of a row to be bound off. When this happens, the following instruction includes the stitch already on the right needle from binding off. For example, if the following instruction is to knit eight stitches, the stitch already on the right needle counts as the first of the eight stitches.

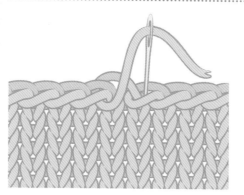

INVISIBLE FASTENING OFF

For a smooth finish to a final round, simply break the yarn and pull it through the loop of the last stitch. Thread it onto a yarn needle and take it under the two top strands of the first stitch, then back into the last stitch and pull it tight until it disappears.

CROCHET TECHNIQUES

Although this is a book about knitting, crochet stitches have been used in a few places, so the basic stitches you will need are explained here. They are quite easy to master, so give them a go.

WORKING IN THE ROUND

When working in rounds, you can start with a ring of chain stitches or with a loop of yarn called a slip ring.

CHAIN STITCHES (CH)

The basic hooking action used to make a chain is used, in various combinations, to work all other crochet stitches.

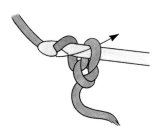

1 Start with a slipknot on the hook (as when casting on in knitting). Hold the slipknot (and later the chain) between the thumb and forefinger of the left hand. Take the yarn over the second finger of the left hand so it is held taut. Take it around the little finger as well if necessary. The right hand is then free to manipulate the hook. With a turn of the wrist, guide the tip of the hook under the yarn. Catch the yarn and pull it through the loop on the hook to make one chain.

2 Repeat this action, pulling a new loop through the loop already on the hook until the chain is the required length. Count each V-shaped loop on the front of the chain as one chain stitch, but don't count the loop on the hook.

Chain ring

Work the required number of chains, then join with a slip stitch in the first chain to form a ring.

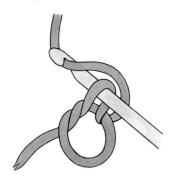

Slip ring

Coil the yarn around two fingers and use the hook to pull through a loop of the ball end of the yarn. Holding the ring flat between the thumb and forefinger of your left hand, catch the yarn again and pull it through the loop on the hook to anchor it (shown above). After working the first round of stitches into the ring, pull the starting yarn end to close the center.

BASIC STITCHES

As well as chain stitches, the following basic crochet stitches are used in this book.

Slip stitch (ss)

Insert the hook into the next stitch, wrap the yarn over the hook, and pull it through the stitch and the loop on the hook.

Single crochet (sc)

Insert the hook into the next stitch, wrap the yarn over the hook, and pull it through the stitch. Yarn over hook and pull it through both loops on the hook.

Half double crochet (hdc)

Yarn over hook, insert the hook into the next stitch, yarn over hook, and pull it through the stitch. Yarn over hook and pull it through all three loops on the hook.

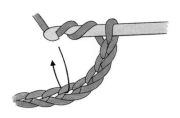

Treble crochet (tr)

Yarn over hook twice, insert the hook into the next stitch, yarn over hook, and pull it through the stitch (4 loops on hook). Yarn over hook and pull it through two loops; yarn over hook and pull it through the remaining two loops.

DECREASING

Just as in knitting, crochet decreases are made by working two stitches together. To do this, start by working the first stitch of the decrease as normal, but stop before you make the last yarn over. You will have two loops on the hook. Now work the second stitch of the decrease. When making the final yarn over, pull the yarn through all of the loops on the hook.

The cream line running around the outside of the Lemon Slice is worked using crochet stitches, including the only crochet decrease used in this book (working two treble crochet stitches together).

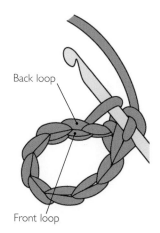

Back loop

Front loop

FRONT AND BACK LOOPS

Each crochet stitch has two strands of yarn that form the top of the chain or other crochet stitch—these are usually referred to as the front and back loops or strands. Always insert the hook under both of these loops when working crochet stitches unless a pattern specifies otherwise.

FINISHING TECHNIQUES

All of the designs in this book are easy to assemble using just a few standard finishing techniques. Here are some tips and suggestions.

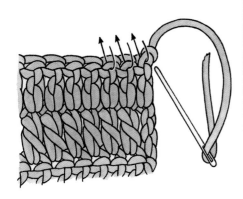

WEAVING IN YARN ENDS

When ends of yarn will not be used for seaming, you may be able to enclose some of them while working the piece. If not, the ends should be woven in on the wrong side after completion. When making any project, read through the pattern first and think ahead, leaving a long end of yarn where it will be useful for sewing a seam.

Use a yarn needle to weave in ends, and always weave in for at least 2in (5cm) to prevent the end from slipping out again. For smooth, slippery yarns, reverse the direction and weave back again for a few stitches. Trim off the excess.

PRESSING OR BLOCKING

Pressing or blocking can be used to improve the neatness of the stitches and to help the finished knitted fabric hold its shape. Both techniques involve pinning the fabric into the correct size or shape. Depending on the fiber content of the yarn and whether the stitch pattern is textured or not, you can either press with an iron or, in the case of blocking, apply water or steam to help set the stitches.

For flat projects, such as the floral block designs, you should always press or block the finished piece. Many of the flowers and leaves are flat items that can also benefit from pressing or blocking, although others are designed to curl and may be better left untouched. The decision of whether to press or block really depends on what you want the finished item to look like—it is entirely up to you.

The three-dimensional items in this book are shaped by stuffing, but even so, a very light press on the right side after completion will smooth the surface and seams.

Pressing

You can press any yarns labeled on the ball band with a recommended ironing temperature (usually natural fibers). Pin out the piece into the required shape or size on a well-padded surface, such as an ironing board or folded blanket. Pin the piece wrong side uppermost if it is textured. Lightly press the knitting, taking care to lift and replace the iron rather than moving it around on the surface. Avoid pressing raised areas of stitches. Some yarns recommend pressing under a damp cloth for steam. If so, allow to dry before unpinning.

Pressing or blocking helps to show off the lovely shape the Maple Leaf.

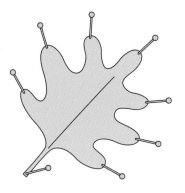

Blocking

Ease and pin the piece into shape on a well-padded surface, then either steam with an iron or spray with cold water, depending on the fiber content of the yarn. Alternatively, the piece can be hand-washed in lukewarm water before pinning out. Always be guided by the ball band of the yarn. When in doubt, choose a cold-water method for blocking synthetic fibers. Allow the piece to dry completely before unpinning.

ADDING A BORDER

A mitered garter stitch border frames some of the square floral blocks in a decorative way, and it is also useful for piecing by making the same number of stitches on all four sides.

To add a garter stitch border, pick up and knit in each stitch of the cast-on edge, then work in garter stitch, increasing one stitch at each end of right-side rows and finally binding off knitwise on a wrong-side row. Noting that it will be necessary to skip some row-end stitches, pick up exactly the same number of stitches along the row ends as well as the bind-off edge and work them all in the same way. By maintaining this pattern of right-side row increases, a border can be made to almost any depth.

The Oriental Poppy block is finished with a narrow garter stitch border. You can add a border to any of the blocks in this book.

Weave in ends at the tips of petals and leaves before moving on to the main project assembly.

SEAMS

Yarn ends are immensely useful for sewing seams, but if a new length of yarn needs to be joined, start with a backstitch rather than a knot. Unless stated otherwise, mattress stitch on the right side is recommended for most projects. When assembling blocks, you may also wish to consider a crochet seam.

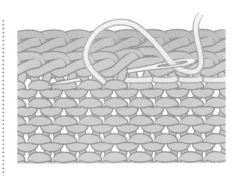

Backstitch

A very firm join can be made with backstitch on the wrong side, taking in two strands of each stitch. This may create a furrow on the right side, especially in stitches such as reverse stockinette stitch.

Mattress stitch

If a textured edge is not required, use mattress stitch (sometimes called ladder stitch or invisible seaming) on the right side. With right sides facing and starting at the cast-on, take the yarn needle under the strand between the first and second stitches of one edge. Repeat at the other edge. Continue working into alternate edges, tightening the stitches as you go.

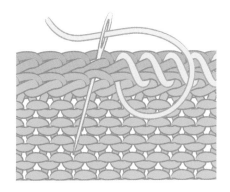

Overcasting

Overcasting creates a flexible seam. With right sides together and working from right to left, insert the needle into the inside loop of the back piece and then the inside loop of the front piece. The result is a very flat seam, but it is not as strong as one taking in two strands along the edge.

Many of the floral blocks in this book have a textured edge made by casting on by the thumb method, binding off knitwise on the wrong side, and then picking up and binding off the same number of stitches along the row ends. In addition to texture, this produces the same number of stitches on all four edges, ideal for overcasting.

Seaming tips

If a new length of yarn needs to be joined for seaming, use matching yarn and start with a couple of small backstitches rather than a knot because a knot can easily slip through to the right side of the piece.

As a general rule, use the darker yarn when seaming items containing different colors or tones.

Take care to sew all seams firmly, especially when making items for children.

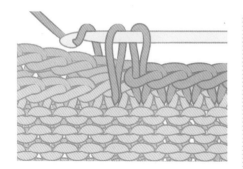

Single crochet seam

Single crochet makes a very strong seam that can work well with knitted blocks. It is easier to work neatly on the wrong side because you have to skip occasional row ends to match the number of crochet stitches on all sides. Place the two pieces together and work a single crochet stitch through both layers of knitting.

Slip stitch seam

This creates a slightly less bulky seam than single crochet, requiring less yarn. Simply work slip stitches through both layers of knitting. It should always be worked on the wrong side because the ridge it makes is not very decorative.

ASSEMBLING THE FLORAL BLOCKS

To assemble the blocks, join pairs until you have strips of the length or width measurement you require. Then join the strips into the finished square or rectangle.

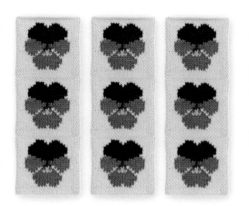

Adding plain squares

Infill squares can be made in stockinette stitch—fold the knitting diagonally from one corner to another to check that the sides match. Or they can be made in garter stitch, knitted from corner to corner by increasing one stitch at each end of right-side rows until the sides are the required measurement and then decreasing one stitch at each end of right-side rows.

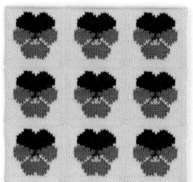

The Michaelmas Daisy block is made using stockinette stitch, while the Cord Leaf block is made using garter stitch knitted from corner to corner. Both can be used as plain squares when designing a block arrangement.

The Loganberry is stuffed with batting.

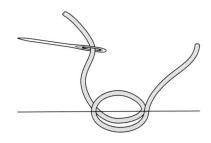

STUFFING

Some of the projects in this book are shaped by stuffing. Leftover matching yarn makes ideal stuffing because there will be no show-through. Either stuff with cut-up pieces of yarn or wind off short lengths of yarn and push these in, one coil at a time.

Alternatively, you can use batting or synthetic toy stuffing, such as polyester fiberfill. Push the stuffing in firmly, one wisp at a time, using it to shape the item without distorting it. Too much stuffing will pack down, whereas too little will never plump up. Don't push the batting in with a pointed implement, but use something like the eraser end of a pencil.

ANTENNAE

A couple of the small critters in this book require yarn antennae. Insert the yarn needle at the position of the first antenna, leaving a yarn end. Bring the needle out at the position of the second antenna, backstitch between the two, then bring the yarn out again at the second antenna position. Trim both ends.

If desired, you can stiffen the antennae by pinning out straight and spraying with a fabric stiffener or strong hairspray. Allow to dry. Bobby pins can also be bent into the shape of antennae (or insect legs) and inserted through the knitting.

This Honey Bee is stuffed with leftover yarn, has wings knitted from fine wire, and legs and antennae made from bobby pins.

WIRING

Some items need a little help to stay in shape, and wiring is the solution. Wire is also used to create the features of some of the small critters in this book. You may also wish to wire petals and leaves to make them easier to bend and sculpt.

You can use craft, jewelry, or florist wire, all of which come in a wide range of colors and gauges (thicknesses). Choose a fine wire, such as 24 gauge (0.5mm), and simply pass the wire through the stitches (around the outer edges of a petal or leaf, for example); you may find it easier to thread the wire into a yarn needle to do this.

Where stronger wire is needed, be careful not to leave a burr when snipping the wire because this will make it difficult to insert. A small file, even an old nail file, can be used to smooth away a burr. Use pliers to twist and tuck the ends of wire safely away.

You can also thread wire through a flower stem to make it bendable, but for adding stronger support to stems for holding them upright in a vase, try inserting clear vinyl tubing (available at hardware and plumbing supply stores) with a couple of pieces of thick wire threaded through.

Caution
Remember that you should never wire an item that is intended for use by children.

POMPOMS

A couple of the flowers in this book require pompoms. Either use a ready-made plastic pompom maker or cut out two rings of cardboard.

1 Place the two rings together and use a yarn needle to wrap yarn around them.

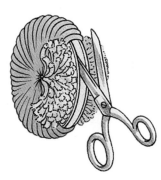

2 Starting new lengths of yarn at the outside edge, continue until the rings are tightly covered. Insert the blade of a pair of scissors between the rings and cut the yarn around the edge.

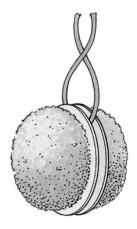

3 Tie a length of yarn around the pompom between the rings. Knot the yarn tightly, slip the rings off, and trim the pompom. Use the ends of yarn from the tie for attaching the pompom to the flower.

The Pompom Puff sunflower features a circle of pompoms made using two colors of yarn.

FELTING

When woollen knitting is washed vigorously in hot water and then rinsed in cold water, the fibers mat together and the knitting shrinks to form a sturdy, dense fabric. The dense fabric created by felting is fabulous for all kinds of sculptural treatments, such as flowers and leaves. Take care, though— once wool is felted, it is felted for good.

For successful felting, choose a yarn that is made of at least 80 percent animal fiber. Pure wool yarn is the best choice—it should shrink by 25 percent or more in the felting process. Wool/synthetic blends may shrink to a lesser degree. Superwash or machine-washable wool will resist shrinkage.

Felted stems and leaves contrast well with unfelted flower heads.

EMBROIDERY, BEADS, AND SEQUINS

Although the designs in this book are perfectly fine left undecorated, it can be fun to add extra special details, such as embroidery, beads, and sequins. There is a huge variety of decorative embroidery stitches to choose from. To make the stitches really stand out, use a double strand of yarn or thread to work them.

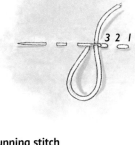

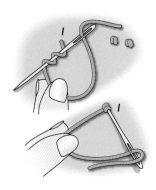

French knot

Bring the needle up at 1 and wind the thread twice (or number of times specified) around the needle tip (top). Holding the thread, insert the needle very close to—but not exactly at—1 and pull through gently (bottom).

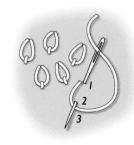

Lazy daisy stitch

This is also known as single chain stitch. Bring the needle up at 1, form a loop with the thread, and insert the needle again at 1. Bring the needle up at 2, inside the loop, and pull through. Insert the needle at 3, catching down the loop of thread.

Running stitch

To work a line of running stitch, bring the needle up at 1, down at 2, and up again at 3. Continue in this way for length required.

Chain stitch

This is worked in the same way as a lazy daisy (single chain) stitch, but point 3 is moved a bit farther away from point 2. Work as many chain stitches as required, then finish with a little stitch to hold the last loop in place.

Sequins and beads

Use "invisible" nylon thread to sew on sequins and matching sewing thread for beads. If the holes are too small for a regular sewing needle, use a beading needle to sew them on.

Beads are best anchored with a backstitch. To sew on sequins for fishscales, start at the tail end and, alternating sequins on each row, overlap them as you stitch. Overlapping them more closely will give a truly scaly effect but will add weight.

The Striped Caterpillar's spots are French knots and the eyes are sequins.

The Sprat has shimmering fishscales made from flat sequins, and larger faceted sequins for eyes.

DUPLICATE STITCH

It is sometimes easier to add small amounts of color afterward, rather than to include them in the knitting process. This technique, also called Swiss darning, is used to make color changes or additions to stockinette stitch. The new color covers the stitch exactly but adds to the thickness of the fabric, so it is better only used over small areas. Use a yarn needle with a rounded point and work from right to left horizontally and from bottom to top vertically.

The Ladybug's spots are duplicate stitches.

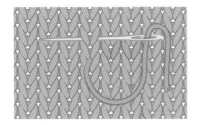

Working to the left

1 Thread the contrast color onto a yarn needle, bring it out at the base of one V-shaped stitch, take it behind the two threads of the stitch above, and bring it out at the front.

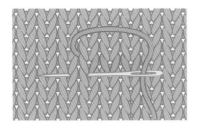

2 Tensioning the yarn carefully, insert the yarn needle in the base of the stitch and bring it out at the base of the next stitch.

Working upward using a yarn needle

Cover a stitch as in step 1 of working to the left, but bring the needle out in the stitch above. Over a large number of rows skip one stitch at regular intervals or the work will buckle.

Working upward using a crochet hook

You can use the surface crochet technique as an alternative for covering stitches from row to row. Using a crochet hook and holding the yarn underneath the work, insert the hook in one stitch and pull a loop through. Insert the hook in the next stitch above and pull a loop through both the work and the loop on the hook. Continue in this way, skipping one stitch at regular intervals.

The veins on the Fig Leaf block are added to the finished piece of knitting using duplicate stitch.

ABBREVIATIONS AND CHARTS

The abbreviations used in this book are listed here for easy reference. Any additional ones are explained alongside the pattern.

c2b	slip next stitch onto cable needle and hold at back, k1, then k1 from cable needle
c2bp	slip next stitch onto cable needle and hold at back, k1, then p1 from cable needle
c2f	slip next stitch onto cable needle and hold at front, k1, then k1 from cable needle
c2fp	slip next stitch onto cable needle and hold at front, p1, then k1 from cable needle
cdd	center double decrease: slip 2 stitches as if to knit 2 together, knit next stitch, then pass both slipped stitches over knitted stitch and off needle
dpn	double-pointed needle(s)
foll	follow(ing)
g-st	garter stitch
k	knit
k1b	knit stitch in row below
k2sso	knit 2 together, slip stitch just made onto left needle, pass next stitch over it, slip stitch back onto right needle

k2tog	knit 2 stitches (or number specified) together
kfb	knit into front and back of same stitch
kfbf	knit into front, back, and front of same stitch
m1	make 1: from the front, lift horizontal strand between last stitch and next stitches and knit into back of it
m1L	as m1, noting that new stitch slants to the left
m1p	as m1, but purl into back of lifted strand
m1R	as m1, but lift strand from the back and knit into front of it; new stitch slants to the right
p	purl
p2tog	purl 2 stitches (or number specified) together
pfb	purl into front and back of same stitch
pfkb	purl into front, then knit into back of same stitch
psso	pass slipped stitch over
RS	right side of work

s2kpo	slip 2 stitches as if to knit 2 together, k1, pass slipped stitches over
sk2po	slip 1 knitwise, knit 2 together, pass slipped stitch over
skpo	slip 1 stitch knitwise, k1, pass slipped stitch over (makes a decrease that slants to the left; this is an alternative to ssk below)
ssk	slip next stitch knitwise, slip following stitch knitwise, insert left needle into front loops of both slipped stitches and knit 2 together (makes a decrease that slants to the left; this is an alternative to skpo above)
ssp	slip next stitch knitwise, slip following stitch knitwise, return both stitches to left needle, insert right needle into back loops of both slipped stitches and purl 2 together
st(s)	stitch(es)
st-st	stockinette stitch
t2L	knit in back of 2nd stitch, knit in front of first stitch, slip both stitches off left needle together
t2R	knit in front of 2nd stitch, knit in back of first stitch, slip both stitches off left needle together

tbl	through back of loop(s)
tog	together
w&t	wrap and turn
WS	wrong side of work
wyab	with yarn at back
wyif	with yarn in front
yo	wrap yarn over needle (counterclockwise) to make an extra stitch
* **	asterisks mark a section of instructions to be repeated
( )	round brackets indicate a group of stitches to be worked together or a stitch count
[ ]	work instructions in square brackets the number of times stated after the brackets

Crochet abbreviations

ch	chain
ch sp	chain space
hdc	half double crochet
sc	single crochet
ss	slip stitch
tr	treble crochet
2tr tog	treble crochet 2 stitches together

Charts are a visual representation of how to work a pattern; the symbols are used to create a stylized picture. It is usually easier to find your place in a chart than in a lengthy set of instructions. All of the symbols used in this book are shown and explained on the relevant pattern pages.

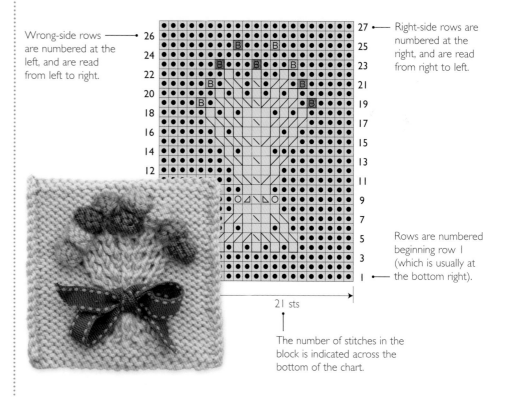

Wrong-side rows are numbered at the left, and are read from left to right.

Right-side rows are numbered at the right, and are read from right to left.

Rows are numbered beginning row 1 (which is usually at the bottom right).

21 sts

The number of stitches in the block is indicated across the bottom of the chart.

Reading charts

Each chart should be read from the lower edge upward, progressing in the same way as the work, with each row of squares on the chart representing a row of knitting. All right-side rows are read from right to left, and all wrong-side rows are read from left to right. The rows are numbered, and in most cases the first and odd-numbered rows are right-side rows, starting on the right.

INDEX

CREDITS

All photographs and illustrations are the copyright of Quarto Publishing plc. While every effort has been made to credit contributors, Quarto would like to apologise should there have been any omissions or errors – and would be pleased to make the appropriate correction for future editions of the book.

Yarn suppliers
DEBBIE BLISS
www.designeryarns.uk.com
www.knittingfever.com

DMC CREATIVE WORLD
www.dmc.com

LION BRAND YARN
www.lionbrand.com

ROWAN AND JAEGER YARNS
www.westminsterfibers.com

SUBLIME
www.sublimeyarns.com